Love and Rage

Kelley Tatro   *Photographs by Yaz "Punk" Núñez*

LOVE & RAGE

Autonomy in Mexico City's Punk Scene

Wesleyan University Press   Middletown, Connecticut

Wesleyan University Press
Middletown CT 06459
www.wesleyan.edu/wespress
© 2022 Kelley Tatro
All rights reserved
Manufactured in the United States of America
Designed by Mindy Basinger Hill
Typeset in Minion Pro

Library of Congress Cataloging-in-Publication Data

Names: Tatro, Kelley, author. | Núñez, Yaz, photographer.

Title: Love and rage : autonomy in Mexico city's punk scene /
Kelley Tatro; photographs by Yaz "Punk" Núñez.

Description: [First.] | Middletown, Connecticut :
Wesleyan University Press, 2022. |

Series: Music/culture | Includes bibliographical references and index. |
Summary: "An ethnography of the contemporary punk music
scene in Mexico City focusing on the aesthetic and political
sensibilities of participants" — Provided by publisher.

Identifiers: LCCN 2022015989 (print) | LCCN 2022015990 (ebook) |
ISBN 9780819580931 (cloth) | ISBN 9780819580948 (trade paperback) |
ISBN 9780819580955 (ebook)

Subjects: LCSH: Punk rock music — Social aspects — Mexico —
Mexico City. | Punk culture — Mexico — Mexico City.

Classification: LCC ML3917.M5 T37 2022 (print) | LCC ML3917.M5
(ebook) | DDC 306.4/842097253 — dc23/eng/20220413

LC record available at https://lccn.loc.gov/2022015989
LC ebook record available at https://lccn.loc.gov/2022015990

5   4   3   2   1

CONTENTS

ACKNOWLEDGMENTS

For the support I needed to research and write this book, I'm grateful to Duke University for providing an Aleane Webb Dissertation Research Fund, Alice Blackmore Hicks Fellows Endowment, Graduate School Summer Research Fellowship, and, after my return from Mexico, a Bass Fellowship for Excellence in Undergraduate Instruction. I also benefited from a U.S. Department of Education Foreign Language and Area Studies grant, secured with the help of Duke's Center for Latin American and Caribbean Studies. North Central College contributed some research funding.

Many thanks to the editors and reviewers of the journals *Ethnomusicology* and the *International Journal of Cultural Studies* for publishing earlier versions of some of my ideas. Material from my 2018 article—"Performing Hardness: Punk and Self-Defense in Mexico City," *International Journal of Cultural Studies* 21 (3): 242–56—appears in chapter 2. Chapter 4 contains a reworking of my 2014 article, "The Hard Work of Screaming: Physical Exertion and Affective Labor Among Mexico City's Punk Vocalists," *Ethnomusicology* 58 (3): 431–53.

Beginning as a dissertation project, this book was shaped in part by a delightful, collaborative committee at Duke University, chaired by Louise Meintjes, and including Paul Berliner, Pedro Lasch, Diane Nelson, and Philip Rupprecht. Their insightful questions and smart suggestions not only helped me think through the material of the dissertation, but also provided a sense of how to make that difficult leap from dissertation to book. I'm deeply grateful to Louise especially, as she has continued to be a tremendous mentor and a wonderful friend, lending her substantial intellectual rigor, writerly creativity, generosity of spirit, and—not least—her sense of fun to all the questions and challenges that have arisen over the years as this project and my postgraduate life took shape.

Academic conferences provided fantastic opportunities to stimulate further thinking, formally and informally. Thanks to Ellen Gray, Marti Newland, and Amanda Weidman for sharing their research on our panel, "Strident Voices: Material and Political Alignments," at the Society for Ethnomusicology meeting in 2014. Anaar Desai-Stephens, Darci Sprengel, Shannon Garland, Matt Rahaim, and Nicole Reisnour were fun and thought-provoking colleagues on the roundtable, "Forming Musical Feelings: Subjectivity, Circulation, and the Political Efficacy of Affect," at the American Anthropological Association meeting in 2017. In 2018, Michelle Tellez, Maurice Magaña, Andrew Green, Livia Stone, José Martínez-Reyes, and Jeff Juris helped broaden my perspective on autonomous organization at our panel for the Latin American Studies Association international congress in Barcelona, "Other Autonomies: Interstitial Spaces of Autonomy in Mexico." I was especially thankful to get to know Jeff a bit before his heartbreaking, too-early death in 2019. It has been lovely to count on Michelle's warm friendship in the years since the panel.

It was an honor to present a lecture at the Music Studies Colloquium at the University of California, Berkeley, in 2015. Thanks especially to Bonnie Wade and Ben Brinner for being kind hosts and engaging companions during that visit. Also in 2015, I had the pleasure of taking part in the Punk Symposium at the Rotunda in Philadelphia, hosted by the Africa Center (now the Center for Africana Studies) at the University of Pennsylvania. Thanks, too, to Joella Bitter and Andrea Bohlman for their thoughtful critiques on a chapter draft during a fantastic weekend writing workshop in Durham spearheaded by Louise Meintjes in 2018. Several more friends helped to wrangle versions of these chapters into greater coherence in writing exchanges, or simply out of the goodness of their hearts. Thanks to Gavin Steingo, Matt Rahaim, Willemien Froneman, Amanda Minks, and Mike Allemana for their thoughtful suggestions. Alan O'Connor provided some valuable ideas early on in this project. Leda Scearce and Melissa Cross contributed mightily to my understanding of vocal function. Thanks to Maritza Urteaga Castro-Pozo for a lovely meeting in Mexico City and helpful correspondence since. It also has been an enormous pleasure and intellectual satisfaction to collaborate with Ana Hofman, our ideas overlapping in such generative ways.

In addition to her guidance in navigating the publishing process, I appreciated brainstorming with Suzanna Tamminen at Wesleyan University Press as we imagined the final form this project would take. Thanks to the anonymous reviewers, especially the generous reader who provided not one, but two sets of constructive, actionable criticisms. Many thanks, too, to Music/Culture series editor Jeremy

Wallach for being such an engaged presence in the revisions process, generously pitching in with many thoughtful ideas. I was in good hands with everyone on the editorial and production teams, with Doug Tifft at Redwing Book Services being especially helpful in advising me on preparing the book's visual aspect.

This book would clearly be far less engaging without the striking photographs supplied by Yaz "Punk" Núñez. In addition to her amazing eye and fabulously dark sense of humor, I have greatly enjoyed the chance to work together, getting to know her more fully through our collaboration. I'm also grateful to Iván Torres for supplementing Yaz's photos with a couple of images of the Biblioteca Social Reconstruir, as it was a key site of sociability and learning during my fieldwork experience. The other images included in the book are mostly taken from my personal collection of fanzines and other ephemera, gathered during my fieldwork period and nicely photographed by Zack Sievers. The beautiful print by Arturo García Bustos (*Sembrador*, 1952) is a well-known image that I'm very pleased to have permission—courtesy of the artist's daughter Rina Alegría García Lazo—to reproduce here.

It was such a privilege to be able to live for almost four years in Mexico City, an experience shaped especially by the time I spent in the punk scene. In the text, I embrace the practice of anonymity to honor my friends' privacy and confidentiality, but also their fierce desire for self-representation. To accord with that practice, I won't single out individuals here to thank them by name, but that does not diminish the huge sense of gratitude I feel in thinking about their many kindnesses to me over the years. I thank them all for sharing their time and ideas in a variety of thoughtful, illuminating ways, opening a fascinating world to me and fostering a deeply engaging learning process that will continue to compel me even when this project is finished. For those who really made it a point to express their respect and friendship, I hope that my deep regard and warm feelings have been and will continue to be evident as well.

In my early days in Mexico City, I was fortunate to form a nucleus of caring neighborhood friends who eased the transition into my new life, especially Rodolfo López Hernández, Eduardo Arcos Reséndiz, and Gloria Mascorro García. Kristin Solli often kept me grounded from afar. Both a friend and a gracious colleague, Luis Alberto Marmolejo Vidal was always ready for probing conversation and to give advice on polishing my language skills. Tomoko Okada and Carlos Sosa Paz have been a supportive, genial presence during all of my comings and goings. In later years, Petra Fischer and Cecilia Bacilio went above and beyond simple hospitality, greatly enriching my brief returns to the city. Though I write a lot about the company of men in this book, Hozeilah Murillo Castaneyra and América Cortés Valtierra have often provided me with some much-needed laughter and female companionship both when I'm in Mexico City and when I'm away.

In Durham, North Carolina, Elizabeth Miehack, Cindy Current, Heidi Halstead, and Sharon Campen helped keep me connected when away and then happily settled again after my return from Mexico. I remain deeply grateful to John and Marlene Rosett for a restorative visit to Montana when I really needed a change of scenery. Ellen Gray has been a valued friend and sounding board for a range of ideas, in the book and beyond. Thanks also to Ericka Adams, not only for spurring me on with my research, but for becoming a trusted confidante as I made some difficult choices. It was a hopeful thing to befriend Mike Allemana during the coronavirus pandemic and a heartwarming one to find that he was a regular, supportive presence as the deadline for this final manuscript closed in. Sarah Sylvain, our friendship puts me in mind of that little tune we used to sing in Girl Scouts—I make new friends, but you remain the gold standard.

Finally, while this book is about big feelings and big ideas, it's also very much about learning. So it seems appropriate to take this moment to thank the many teachers who have guided or partnered with me, whether formally or informally. Thanks especially to my mother, Jeanne Tatro, for fostering my love of language and reading at an early age, and my late grandfather, Ralph Souza, for encouraging me to be curious about the world around me. I was almost always fortunate to find skilled, enthusiastic teachers and professors in the many classrooms, rehearsal halls, and libraries I've frequented over the years, but I've also learned enormously from people around me, such as those who were eager to show me what life was like for them in Mexico City. During the long period of researching and writing this book, I lost one particularly treasured mentor and friend, Kató Havas, whose sharp intelligence, fluent musicianship, and absolute ardor for life remain deeply inspiring. I remember Kató especially, while extending heartfelt gratitude to all my teachers. Thank you for demonstrating how to move through the world in the best way I've yet encountered—with the curiosity, open-mindedness, passion, and tenacity of the lifelong learner.

A NOTE ON THE ILLUSTRATIONS

Filmmaker and photographer Yaz "Punk" Núñez is a graduate of the Centro Universitario de Estudios Cinematográficos of Mexico's Universidad Nacional Autónoma de México (UNAM). As she says of her fascination with the visual,

"Si pudiera contarlo con palabras, no necesitaría cargar con una cámara." ("If I could say it in words, I would not have to carry a camera.") I find that her photos do say a lot about life in Mexico City through her arresting and sometimes surprising observations.

I have been enjoying Yaz's photos for years on Facebook and Instagram, and we began speaking informally about a collaboration for my book project a long time ago. However, some obstacles presented themselves. Until more recently, Yaz did not own a decent camera, but was snapping pictures on a cheap cell phone. As a result, most of the images she provided for this book date from 2017 to 2020, which means that many are newer than the fieldwork experiences I describe in the text. Certainly, the cityscape has changed over time. Our approaches are also different. Yaz doesn't shy away from capturing people's faces in her images, while I prefer to keep people anonymous in my writing. In the captions to her photos, however, Yaz also refrained from naming people, not wanting—as she put it—to cast any individual in the role of protagonist.

Ultimately, Yaz's photographs are not meant to illustrate the text, but provide her own perspectives on life in the city and its punk scene. She has drawn the photos from a collection she calls "Crónicas de Ozías" (Chronicles of Uzziah), an obscure figure from the Old Testament, a king who was punished for disregarding God's will.

Love and Rage

PROLOGUE

Anarchist punks from the country and city
Anarko punks searching for equality
Anarchist punks from the country and city
Anarko punks sowing liberty
Desobediencia Civil, "Anarko Punks" from their album
No hay libertad sin desobediencia
(There is no liberty without disobedience), 2001[1]

While singing about the seemingly bucolic agricultural metaphor of sowing, the four musicians of Desobediencia Civil create an intensely distorted sound that conveys an incandescent energy. This happens despite the song's relatively slow pace and its unusual verse-chorus format, which includes a surprisingly catchy, anthem-like chorus with repeated lines and internal rhymes. The vocalist screams the awkward lyrics in a hoarse, gravelly voice that occasionally breaks at strategic points, a delivery that underscores the difficulty and emotion of his task. Supporting his message, the guitarist, bass guitarist, and drummer generate a harsh, powerful, static-filled sound, which challenges but ultimately doesn't overpower the voice. Together, they paint an image of a hardworking "anarcopunk," alloying punk sounds to historical anarchist iconography of *tierra y libertad*: "land and liberty."

Delivering politicized language and imagery through ear-splitting, body-pounding sonic intensity is key to the process of "sowing liberty" in the context of Mexico City's punk scene. However, many people I met in the scene, whether musicians or not, talked more about their politics than about music. Clearly, music was important to everyone, as punk shows were highly anticipated social events; bands were always in formation and re-formation; punk recordings formed the

FIGURE P.1. A *tianguis* in the Iztacalco municipality
of Mexico City. Photo by Yaz "Punk" Núñez.

soundtrack to many everyday activities; and groups of scene participants might burst into impromptu street sing-alongs when together, demonstrating an impressive repertoire of songs. But often, people emphasized that punk was more than music, a lifestyle choice—a common view in punk scenes globally (Dunn 2016; Bestley et al. 2019).

I first experienced the song "Anarko Punks" through a home-burned CD recording that I bought from a band member at one of Mexico City's many street markets. My own handwriting identifies the band's name in red marker on its surface. Previously, the blank CD-R disc had been wrapped simply in a slip of photocopied paper with the album's cover art, featuring an eerily anonymous person in a gas mask ready to throw a Molotov cocktail, along with the barest of information about the recording and the band, tucked into a cheap, crinkly plastic sleeve. I had been told that this humble object was a key recording in

Mexican punk, something I needed to acquire if I was to learn about the local scene. Learning more about street vending would also turn out to be essential to my understanding.

You can buy virtually anything in Mexico City's street markets, from everyday necessities to specialized items to black-market goods. Some offer an overwhelming mix of everything all together, perhaps internally cordoned off into sections, while others are exclusively themed by the type of products offered within them—markets dedicated to flowers, clothes, or even musical instruments. Not only does street vending provide a hardscrabble livelihood for millions in Mexico's tough, inequitable economy, but it's also a link to the past, a tool of cultural expression and exchange. Crowded, colorful, open-air markets have existed in some form since pre-Hispanic days, when the city was known as Tenochtitlán, a stronghold of the Mexica people, established around 1325. The street markets are still called *tianguis* today, the word derived from the Indigenous Nahuatl term. The markets are not only open-air but also mobile, set up and torn down once per week. The tianguis where I bought the Desobediencia Civil CD and made my first contact with Mexico City's punk scene was a particularly distinctive one, called the Tianguis Cultural del Chopo (Chopo Cultural Market). Enjoying a hard-won longevity, it was founded in 1980 following a period of especially intense repression of youth culture.

Because of its contested history and continued significance for the social and artistic life of Mexico City, el Chopo (as it's more informally called) is more than just a marketplace. It's a centrally located cultural institution where people go on Saturdays, not only to buy music paraphernalia and to hear live bands but also to socialize, plan, and organize. Located in the Colonia Guerrero neighborhood, not far from Mexico City's central plaza, the market is a weekly gathering place for people from all over the city and its vast metropolitan zone. Linked historically to rock music in particular, the tianguis also draws plenty of tourists looking to spend a bit of cash in its *puestos* (booths). Each week, certain vendors, who have been granted a fixed spot in the exclusive ranks of Chopo merchants, construct and later deconstruct their booths from metal rods, stretching colorful tarps over and weaving electrical wires into their skeletal frames. Inside these small, shady spaces, vendors usually display a riot of merchandise.

Entering the street where the market begins, at the spot where the puestos start to dot its edges, there is often a small visual arts exhibition or a workshop in progress in the so-called "cultural corridor." A permanent brick-and-mortar shop at the side of the road often places its speakers at the entrance of the building, pumping classic rock outside and in. Several people station themselves just past this juncture to give out fanzines or fliers for events, clubs, and music lessons. Others chant their offerings of food and drink for sale. "Güerita!" several vendors cry out to me, cozying up "white girl" with its diminutive form, glossing my fair skin and foreign appearance as clues that I in particular have come with money to burn.[2]

Sometimes I would heed their calls and give over some coins in exchange for a print or a fanzine. But as a regular market attendee for a time, I often continued doggedly along, making my way slowly through the tight crowd, working my way to the very back of the market space. As I moved purposefully through the market, the street became ever more crammed with an unbroken string of puestos selling everything from Doors compilations to handbags made of old records and fake fur. Among the many LPs, compact discs, cassettes, musical instruments, and band T-shirts, there are also a great many things for sale that help people maintain their alternative identities, from clothing to piercing services to a variety of knickknacks for the home. Some vendors advertise their wares aurally, playing metal or ska or various other genres from small speakers wired up in their booths, adding another layer to the dense sonic texture of a busy city overlaid with the sounds of a busy marketplace.

At the back of the market, there is an open space for musical performance off to the left. Toward the right of the live music area, another small space fills with dozens of people participating in the time-honored Chopo tradition of *trueque*, swapping their unwanted goods for the cast-off treasures of others. Here, too, at the very back of the tianguis, in raggle-taggle rows on the asphalt, sometimes snuggled right up against the one portable toilet that serves the entire market, is the Espacio Anarcopunk (Anarcopunk Space). Unlike the majority of authorized market vendors with shaded booths, the people in this section arrange their merchandise on blankets on the ground. Through concerted collective effort that took a few years to accomplish—gathering first the will, then the funds, settling logistics—they now have a communally owned tarp that they stretch overhead, eliminating a previous need to bring umbrellas or wear broad-brimmed hats. The tarp is useful to ward off both the searing afternoon sun, which feels particularly powerful at the city's high altitude, and the torrential rains that quickly soak through clothing in the afternoon showers of the rainy season.

Many of the people who participate in Mexico City's punk scene also participate in markets like these, or even more informal ones, during the weekday. Street vending is for some their primary occupation, or it's one among several

FIGURE P.2. A panoramic view of Mexico City from
the south. Photo by Yaz "Punk" Núñez.

jobs that they do to get by. My friends in the punk scene like the Chopo market because it can be more lucrative than other tianguis, even if it's also more restrictive and, some allege, more disorganized. However, not only must people who participate in Mexico City's punk scene hustle to get by in a difficult economy, but they also disapprove of the economic system, with most identifying as anarchists and anti-capitalists.

And yet the Chopo is not just a hustle, even if a pervasive punk cynicism may sometimes make it seem so. Browse the merchandise available for sale here in the Espacio Anarcopunk, and you'll find many affordable used books, documentaries on DVD, fanzines, and, of course, recordings of punk, both of local and international bands on CD, sometimes on cassette, and occasionally on vinyl. Though an item of dress may find its way into the mix—patches for sewing onto clothes are the most popular, though maybe a set of spikes for a jacket or a belt might appear—there is generally less *cháchara* (junk) than you'll find in the rest of the market. Many people who participate in the punk scene like to make use of the knowledge they've worked hard to gather, trying to do good as they get by, sharing what they believe to be important information through the stuff they sell or trade. This forms part of a belief enacted through a constellation of practices referred to as *autogestión*, an important term in local leftist politics that signifies—for lack of a better English-language term—"self-management."[3]

One day in the Chopo market, I received a welcome lesson on the term *auto-gestión* when someone handed me a small pamphlet. The tiny, black-and-white photocopied booklet, measuring about a quarter of a book page with only four pages of text, has no overtly punk imagery. Titled "Autogestion [*sic*]: Un proyecto de practica cotidiana" (Autogestion [*sic*]: A project of everyday practice), the pamphlet attempts to lay out a working definition of autogestión as the "functional mechanism" of anarchism:

> We understand as autogestión all the options for social and community self-organization, where the community itself, whether it be syndical, cooperative, campesinos [farmworkers], women, retired people, marginalized people, or whatever other oppressed social sector in our society takes in its own hands the task of assuring its necessities.

The pamphlet's anonymous authors, identified only as members of the collective organization Acción Libertaria (Libertarian Action), then continue on to group several key practices within the rubric of autogestión, including direct democracy, direct action, mutual aid, outreach, and training.[4] According to members of the collective—a locally preferred form of social organization—tens of thousands of these pamphlets have been freely distributed over the years since it was first produced in the early 1990s, educating many about how to understand the all-important concept of autogestión in local anarchist thought. Some anarchists insist that anarchism is about order, not chaos. It's about imagining new, better ways to organize social and political life. The practices of autogestión are the tools for preparing individuals and, through them, groups of people to do that everyday, painstaking reorganizational work.

This emphasis on everyday effort might come as a surprise for people who are unaware of anarchism as a diverse body of political thought and practice—who, moreover, tend to associate "anarchy" with chaos or violent revolution, a questionable popular usage of the term. An old chestnut in local and global anarchist political thought and writing is encapsulated in the phrase "propaganda of the deed," highlighting an emphasis on action and a fundamental belief in the inseparability of theory and practice.[5] While in recent decades, the international news media has contributed to stereotypes that link anarchist action with spectacular acts, like black blocs and Antifa tactics, the slow, mundane, uncertain processes of autogestión count as propaganda of the deed.[6] As much as anarchism is about

FIGURE P.3. Pamphlet defining *autogestión*, created by the collective Acción Libertaria with the Biblioteca Social Reconstruir. Photo by Zack Sievers.

taking action, this may include unremarkable but important everyday actions, including generating new thought: stimulating new ideas, nurturing them into life.

An attitude shaped by the practices of autogestión was evident even on my first visit to the Espacio Anarcopunk. Here, vendors pressed me to take, not buy, material: a free broadsheet, fliers for punk shows, and a DVD documentary that I was exhorted to watch and return another week. In fact, the broadsheet, titled *La revancha del ahuizote* (The revenge of the ahuizote, from the *ahuizotl*, a fierce mythological creature from Mexica lore), should have been available for *coóperación voluntaria*, for whatever contribution I wanted to make. However, in this case, the paper and other materials were simply pressed on me, without anyone asking for a donation.

Despite having no previous experience with punk scenes in Mexico or elsewhere, I was intrigued enough to keep going back to the Espacio Anarcopunk, initially with the pretense that I needed to return the DVD. But really, I wanted to learn more about how people in the local punk scene imagined the link between their music and their politics. Having written previously about experimentalism in music, performance art, and education, I was soon fascinated by how local punk-scene participants invoked autogestión within and beyond the context of musical performance, framing it in a way that resonated with my love for experimental practice while emphasizing its more overtly political ends. I had also done previous fieldwork with Mexican migrant communities, and indeed had grown up in and around a port city in the United States with a rich history of migration, fostering my deep interest in the entanglements of class, gender, migration, and acculturation. These themes, combined with my healthy appreciation for unusual and strident sounds, coalesced in Mexico City's punk scene. Soon, I was going to punk shows, attending meetings, tagging along at protests, reading at *fanzinotecas* (libraries of zines), checking out squats, and otherwise learning about Mexico City's punk scene, about Mexican politics through my new friends' eyes, about anarchism, and many other topics of significance to them—and, increasingly, to me.[7]

Emphasizing the importance of the small document on autogestión in my experience, I call it a "seed," invoking a powerful body of metaphors—*semillas* (seeds), *sembrar* (to sow), and the *sembrador* (the sower)—that circulates in Mexico City's punk scene, as well as among leftists and anarchists in Mexico and in Latin America more broadly. I use the seed metaphor to highlight key events, objects, sounds, or interactions that contributed greatly to my learning. Still, despite many pleasant experiences I had during my ethnography, the seeds I provide from my time in Mexico City's punk scene are not soft, fluffy spores alighting peacefully on the rich loam of consciousness. Instead, many have impenetrably hard shells, burrs, and sharp edges. They may have arrived in the form of distorted, powerful, high-decibel sounds. Or perhaps they were communicated through disturbing, confrontational, crude black-and-white imagery. Some seeds may be intense, brusque, even aggressive interpersonal encounters. Participants in the punk scene are not necessarily the easiest people to get to know. And often, seeds in Mexico City's punk scene are sown with *rabia*, with the rage of a consciousness awakened to myriad violations of social justice, by sowers who may willfully attempt to provoke an intensity of anger equal to their own. In the process, some speak of simultaneously igniting the love of friendship and solidarity, tying together *amor y rabia*: love and rage.

This is a tough kind of love. And sometimes, participants in the punk scene appear to forget about the love side of the amor-y-rabia equation, letting their anger flame out of control. Malicious gossip in the scene is rampant. Feuds between collectives and individuals are common. Punk shows and sleepy hangouts alike become theaters for street fighting. But how can people successfully combine a feeling as potentially destructive as rage with a broad, generous love that seeks to create a new model of liberty for all people? How should they collectively create better, more equitable relationships among themselves? This is particularly hard to imagine in the context of Mexico City today, still struggling with the legacy of colonialism and decades of ruinous neoliberal economic policies. Add to those problems the ravages of emigration and the so-called "drug war" on the fabric of Mexican society everywhere.

But what is important is their aspiration to radical change, which entails a significant amount of discussion, experiment, and debate. In this, they are inspired not only by witnessing struggles of punk-scene participants in other parts of the world but also by global and local histories of anarchist politics and by their own activity in various social networks, including social movement networks. The notion that feelings of love and rage together may motivate meaningful, grassroots political action is not unique to Mexico City's punk scene. It's an idea that has been embraced by various activists addressing diverse causes globally, as well as by anarchists in Mexico City specifically.[8] But in Mexico City's punk scene, this key pairing is understood to occur at least in part through participation in punk music and performance. Punk aesthetics and practices are fundamental aspects of the autogestión that occurs in Mexico City's punk scene, stimulating affective practices and networking behaviors that may also extend beyond it.

In this book, I reimagine the metaphor of sowing as a method for ethnographic writing, symbolizing the intense learning process I underwent while spending time in Mexico City's punk scene. Highlighting the key anecdotes and other materials that germinated my process of understanding, in each chapter I offer seeds to guide the discussion, delving into their genetic material while also providing further support as to why they have the power to propagate new ways of thinking. Though the metaphor of sowing is unavoidably pastoral, I emphasize the grit that is the medium for germination, the uncertainty of that process, and the unflagging care needed to realize it.

I also recognize and value the contradictions within this metaphor, tensions that were less apparent in the conversations of my punk-scene friends. Among other things, the seed metaphor reproduces a traditionally gendered view of the learning process, with a sower, usually imagined as a male farmer, tilling ready, if inert and passive, soil.[9] The figure of the sembrador is also typically a solitary one, reinscribing not only conventional binaries between masculine activity and feminine passivity but also the hierarchical relationships of patriarchy. A common complaint among friends in the punk scene is that any one person is attempting to *protagonizarse*—to paint himself as the protagonist of what is actu-

FIGURE P.4. Print titled "Sembrador" (from the series *Testimonio de Guatemala*), representing the soil as an active partner in the learning process. Linocut (30 × 40.3 cm.) by Arturo García Bustos, 1952. Courtesy of Rina Alegría García Lazo.

ally a shared story. Yet the rugged individual sembrador, no matter how humble a peasant figure he may appear, is still a hero of sorts. As I have indicated, there are many contradictions at work in Mexico City's punk scene. The hierarchical, gendered nature of the seed metaphor is entirely of a piece with these dynamics.

However, the embrace of autogestión also requires that people see themselves as active learners, contradicting the passivity inherent in the seed-and-soil metaphor. While providing the high points of my ethnographic learning process, I intend that the "seeds" will also serve as a consistent, if subtly ironic, reminder of the contested nature of punk-scene sociability. And to begin, I flip the script to play the *sembradora* myself, recalling the key moments, objects, and sounds that I shared with participants in Mexico City's punk scene as they worked hard, in places directly understood as informal workplaces like tianguis, but also in punk shows, in collective organizations, and in various other attempts to power the processes of autogestión.

ONE

Sowing

SEED: DEFINING PUNK

One day in March 2009, I tagged along with a group of punk-scene participants as they set out to panhandle on a Saturday evening at the Glorieta de Insurgentes, a popular reunion point encircling a metro station along the city's pink subway line, which threads through some of the more upscale neighborhoods in the city. As it turned out, my companions didn't seem too serious about accumulating spare change. Instead, they asked for handouts as a tactic to approach people their age perceived to be better off than they were, initiating teasing banter with them as the idle evening's entertainment.

Not that long before, Mexico's "punks" had been featured in a series of negative national and international news stories that accused them of aggressions against a new subcultural figure: the "emo." Supposedly, emos were highly sensitive teenaged kids who listened to a particularly emotional strain of post-punk and blurred gender norms with their androgynous appearance. It wasn't long after we boarded a crowded bus en route to the metro station that talk shifted to the controversy. "Rockers" might have been among the aggressors, but not real punks, my friends said. Someone laughingly pushed my hair over my eyes to see if I might be harboring secret emo tendencies. Another mockingly checked the insides of my wrists and arms for signs of cutting, self-harm supposedly another potential sign that I might be an emo.

But as the bus rolled slowly along, the conversation shifted to who "punks" were. I had the sense that the loud conversation was for my benefit, but also for the benefit of the other passengers. Many, I noted, eyed my friends with visible unease while we claimed our seats. The discussion became particularly heated when the topic turned to the hated term "urban tribes," coined by French sociologist Michel Maffesoli and adopted by several academics and journalists who wrote about the "punk-versus-emo" story. As we descended from the bus, one friend summarized his opinion: "Punk is a movement, or maybe a counterculture. Anything but a fucking tribe." Underscoring their ridicule of the term, another friend told us to don our feathers and then began to hop and twirl down the sidewalk, whooping and dancing like 1940s Warner Brothers cartoon representations of Native Americans.

NETWORKS

Is punk a social movement? In fact, the assertion can prompt scornful rejections from some who participate in Mexico City's scene. But it was an idea voiced affirmatively often enough to make me take note.[1] Others validated the idea that the punk scene was part of a larger counterculture, recommending that I read José Agustín (2008), a local author who also presents this perspective. By negating that "punks" were members of an urban tribe and proposing alternatives, my companions confirmed that they're well aware of all the theorizing out there about subcultures, scenes, and other terms that intersect variously with youth culture studies and, more recently, an emerging "punk studies." People I encountered debate and often reject most of these terms, except for "scene," because they themselves refer to *la escena punk*. In accordance with that local preference, as well as with many scholars, I also adopt the term "scene" (O'Connor 2002; Bennett and Kahn-Harris 2004; Bennett and Peterson 2004; Baulch 2007; Taylor 2012). However, as some scholars have noted, punk may best be described as a field, drawing upon Pierre Bourdieu for a useful model, which allows for the coexistence of various types of practices within the field while also mapping nicely onto "scene," a more colloquial term embraced by people in punk scenes globally (O'Connor 2016; Dunn 2016).

In addition to field and scene terminology, I also embrace the concept of the network to describe punk in Mexico City, a term that brings attention to the interpersonal and inter-group relationships that are actively networked both within and beyond the punk scene itself. Through the idea of the network, I gesture to the activities that link people not just locally but transnationally, and highlight the work involved in creating and sustaining these many relationships. As Bruno Latour (2007, 143) has pointed out with his wistful neologism the "work-net," always emergent, unstable networks require constant care in their never-ending construction.[2] The highly visible, historiographical quirk of fixation on the question of what punk is among scholars, journalists, and others helps fuel debate and dissent in Mexico City, as many scene participants feel compelled to weigh in and define themselves.

Certainly, Mexico City's punk scene—as a scene, a field, and a point along various intersecting networks—is a setting for an affectively charged, sometimes fractious series of interactions. The disparities in ideas, experiences, and practices among local punk-scene participants provide material for a related discourse over what it means to be punk, including disagreements about best listening practices and musical preferences, dress and grooming styles, political opinions, degrees of involvement with social justice issues, forms and frequency of drug-taking, involvement with friendship groups, political organizations, or social collectives, type of work or study one pursues, and more. But there are also points of commonality that link people who participate in the local scene. In general, participants tend to be from more economically marginalized parts of the city, especially the metropolitan zones that ring the central core of Mexico City proper (Castillo Berthier 2004; Feixa 2006; Agustín 2008; Poma and Gravante 2016).

One overlapping network of people to whom punk-scene participants often feel especially connected is called *la banda*, a term that denotes a certain solidarity among economically marginalized young people in the city broadly—a designation I'll explore more fully in chapter 3, contrasting it with *fresas* (literally "strawberries"). This second term is a disparaging name for more economically privileged people, like those who might pass through the Glorieta de Insurgentes on a Saturday night, headed for more middle-class entertainments like movies, clubs, or restaurants (Valenzuela 1998; Urteaga Castro-Pozo 1998; Castillo Berthier 2004).

In addition to sharing a sense of economic precarity, punk-scene participants are also largely alike in sex and gender identity, being overwhelmingly male, straight, and cisgender. Women have been participating in Mexico City's punk scene since it began, but with difficulty and in far smaller numbers (Urteaga Castro-Pozo 1998; Estrada and Palacios 2004). Individuals who openly identified as members of the LGBTQ+ community were rarer still during my initial time in the city, though during later visits tolerance for diverse sexualities and gender identities seemed to be increasing, partly through the influence of Martín Crudo (also known as Martín Sorrondeguy), who has been touring in Mexico since the 1990s as vocalist of Los Crudos, a Latinx punk band renowned worldwide. More recently, he has appeared in Mexico City with his band Limp Wrist, which draws attention to the presence of LGBTQ+ issues via punk performance (Mondini 2016).

Over the course of over ten years of fieldwork, I met participants in the punk scene who ranged in age from their late teens to their fifties, making it clear that age is not necessarily a unifying characteristic among those who comprise Mexico City's punk scene. In my early days, street socializing was an effective strategy to meet many new people. Then, I encountered more very young people than I would later, when I began to spend less time at the Chopo and in street sociability, instead privileging collectives, clubs, tianguis, and other spaces where people long associated with the punk scene spent significant time. In fact, it became increasingly apparent over the years that my own closest collaborators in the punk scene were my age-mates, men and women who, like me, were in their late twenties and early thirties when my fieldwork began, and in their late thirties and early forties at the time of this writing. As older scene participants, many had been able to accumulate greater economic and cultural capital than younger participants, amassing not only longer memory and deeper experience but also better gear and burnished reputations, in some cases. Though much writing on punk continues to be framed by youth culture studies, my own experience accords with scholarship emphasizing that punk scenes are not dominated by the very young (Muggleton and Wienzierl 2003; Bennett 2006; Bennett and Taylor 2012; Marciniak 2015a; Poma and Gravante 2016; Magaña 2020).

Subtler negotiations around local "punk" identities filter through musical preferences and stylistic choices. The fact that punk went underground and hardcore in the 1980s (see chapter 3) did not eradicate all of its original punk rock meanings, practices, sounds, and symbols. Over the course of the 1980s and to the present, metal has become an influential body of sounds and practices within the punk scene as well, adding more layers of aesthetic and political possibilities (Kahn-Harris 2007; Waksman 2009; Wallach et al. 2011; Castillo Bernal 2015).

To some extent, all participants in the punk scene listen to one another's music, but a preference for one subgenre or another is a factor that shapes an individual's participation. The continued vibrancy and relevance of 1970s punk

FIGURE 1.1. Old-school punk style in the *centro histórico* during the 2019 march in remembrance of the massacre of October 2, 1968. Photo by Yaz "Punk" Núñez.

rock and hardcore punk is especially evident among lesser-privileged participants in Mexico City's punk scene, who often live far out in the metropolitan zone and survive on the most precarious kinds of informal labor, while an interest in more overt metal-punk crossover styles may signify someone who has a somewhat higher class positioning. Those who prefer newer, metal-punk crossover aesthetics are often better linked to the global punk scene, helping to sponsor do-it-yourself tours by foreign musical guests. On the other hand, those who adhere to an older punk-rock aesthetic, "destroy punks" or "rockers," may be frowned upon for their supposedly self-destructive practices, viewed as holdovers from the early years in the 1970s and 1980s, when Mexico City's rock and punk scenes struggled to survive in the face of intense government and cultural repression.[3] Meanwhile, some people have referred to more politically conscious "punks" as "anarcopunks" or "radicals," which may include those who listen to hardcore exclusively or people who like metal-inflected subgenres as well.[4]

These categories of "rockers" and "destroy punks" versus "anarcopunks" and "radicals" not only attempt to delineate a divide between those who engage with music for hedonistic pleasure and those who use it as a political tool, but they also serve to emphasize the contested nature of anarchist politics among those who consider themselves to be politically aware and active. Recent developments in social movement organization and its intersections with certain anarchist practices are more attractive to some participants than others, who cling to older models of anarchism rooted in other local traditions. In contemporary Mexico, as well as globally, there are many models and many ways to think about the nature and relevance of social justice organizing, including a number of anarchist collectives in Mexico City that interface to greater and lesser extents with the punk scene.

Such political ambiguity also helps to fuel tensions within the punk scene and thus the necessary debates around what punk is and who gets to define it. While some participants decry this constant tension, attempting to mediate it explicitly, I argue that for those who engage in more overt political activity and even for those who talk more about politics than engage in any real action, the networked dispersal of the scene can make it easier to fly under the radar, carrying out individual projects in relative peace. Nevertheless, various authors have noticed "punk" participation in social movement activity in Mexico, with G. M. Joseph and Jürgen Buchenau writing:

> Like the EZLN, the APPO (Assemblea Popular de los Pueblos de Oaxaca) initially included members of the old Marxist Left, who eschewed a vanguardist strategy; representatives of new social movements (e.g., women, students, neighborhood and environmental groups) who opposed neoliberalism; broad support from the state's Indigenous communities; and a sprinkling of countercultural and fringe elements (like anarchopunks) [sic]. (2013, 210)[5]

Throughout this book, I choose not to call people "punks" at all. Though many of the people I know in Mexico City's punk scene do identify as such, I also know many who reject the term, including several people who went fairly regularly to punk shows, participated in anarchist collectives, and counted "punks" among their own tight-knit social circles. For some, rejecting the term "punk" means rejecting identifying labels. Others deny the classification because they believe that the word is an ugly one, grounded in the continuing repression of young people. Some are skeptical about the aggressions that occur within the punk scene itself and want to distance themselves from them. Most of my women friends who are involved in the scene do not choose to call themselves punk, despite attending plenty of shows and other events.

Likewise, I do not identify as "punk." Several scholarly works on punk have been written by people who identify as punk themselves, some of them even de-

FIGURE 1.2. An "anti-monument" to the 43 disappeared students
from Ayotzinapa, created and installed by their families in the Paseo de la Reforma
near the city center. Photo by Yaz "Punk" Núñez.

scribing themselves as "punkademics" (Furness 2012; Greene 2012, 2016; Bestley
et al. 2019). Emphasizing their personal histories in punk scenes and sometimes
adopting a brusque, profanity-laced writing style meant to evoke punk on the
page, some of these authors use such tactics to frame their research as authentic,
without necessarily providing much discussion about the challenges of navigating the insider-outsider relationships of a "native" ethnographer or an interested
cultural studies writer. In contrast, I began with no deep-seated feelings about
punk as music or as a lifestyle. Despite the term's inelegance, I prefer to call
everyone "punk-scene participants," a descriptor that happens to fit me as well.[6]
Given the fact that this book is also about the importance of affective ties like
love and rage, I also embrace the term "friend" to refer to people I came to know
in the punk scene, rejecting more common, if contested, ethnographic terms like
"interlocutor" or "collaborator" (Rohrer 2014; Carspecken 2018).

Sowing **17**

Among the many forms of difference animating contentions about what punk is, what it means to live a punk lifestyle, and who belongs to the local punk scene, I next describe one commonality: the city itself, with its distinctive pleasures and its profound challenges for all who live and work there.

MONSTER CITY

They call it "el DeFectuoso," the defective one.

Of the several ways that Mexico City residents have nicknamed their city, "el DeFectuoso" attempts to succinctly communicate the intense and frequently difficult quality of life in the megalopolis. More cynically than lovingly bestowed, the nickname provides an alternative gloss on the bland and innocuous "D.F.," short for the Distrito Federal, formerly the large, sixteen-borough heart of the immense city, the seat of Mexico's federal government. The term often has been used to underscore general, systemic city problems from traffic to state corruption, as well as trying everyday encounters with overpopulation, water shortages, air pollution, violence, and petty crime. The name speaks residents' dismay at their often frustrating environment, and their resignation. "Así es" (So it is), people sigh. For some, there is a hint of pride in their resilience, a sardonic satisfaction that they can get by in a city also frequently called *ciudad monstruo* (monster city), not just for its monstrous, chaotic sprawl but also for its often brutal history, still visible and visceral (Ross 2009; Villoro 2021).

At its heart, the Metropolitan Cathedral tilts crazily over the ruins of the Templo Mayor, cheek by jowl with the National Palace, formerly the home of Moctezuma, then Hernán Cortés, and now the symbolic seat of Mexico's executive power. All of these landmarks line the massive space of the Zócalo, the gigantic public plaza where demonstrators frequently gather and agitate against a paternalistic and often repressive government—a symptom, some argue, of a "violent democracy," in which electoral reforms have not led to the calm, regular civic life associated with such systems by political scientists.[7] In the densely populated capital, many residents have hardened themselves to the myriad of trying elements that shape their lives, seeing each problem as intertwined with the snarled fabric of a defective city perpetually knit by conflict and conquest.

On January 20, 2016, however, the Distrito Federal began to disappear. Officially, this was an administrative move designed to further distance the city from the federal government, reorganizing local government and possibly granting it more autonomy.[8] Though by 2018 the Distrito Federal became fully obsolete, that process did not alter the enormity of Mexico City's area and population when considered in their traditional totality, including its vast metropolitan zone that stretches into two neighboring states. Mexico City has long been the biggest urban area in the nation—and, by some measurements, among the three biggest cities in the world—while also being the hub of the federal government. Like many such cities globally, this entanglement has caused perks and problems for residents, the problems exacerbated by the city's historic lack of independence from the national government. After all, it was not until 1997 that the mayor of Mexico City was elected rather than appointed by the president, a change finally accomplished in the waning years of total PRI dominance of the nation's politics.[9] In 2016, Mexico City—as the metropolis has long been known to the rest of the world—officially became Mexico City to Mexicans themselves, or la Ciudad de México, abbreviated with a vaguely Roman numerical cool as CD.MX.

Arguably, this graphic hipness may be one reason for the name change: to rebrand Mexico City at home as well as on the international stage. Since the mid-twentieth century, Mexico City has been anxious to assert itself as a cosmopolitan global capital on par with New York, Paris, Tokyo, and other grand cities of international cultural importance. Mexico City's lust for recognition has been the impetus for several monumental civic projects in recent decades, though many see such efforts as attempts at gentrification and greater control over the population. Rubén Gallo frames civic projects carried out in recent decades as a desire to curtail the messy vibrancy of Mexico City—"unplanned, chaotic, crowded, and as heterogenous as it gets"—into a so-called "generic city": uniform, modern, with the clean lines and, importantly, the major expressways that replace the street, the plaza, and other civic spaces in an effort to contain an exuberant and potentially rebellious public.[10] As such, development projects often repeat past failures to address the city's most pressing needs at crucial periods (Davis 1994, 2009).

In the middle of the twentieth century, Mexico City's population and size expanded exponentially as migrants poured in from the countryside, many hoping to find work in the rapidly modernizing capital. The quick expansion of the city resulted in an under-planned, overstretched urban area, in which city planners attempted to confront the enormous influx of new arrivals into their industrializing city with a toolbox inspired by European modernists like Le Corbusier, whose urban planning strategies were no match for the social conditions playing out half a world away.[11] As in other Latin American nations, Mexico City's outskirts were settled in part through "land invasion" by migrants from the countryside who slowly built up their own neighborhoods in unused land ringing the urban centers.[12]

While shantytowns began to form in and around the nucleus of the Distrito Federal in the 1960s due to this migration, a series of economic crises in the 1970s and 1980s contributed to increasing poverty and wealth disparity in the capital. Around the same time as another devastating financial crisis in 1994, which drastically devalued the peso, driving down the buying power of wages and increasing foreign debt and dependency, renowned urban planning scholar Diane E. Davis summarized the city's situation: "Glorious Mexico City, once known as the city of palaces, is now gasping for breath in a sea of people, poverty, and pollution" (1994, 1).

Though there are so-called *colonias populares* (popular neighborhoods, a euphemism for less economically privileged neighborhoods) in the city center, various forms of inequity play out most visibly between the center and the metropolitan zone. This is the enormous area most densely and haphazardly occupied by waves of migrants to the city relocating from rural Mexico in search of work and opportunity, the area rarely on tourist itineraries, having a much rougher and less well-maintained appearance that is markedly different from the impressive architecture, broad thoroughfares, and cultural landmarks comprising the *centro histórico*.

In most of my time in Mexico City, I lived in "popular neighborhoods" in the Distrito Federal, though my interests in the punk scene often took me into the metropolitan zone, to the municipalities of Tlalnepantla, Nezahualcóyotl, and especially Ecatepec. While I spent a great deal of time in those areas, friends in the punk scene and beyond it actively discouraged me from attempting to live there. As a light-skinned person, I might blend in a bit in the wealthier parts of the city, but my appearance immediately marked me as a foreigner to most observers in the metropolitan zone—a legacy of class and colorism that directly impact the city's geography and demography. This hyper-visibility in the outskirts of the city made me vulnerable to unwanted attention and potentially to an increased threat of robbery, assault, or abduction.

On long journeys from my relatively privileged neighborhoods in the city center to the metropolitan zone, I became familiar with the many differences that played out between these areas in what are virtually two versions of Mexico City. The differences were evident in the look of them, in the simple cinder-block buildings and dry, dusty streets of the metropolitan zone, where the endemic drought that plagues the city often hits hardest.[13] During the peak of severe winter

FIGURE 1.3. A view of Colonia La Raza in the Azcapotzalco municipality of Mexico City. Photo by Yaz "Punk" Núñez.

FIGURE 1.4. A view of Colonia Pantitlán in the Iztacalco municipality of Mexico City. Photo by Yaz "Punk" Núñez.

droughts, water was still available in my central neighborhood, while in some of the city's outer regions, those who had taps saw them run dry. Merchants inflated prices on bottled water, and there were fights greeting the arrival of water trucks. And yet the rainy season poses its own challenges for people in the outskirts of the megalopolis. When the heavy rains come in the summer months, the streets in the historic district might flood a bit, but that floodwater quickly recedes rather than rising and rising until it inundates homes and ruins property, as it too often does in places like Ecatepec, a suburb nicknamed "Ecatepunk" for the many punk musicians and fans who live and gather there.

Other infrastructural improvements happened at a pace vastly different in the city's center versus its outskirts. Over the course of my years in Mexico City, the local government slowly began to repair worn-out pavement and install ramps on sidewalks to make them accessible in my working-class neighborhood, while in the metropolitan zone, they remained poorly maintained, with gaping holes, dangling power lines, and ripe-smelling trash heaps.[14] When the government forcefully took over the city's electrical supplier, wresting it from the control of the Sindicato Mexicano de Electricistas in a highly controversial move that many read as union busting, my neighborhood experienced short, hours-long outages, compared to the days-long blackouts reported elsewhere. Armed hold-ups on public buses were also fairly routine in the metropolitan zone and far less frequent in the central part of the city.

Security measures were generally far more evident in the Federal District than in the metropolitan zone, accomplished with the state's heavy hand. Such tactics—such as the installation of thousands of security cameras in upscale parts of the city, and a large, highly visible, and highly armed police and military presence—provide a daily, chilling reminder of the violence of contemporary Mexican life. Many Mexico City residents were on edge during my early fieldwork and would become more so during my stay in the city, as meanwhile the so-called "drug war" escalated across the country. The Distrito Federal briefly became known as a haven away from the violence of then-president Felipe Calderón's militarization of the drug trafficking conflict. For a time, reports circulated that some Mexicans living in communities plagued by cartel violence were moving to Mexico City, a place that had long been feared for its own high levels of violent crime and delinquency (Davis 2010).

Despite the city's somewhat improved reputation, grisly crimes related to drug trafficking did occur there over the course of my stay, prompting fears that it was only a matter of time before a full-blown "war on drugs" hit the capital. During

FIGURE 1.5. Trash heap with doll. Photo by Yaz "Punk" Núñez.

my fieldwork period, these fears were also fueled by the noticeable increase of violent cartel-related activity in formerly tranquil places, from tourist zones like Acapulco to the bustling metropolis of Guadalajara. Additionally, in the city's metropolitan zone, municipalities like Ecatepec became some of the most dangerous places for young women in the country, with rates of *feminicidios* (femicides, the targeted and usually unpunished murder of women and girls) rivaling those of the more infamous Ciudad Juárez (González Rodríguez 2012). Neither was Mexico City a safe place for journalists.[15] The day before my return to Mexico City in 2015, photojournalist Rubén Espinosa and four companions were tortured then shot to death in the middle-class Navarte neighborhood. As I prepared for another trip, in July 2017 a drug kingpin was killed in Tlahuac, one of the city's outer delegations, while in August, at a bar in the city's center, a shoot-out occurred, with most people interpreting it as an episode of cartel-related violence.

Though city residents may have worried about the possibility of various types of crime and violence, their days were always bustling with activity, creating an exciting, dense sonic and visual environment. Music wafted out of small restaurants and shops and thumped from passing cars and microbuses. Food carts crowded the streets and hungry customers huddled around, chewing and chattering. Street vendors called out their wares (Rasmussen 2018), while *tortillerías* contributed the distinctive creaking of their machinery, and butcher's shops

FIGURE 1.6. Sharply dressed men in an arcade in the neighborhood called La Ronda. Photo by Yaz "Punk" Núñez.

filled the air with the clang of cleavers and the crackling of boiling oil. Tamale sellers circled on bicycle carts, their small speakers playing an iconic recording used all over the city, featuring a singsong, nasal promise of delicious Oaxacan-style tamales. Tractor-trailers thundered by at all hours or idled in the street. Men selling tanks of cooking fuel roamed the streets ahead of heavily stocked trucks, bawling out "Gas! Ga-aas!" In the late afternoons, enormous crowds of teenaged schoolchildren congregated on street corners, testing out the volume and importance of their voices.

But apart from the occasional street food vendor, often located near major metro stations, the streets became dark and eerily still at night. As some of my own friends counseled me, staying home after dusk was one of a many-pronged approach that city residents took to avoid personal encounters with the insecurity and violence that pervaded the city. Renowned Mexican author Paco Ignacio Taibo II also notes the contrast between city life in day and night:

> I've said many times that statistics reveal a surprising city: one that has more movie theaters than Paris, more abortions than London, more universities than New York. Where nighttime has become sparse, desolate, the kingdom of only a few. Where violence rules, corners us, silences us into a kind of autism. Shuts us in our bedrooms with the TV on, creates that terrible circle of solitude where no one can depend on anyone but themselves.[16]

While participants in Mexico City's punk scene are highly impacted and so highly aware of the difficulties of city life, particularly in its metropolitan zone, many would emphatically deny Taibo's conclusion. In fact, as I will describe, the punk scene functions in part as a training ground that helps its participants confront these challenging realities, encouraging them not to isolate themselves but ideally to draw together to provide for their own needs when the government neglects or represses them, or when criminal groups attempt to exploit them.

SEED: NO ONE TO CALL

On the night of the U.S. presidential elections in 2008, some local neighborhood friends invited me to a little storefront café where we often met, to watch the returns together. Compelled by the activity, we ignored the lateness of the hour and even some faint popping sounds, which seemed to come from several blocks over.

> Suddenly, two men descended into our space, one aiming a gun at us, and both barking orders to lower our eyes and hand over our things. Once they ran off, one friend set out on foot, following their path, hoping to find what they would believe useless: discarded keys, backpacks, and empty wallets. Meanwhile, the owner of the café shakily lowered the metal curtain that provided security for the space, enclosing us. No one even mentioned calling the police.

LOVE AND RAGE IN A CLIMATE OF *DESCONFIANZA*

Most of my friends and acquaintances in Mexico City, including those who had nothing to do with the punk scene, explicitly distrusted and even hated the police. In addition to episodes of police brutality that some endured, many more had experienced their legendary corruption in the form of bribes, the famous *mordida* (bite) that often would be demanded in an encounter with the police, such as at a traffic stop. Due to elevated levels of crime and violence across Mexico City since the economic crises of the 1970s, 1980s, and 1990s, people had adjusted to a sense of insecurity in their daily lives. However, during my residence in the city—which began two years after the inauguration of President Felipe Calderón's so-called "war on drugs," a time when episodes of extreme violence were increasing exponentially all over the country—I witnessed a new twist on the mistrust of police and government, one colored by concerns about cartel violence; the availability of firearms; the militarization of Mexico's security forces; judicial corruption and criminal impunity; and the degree to which members of the federal, state, and local governments, including the police, were intertwined with the cartels.

It was commonly asserted that the "soft dictatorship" of the PRI government had managed to contain the power of the drug cartels through patterns of coexistence and cooperation with them, decades-long habits of corruption that served to keep the cartels in business, but with less need to display their power through violence. While the PRI continued to have a strong presence in the country and in specific states after the election of the PAN presidential candidate (from the right-wing Partido de Acción Nacional) to the federal government in 2006, the breakdown in the PRI's dominance and its codependence with black-market forces appeared to be at least one cause of the surge in cartel violence in the early years of my fieldwork. While we witnessed truckloads of masked, highly armed, black-clad soldiers appearing inexplicably on streets within the Distrito Federal, and machine-gun-wielding security guards patrolling everything from the ATM to the pharmacy storefront, friends also told me to beware of certain street vendors, who were believed to work for the "mafia." Punk-scene acquaintances ruefully recounted that their neighbors listened to *narcocorridos* (songs about drug trafficking) at high volume. People distrusted the government, the military, and the police; in addition, many distrusted everyday encounters with ordinary people, as it was not always certain who was involved in working for organized crime. In fact, commentators have pointed to hardscrabble economic conditions as a major reason for the power of the drug cartels across Central and North America (Gibler 2011).

Though Mexico's recent history provides a particular context for pervasive mistrust among its populations, anthropologists in other Latin American contexts have also noted similar attitudes and behaviors among their interlocutors, especially in urban areas. Daniel M. Goldstein has theorized *desconfianza*, a generalized mistrust that he encountered among residents of Cochabamba, Bolivia, where migrants from the country's rural altiplano settled in unused outer zones of the city. Such new arrivals frequently were accused of violence and criminality, in addition to bearing the stigma of living in makeshift neighborhoods, many of them illegal or semi-legal land invasion settlements. According to Goldstein, residents of these *barrios*, used to being treated like criminals, learned to mistrust outsiders even if they seemed to come for ostensibly harmless reasons. For

FIGURE 1.7. Riot police on Calle 5 de Mayo in 2017. Photo by Yaz "Punk" Núñez.

example, visitors might claim to be in the neighborhood for census taking but then help implement higher taxes based on the information gathered (Goldstein 2002, 2004, 2016). On the other hand, some visitors could bring good fortune to the neighborhood, provided that they were given the correct understanding of its needs. Goldstein recounts the various ways that community leaders were at times able to attract attention from the city government or non-governmental organizations to create pilot projects in the neighborhood, programs that would help improve living conditions. Ultimately, Goldstein theorizes desconfianza as not simply a response to insecurity but also as a political stance, a shrewd, quid pro quo attitude that shaped residents' behaviors when confronted with unknown outsiders, like gringo anthropologists, whose ability to bring positive or negative attention needed to be investigated and, if possible, directed.[17]

Goldstein's experience struck many chords with my own. While I often noted the desconfianza that played out between Mexico City residents generally, that mistrust was even more marked among participants in the punk scene. Their mistrust was shaped not only by the experience of living in the metropolitan zones—many of which, like the suburbs of Cochabamba, are commonly considered to be among the most unruly, lawless parts of the city—but also by their belief in autogestión, with its concomitant desire for self-fashioning. While there were a few scene participants who were unbothered or even a bit flattered to see strangers with cameras snapping pictures of "punks" in the street, many people complained about this stereotyped attention. For some, this desconfianza was founded in an even more granular local history.

In the 1980s, academics, journalists, artists, and government representatives had become involved in the nascent punk scene, creating a particular mistrust of those who looked to extract information or cooperation from scene participants for their own, sometimes dubious, purposes (see chapter 3 for more on this). Storytelling about the history of punk in the city was risky business even for people who had been a part of the scene in previous decades (Detor Escobar and Hernández Sánchez n.d.; Detor Escobar 2016). Many of my friends had a strong sense of ownership of their images and their stories and were not pleased when people attempted to appropriate these. Desconfianza in Mexico City's punk scene, as among Cochabamba residents, is a politicized position based on the desire to shape their own self-representations to one another and to outsiders, as well as a generalized response to violence and insecurity.

Additionally, participants in Mexico City's punk scene tell of their valorization of "energy," of "rage," and of "solidarity," appreciating intense feelings that play out in many of their interpersonal exchanges, training them to enact a politics created through autogestión and embracing an aesthetics of noise, contrast, and confrontation. This was not an environment in which I could always foster marvelously intimate and cozy relationships. Even among the friendships I've developed after years of participation in Mexico City's punk scene, some of them remain prickly, on edge, prone to teaching me more through discomfort, breakdowns in communication, disagreements, evasions, and even outright conflict than through harmonious friendships and direct participation in my research.

Certainly, I never experienced the kinds of warm, magical moments that some ethnomusicologists mark as pivotal arrival points in their research, when friendships honed through musical performance deepen the ethnographer's knowledge and make intellectual goals—and even recording equipment—invisible.[18] Despite being a highly trained and versatile musician, I didn't play music with my new friends and cannot lay claim to the kind of authority that musical integration might lend me.[19] Instead, my experience, unfolding in the context of the generalized desconfianza that I witnessed, throws into relief pervasive ideas about trust and authority that lie beneath the ethnographic endeavor, particularly as it plays out among ethnomusicologists. Along with scholars like Matthew Carey, it became necessary for me to examine the assumption that trust is something that ethnographers should be seeking in the field, or could secure through musical performance, particularly in a network of fiercely anti-authoritarian people who explicitly link their musical performance to their actions as political subjects in a fraught environment.[20]

For friends in the punk scene, desconfianza lives uneasily along with scene discourse that celebrates friendship and solidarity. The processes of autogestión, however, are meant to build up not only the self but also the bonds of community. And though scene participants may privilege their discussion of politics in many cases, aesthetic practices are key to this scene sociability. In the chapters that follow, I illuminate how musical and other social practices help strengthen the bonds that fight a pervasive desconfianza, and how at times they fail.

Of course, the relationship between aesthetics and politics is a complicated one. Local punk-scene participants may have trouble keeping the love-rage duality intact, but it is in the process of autogestión—encouraged in large part through punk sounds, imagery, and practices—that they attempt to do so. Through an engagement with punk aesthetics and politics, participants fashion themselves into tough subjects who can withstand the difficulties of their environment, eyes open to all the infuriating problems that surround them.

In this account, I follow the guidance of friends in Mexico City's punk scene who frequently use the term *rabia* to discuss highly valued affects that occur during key practices around punk and its performance. This is in keeping with many previous books on punk in various global locations, which privilege the anger that scene participants experience while navigating challenging environments or that they express through contentious lyrics, purposefully crude musical aesthetics, or unusual sartorial choices. The rage that "punks" are understood to voice through their aesthetics often informs more or less critical representations of punk as resistance, rebellion, or even revolution.[21]

While recognizing the importance of rage, however, I also pay careful attention to how love and intimacy frame relationships between scene participants. In this, I follow friends in the local scene, though they don't always privilege the term *amor* (love) per se. Instead, they draw attention to the importance of their long-lived friendships, sometimes with men and women they have known since early childhood.[22] While these are often conflicted relationships, as people change but remain in the same difficult place over many years, *amistad* (friendship) is key to sociability in the punk scene and ultimately enveloped me in its complicated embrace as well.

In addition to repeatedly remarking on their strong friendship ties, scene participants maintain a long-standing, pervasive discourse about *solidaridad* (solidarity), a term that can mean anything from the strategic social cohesion among trade unions to something akin to a universal love that should ideally ground moral behavior.[23] This solidarity discourse is a key element in arguments about the politics of punk and the lifestyle that participation in the local scene demands. However, I frequently saw attempts at solidarity fail in the often-conflictive interpersonal dynamics of Mexico City's punk scene. Friendships usually lasted, though, even when they required tortured mediations of personal differences. While local punk-scene participants may aspire to solidarity among themselves and with people of other social movement networks, I believe that a more complex web of affective experience knits relationships among punk-scene participants. For me, "love" stands in for these two powerful, affectively intense types of relationships circulating within the scene: friendship and solidarity. In turn, I use love and rage as twinned concepts that together provide a lens for viewing the links between punk-as-sound and punk-as-politics.

Attempting to keep both love and rage in the picture as I describe what punk is, what it sounds and looks like in Mexico City, and what its political significance is for people who participate in the scene, I consider the razor's edge that exists between intimacy and violence. "Punks" in the city have frequently been charged with violence and disorder, even as the city itself provides many of its own forms of violence for them to endure. Participation in the punk scene trains individuals and groups to confront the violence of their environment, and that same training may be productive or counterproductive when it comes to fortifying the bonds of good feeling. Following an "affective turn" in the humanities, social sciences, and in ethnomusicology specifically, I investigate discourse about feelings that circulate in the scene, how they are prompted by sonic and other embodied experience, and how they overlap—or don't—with the kinds of states that people report feeling as part of their lives in other social and political contexts (Brennan 2004; Mazzarella 2009; Gregg and Seigworth 2010; White 2017; Hofman 2015, 2020; Graber and Sumera 2020; Gray 2021).

Ultimately, I place these conversations about love and rage in the service of an exploration of music in political subjectivity and social movement cohesion. In Mexico City's punk scene, this means engaging deeply with rich and varied histories of anarchism in the city, country, and Latin American region, as well as with punk as a global phenomenon. While some punk-scene participants around the world are interested in anarchism, its local histories are deep and distinctive, providing concepts and imagery that ground a particular intersection of punk practices with autogestión, a term that shares ground with the idea of DIY and yet is far more detailed, specific, and grounded in local anarchist histories (O'Connor 2002, 2003; Dunn 2016; Poma and Gravante 2016; Bestley et al. 2019; Greene 2016; Magaña 2020).

SEED: AN INFLUENTIAL SEMBRADOR

The sower of ideals must struggle against the masses, who are conservative, against institutions, which are likewise conservative; and alone, surrounded by the comings and goings of a herd that does not understand him, he walks through the world not hoping for any reward more than fools slapping him in the face, tyrants throwing him in jail and, at any moment, the scaffold. Yet nevertheless, as long as he can sow, sow, sow, the sower of seeds will continue sowing, sowing, sowing . . .

Mexican anarchist Ricardo Flores Magón,
"Sembrando" from Regeneración (November 5, 1910)[24]

ANARCHISM, AUTONOMY, AUTOGESTIÓN

Many of my new friends loved reading, but books in Mexico City are expensive and public lending libraries are almost nonexistent. There is a huge market for used books, particularly among street vendors and their clients, but, of course, the availability of specific titles is always a matter of luck. Online shopping was not a popular option among people I knew, as some people didn't have regular internet service. Friends complained, and I could confirm their charge over time, that titles pertaining to anarchist political history and theory were particularly hard to come by, as many were rare, out of print, or had never been printed locally. The same nineteenth- and early twentieth-century classics—by Malatesta, Tolstoy, Kropotkin, Bakunin, Emma Goldman, and Ricardo Flores Magón—seemed to circulate most prominently.[25] Autogestive organizations in the city, such as Ediciones Antorcha and Hormiga Libertaria, attempted to ameliorate the situation, creating editions of foundational texts, increasingly in online versions.[26] But for me, reading up on anarchism took time and patience and was always easiest when I could make use of my privilege of access to a vast research university library network during brief periods away from Mexico, or the ability to buy cheap books to bring back with me.

Having been told multiple times that I needed to know more about Ricardo Flores Magón, I easily acquired a compilation of his writings while in the United States, and almost immediately the metaphor of sowing leapt off the page. As I learned, Ricardo Flores Magón was a key figure in Mexican political history, having been among those who helped to precipitate the overthrow of dictator Porfirio Díaz, the act that sparked the Mexican Revolution (see Carbó Darnaculleta 1997; Gonzales 2002; Bufe and Verter 2005; MacGregor and Blanquel 2008; Joseph and Buchenau 2013; Akemi et al. 2017). A prolific author and organizer who agitated against Díaz and for worker and campesino rights in a series of political broadsheets like *Regeneración*, Flores Magón was considered a nuisance by the Mexican and u.s. governments. He was pursued on both sides of the border, repeatedly imprisoned, and eventually he died under suspicious circumstances in Leavenworth Penitentiary in Kansas in 1922. But before his ultimate exile and death, he had become an important voice, leaving behind a profound legacy and impressive body of writings, a huge influence on the tradition of anarchism in Mexico. Recognized as a key thinker in his own time, Ricardo Flores Magón created a collection of works that were published in Mexico City in two volumes under the title *Semilla libertaria* (Libertarian seed) in 1923, soon after his death.

FIGURE 1.8. The tomb of Ricardo Flores Magón in the Rotunda of Illustrious Persons, Mexico City. Photo by Yaz "Punk" Núñez.

Sowing was an important metaphor for Flores Magón because ideas and images of the land run deep in the history of political resistance in Mexico. Punk-scene participants are drawing from a long tradition when they affirm the unity of country and city dwellers in pursuit of freedom (see the lyrics to Desobediencia Civil's "Anarko Punks," cited in the prologue). This country-city collaboration was important for the initiators of the Mexican Revolution, as they participated in the slow process of organizing against and ultimately overthrowing Díaz. Then, anarchists and other revolutionaries strove to demonstrate to the workers in the cities how much they had in common with their oppressed counterparts in the countryside, uniting the anarco-syndicalism of the urban environment with something akin to an anarco-communism in the rural environment, based on the collectivist traditions of certain Indigenous populations.[27]

Land reform became one of the key issues of the Mexican Revolution and its aftermath, as the rebels not only demanded basic freedoms for all the nation's citizens but also, and importantly, agitated for the redistribution of land that had been appropriated—first by the Spanish crown and the church, then by local elites, and then by foreign businessmen with the consent of Mexico's governing class. For many, "Tierra y libertad!" (Land and liberty) became their rallying cry. Seed metaphors became popular in anarchist literature in Mexico, and the figure of Ricardo Flores Magón as sembrador remains a touchstone not only for Mexican anarchists but also for academic historians and other storytellers (Muñoz 1963; Lomnitz 2014).

This rich political history colors local punk-scene participants' claims to an anarchist politics. Many people who participate in punk scenes around the world talk about their anarchism, but the context of those claims is substantially different as they represent vastly different political systems (Wallach 2008; Marciniak 2015b; Dunn 2016; O'Connor 2016; Bestley et al. 2019; Magaña 2020). In Mexico City, the link between punk and anarchism is based on an especially deep well of traditions of anarchist thought and activity over the course of not only the country's but also the city's history. In addition to the anarchist elements that contributed to the Mexican Revolution and its aftermath, Mexico City also experienced a significant immigration of anarchist Spanish Civil War exiles in the 1930s and 1940s. In fact, Mexico was one of just a few countries that willingly offered refuge to Spanish exiles (Lida 2009; Pla Brugat 1999). Anarchism appeared to recede by midcentury, but its influence became visible once again in the social movements of the 1960s and onward (Carr 1983; Hodges 1995; Draper 2018).

Despite some populist concessions early in the twentieth century, Mexico's post-revolutionary government never did truly achieve lasting, fair land reform, nor real equity for working people, with the nation's Indigenous populations continuing to suffer disproportionately on both counts. It was this state of affairs, in addition to growing outrage over corruption and electoral fraud in the PRI, that prompted what was arguably Mexico's next revolution, the Zapatista uprising of 1994, a rebellion that also ultimately drew together people from various walks of life—not just from the countryside and the city, but from around the world. While it began as an armed insurgency, the Ejército Zapatista de Liberación Nacional (EZLN, or Zapatista Army of National Liberation) quickly morphed into a largely peaceful and extensive solidarity network through an impressive media and grassroots campaign, bringing together Mexican civil society and activists from around the globe (Vodovnik 2004; Khasnabish 2010).

Participants in Mexico City's punk scene were among the many in Mexico and elsewhere who learned from the Zapatistas; APPO-affiliated social movements in Oaxaca after 2006; activists in solidarity with the Atenco "Frente"; anti-globalization protestors; and other social movement groups in Mexico who made use of anarchist or communitarian practices, making their influences multiple as they sought to create broader solidarities with punk-scene participants and activists in other parts of the world.

Participating in Mexico City's punk scene means learning about those traditions and the ideas that created them, while also experiencing them through harsh, noisy, confrontational punk aesthetics shaped by the sounds, images, and practices of punk as an evolving global music genre as well as a local one. Ideally, it means turning oneself into the ready soil in which the seeds of such learning may grow, a more sustained and conscious process than it may seem. Along with anarchism, autogestión is a ubiquitous concept in Mexico City's punk scene, a strange word with a strange history, a blend of Latin and Greek root words, a mixture of uncertain provenance.[28]

Though the word *autogestión*, roughly translated as "self-management," shares some common ground with the Anglo term "DIY" (do-it-yourself)—a mantra familiar to punk-scene participants in many other parts of the world—it's also a term that speaks more broadly, directly engaging the history of anarchism in Mexico and encapsulating different thoughts about what it is that needs to be done and how, by people who have been oppressed by their government.[29] Alan O'Connor traced the adoption of the term "DIY" into global punk scenes over the course of the 1980s, as the music industry gave up on punk music and scene participants themselves had to learn how to make and distribute recordings. It has since acquired a broader significance, indicating a broader orientation to independence and anti-authoritarianism (O'Connor 2008; Dunn 2016; Bestley et al. 2019). The term "DIY" is used occasionally in Mexico City's punk scene, but with far less frequency than the homegrown and more richly significant term *autogestión*, which may refer to specific practices of self-management that are invoked by people outside of the punk scene as well as within it, including outreach, training, mutual aid, direct democracy, and direct action (see Figure P.3).

Of the various practices of autogestión, outreach, training, and mutual aid exercises are the most clearly expressed through events in the punk scene, including activities around musical performance. Some people may attempt to create instances of direct democracy and direct action, but these are more disputed notions that can cause heated debate, with direct democracy being particularly hard to negotiate in any context (Polletta 2002; Juris 2008; Graeber 2009). While certain punk-scene practices stimulate rabia, various experiences led me to question whether that same oppositional stance is always helpful for sustaining the love of friendship, let alone achieving the love of solidarity that aid people in pursuing practices of autogestión like direct action and direct democracy. In addition to the breakdowns in good feeling that I witnessed in my fieldwork, Maurice Rafael Magaña has noted some difficulty in accomplishing solidarity between anarcopunks and other social movement participants in his ethnography of Oaxacan social movements since 2006. A "punk" presence earned respect on the barricades that provided self-defense for protestors but was less appreciated in complex negotiations among people who had different approaches to social movement organizing (Magaña 2020, 20).

Among different organizational approaches, one increasingly prominent approach to social movement organizing in Mexico, Latin America, and beyond is called "autonomous organization" (Stahler-Sholk et al. 2014). "Autonomy" in this context refers to a certain operational freedom from the state that may be achieved when social groups work together to ensure their own needs or rights, rather than petitioning them from governments. Because the focus in this type of organization is on the community itself instead of on its exchange with the state, autonomous politics may be contrasted with a politics of protest, demand, or dissent (Shantz 2011). Its roots are intertwined with anarchist theory—whether or not groups that embrace it employ that term—and it may be imagined as a desired outcome of autogestión. Autonomous organization is not necessarily neatly opposed to more traditional forms of protest. And certainly, both forms require that people cooperate in the pursuit of common goals. Yet there is a recognition that achieving autonomy often requires a hyper-awareness of organizational processes like direct democracy, something that can feel tedious to people more accustomed to other forms of advocacy.

Like love and rage, dissent and autonomy form a useful conceptual pairing, the two terms implicated within one another, shedding light on one another even if, on the surface, they may seem to be opposed. In this book, I investigate how a "taste" for rabia reflects changing aesthetic and affective practices in the punk scene since the music's arrival in Mexico City, exploring when it does or doesn't line up with key ideas about social movement organization, themselves in a great deal of flux during these decades.[30] I explore how love can be stimulated through punk-scene practices, helping ensure solidarity and cooperation within and, ideally, beyond the punk scene. For some participants, this affective experience may involve consciously reaching toward autonomy, imagined in various ways, as they enact the processes of autogestión.

MY PUNK-SCENE PARTICIPATION

Because of the desconfianza that I recounted earlier, many people I encountered in the punk scene resisted the possibility of active participation in my ethnography—at least as I initially imagined it. No one ever suggested that I should not come and take part in punk-scene events and activities, though some people remained wary of my presence. But when I mentioned my desire to do interviews among them, some people laughed outright. Many more simply ignored me.

However, there were always people who enjoyed my company, and many became genuine friends. They and others made a habit of indirect forms of participation in my learning, giving or loaning me materials, sharing opinions about contentious issues argued in the punk scene, or pointing out events that might be of interest. People invited me on outings to learn something they found important or engaged me in debates about issues they thought I might know something about. Some would question me if I failed to turn up at an event, or if they sensed that I seemed bored or inattentive to the action around me. Ultimately, I decided not to pursue the more formal methods of a typical music ethnography, such as structured interviewing, out of respect for punk-scene participants' deep desire for self-definition, their wariness of academic, journalistic, and governmental interventions into punk-scene sociability, and their abhorrence of the hierarchies all too often reproduced by the interviewer-respondent dynamic.[31]

Participant observation was a perfectly fine practice, however, since it meant that I showed up regularly and took part in whatever was on offer. Rather than incessantly posing questions or subtly trying to direct conversations into the channels that most interested me, I hung out, tagged along, listened closely and carefully, took detailed notes at home, watched for patterns that emerged, and answered questions about my own musical preferences, my experiences as a North American in Mexico, my politics. I contributed where and how I could to the knowledge sharing that was such a key part of life in the punk scene, as well as to the intense and often conflictive sociability around me. In return, I was variously treated as a curiosity, a nuisance, an interloper, a friend, a patron, and a potential love interest as together we negotiated my relationship to the scene, a process of negotiation not dissimilar to those that integral members of Mexico City's punk scene also undergo while they constantly question and contest definitions of punk, anarchism, and more. This "deep hanging" was a way to explore alongside my new friends through a process that did not place me in the role of extracting the knowledge that I most wanted, but rather encouraged a more organic learning.[32] Because of this style of inquiry, I keep my interlocutors anonymous, using only pronouns and obscuring or changing personal details if I believe they might be of use in identifying individuals.

I obtained the seeds that germinated my own process of learning in a variety of musical and social events in various parts of the city, in fieldwork that occurred most intensively from late 2008 through 2011, when I only left the city for brief, weeks-long periods of visits to family and friends. Since then, I have returned to Mexico City for shorter periods, in the summer months of 2015, 2017, and 2018. My most intensive period of research coincided with the presidency of right-wing PAN president Felipe Calderón and his escalation of the so-called "war on drugs." This period was also difficult for coming after a particularly hopeful, fruitful period of intense activism in the punk scene and beyond—including solidarity with Atenco and anti-globalization protestors—from the mid-1990s to the middle of the first decade of the new millennium, years that ended in fierce repression in Mexico and in other places around the world. People told me repeatedly during that initial period from 2008 to 2011 that the punk scene was in decline, that events hardly occurred anymore compared to their previous frequency, that people had no loyalty to the scene anymore, that shows had become about nothing but hedonistic pleasure.[33] In this dark moment, the pitfalls of using music as a source of social cohesion were especially evident.

In later years, the scene appeared to be flourishing better and better with each visit I achieved. After several years of hearing my friends complain about the lack of spaces for punk-scene sociability and a relative decrease in activity, by 2015 the scene's energy was clearly increasing. By 2017, a veritable resurgence in scene activity—from increased musical performances, new spaces, new collectives, new fanzines, new bands, and more—was remarked upon by many. Perhaps in a parallel development, greater numbers of young people from more privileged social backgrounds had become visibly interested in punk in more recent years, resulting in new terms for them, such as "happy punk" or "hipster punk," with locations and events that more clearly catered to their tastes.

In addition to the changing social and political context in the new *sexenio*, which saw the reinstallation of the PRI in presidential power beginning just a little while after I left the country in November 2011, other aspects of my participation in the punk scene have changed.[34] For one thing, in the long arc of time since I began the project, my friends and I have all gone through momentous life changes. In our late twenties and early thirties in 2008, we were in our late thirties and early forties in 2018. The same faces are still around. But several of us have new responsibilities. Most notably, some have become parents. I published some articles and became a tenure-track professor for a time. While we sport visible signs of age, with our gray hair and the depth of the lines around our eyes, I would argue that we've collectively mellowed too. In what I'm certain is a related development, our friendships have grown richer over the years. On a return visit to the city one day in August 2017, I reminded a friend that the last time I saw him, we had argued. He disagreed with this characterization, so I rephrased. "Tuvimos una charla intensa," I said, reframing our heated exchange as an intense conversation. Yes, he assented, and then offered, "Me gustan las charlas intensas." I had to admit that I liked them too. We always have several of them—whether heated to the point of what I would call an argument or not—whenever I return.

While my first contact with the punk scene occurred in November 2008 at the Chopo market, increasingly I visited punk-scene friends at other markets as well, as they drew my attention to the importance of labor issues, inviting me to come to their workplaces, literally in the city's streets and sidewalks. Despite the survival of the Chopo as a prominent institution, finding meeting places continues to be an issue even today—though during my last period of fieldwork, there were a few clubs or cultural centers where people could go regularly for concerts or meetings. Music clubs are often in danger of closure, charged by police with disturbing the peace, improperly selling alcohol, or a whole host of other administrative problems. Indeed, there were clubs associated with punk that remained *en clausurado*, city notices taped to their doors, for large chunks of my initial period in the city. One club, however, was a regular place to find punk shows during my early years, a space then called El Clandestino, in Ecatepec.[35] Many other punk shows happened as one-offs in various locations, from clubs like El Under or El Gato Calavera, to *ocupas* (squats) like the now-defunct Chanti Ollín in the city center and Casa Naranja in Tlalnepantla, to a site loaned by Hare Krishnas in the centro histórico. More recently, a club called El Mundano opened not far from the iconic Torre Latino downtown, catering to all kinds of people but including many events of interest to the punk scene. At the time of this writing, during the coronavirus pandemic, many of the venues that had opened in recent years are now closed.

The Biblioteca Social Reconstruir remains open, however. There, having offered myself as volunteer labor several years ago, I catalogued deteriorating newspapers from the Spanish Civil War era before, just weeks later, the library was evicted from its space, only reopening in 2015.[36] I also spent time in the Auditorio "Che Guevara," a contested space on the main campus of the Universidad Nacional Autónoma de México (UNAM), which has been occupied by various people, including some with ties to the punk scene, since the university strike of 1999. In that space, I browsed an extensive collection of fanzines in its fanzinoteca, attended musical events, ate in the vegetarian dining room, attended the occasional workshop or meeting, and simply hung out socializing in front of the building as students passed, some throwing mistrustful glances in our direction.[37] As in many of the spaces I frequented, some people in these places identified as punk and some people did not. However, they were almost always reliable for finding a good handful of my new friends in the early days of my research.

Saturdays after the Chopo market were also occasions for further learning in my earliest days of fieldwork, when I did the most street socializing. Whether or not there were organized events scheduled for late Saturday afternoon or evening after the tianguis wound down, generally between four and five o'clock, the Chopo was almost always a prompt for further socializing. A few cantinas and bars on the edges of the market space do a brisk business on Saturdays from post-Chopo patronage, blaring music above the din of the tightly packed crowds and perhaps serving meager snacks to those who are lucky enough to have found unoccupied tables. Outside these establishments, legions more congregate on the street, stealthily sipping from *caguamas* (liter bottles of beer) as the police pass again and again, hard faces set and eyes glaring in an attempt to intimidate the crowd. Here, the post-Chopo population might pore over what they picked up at the market, looking at fanzines and recordings they bought or traded, or perhaps continuing with an even more informal bit of exchange. Absent the music spilling out of the Chopo's puestos, people sometimes take to musical performance themselves, aided by friends carrying guitars. These informal singing sessions developed on occasion into full-blown street sing-alongs, with a throng of people gathered around the guitarist, shouting song after well-known song into the night (see chapter 4).

Later, there could be a wide variety of other Saturday-night entertainments or, occasionally, no action at all. When we were in luck, perhaps an anarchist collective offered a lecture, followed by a party lubricated with the sale of *pulque*.[38] As I became more involved in learning about anarchism, I frequently attended lectures, parties, and other meetings created by anarchist organizations, such as those sponsored by CAMA, the Colectivo Autónomo Magonista, the Cruz Negra, or the Federación Local Libertaria, an umbrella group for several smaller anar-

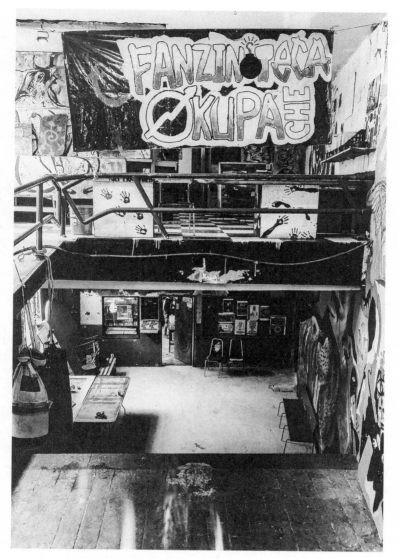

FIGURE 1.9. The vegetarian dining room and fanzinoteca at the Okupa Che, a squat on the main campus of the Universidad Nacional Autónoma de México (UNAM). Photo by Yaz "Punk" Núñez.

FIGURE 1.10. The facade of the Biblioteca Social Reconstruir. Photo by Iván Torres.

chist collectives. Various organizations in the city might offer an occasional free film screening, or perhaps another punk collective procured a projector for that purpose. Someone may have heard of a house party or an event in a club or squat that sounded appealing. Shows were often attended after a few hours' socializing in the vicinity of the Chopo, the area clearing around nine o'clock when the larger of the nearby cantinas closed, if there had not been some incident—a large-scale brawl or confrontation with the police—to cause an earlier end of service.

Saturday night's musical offerings were generally advertised as starting somewhere between four and nine o'clock, but on-time arrival is unwise, as things often didn't even begin to get underway until at least two or three hours after the promised time. If there were no shows and slim pickings generally, the post-post-Chopo crowd in my early years might have moved to the Plaza Garibaldi, famous for its wandering mariachi bands and for being the one place in the city where the public could drink openly outdoors. Since my first stay in Mexico City, however, this space has become far more decorous as the city slowly gentrified what had become a fairly seedy, rowdy, crime-prone space, repaving the plaza and erecting a chic, modern museum of tequila and mezcal with a high-priced bar on its roof. In my early experience, before the gentrification process, when public transportation became scarce past midnight, the party in the plaza might have continued until morning, something far less likely in the neatly clipped plaza with the well-heeled patrons of today.[39] Still, Saturday afternoons at the Chopo during my initial fieldwork period often lasted until or through Sunday, participants using the tianguis as the catalyst to a weekend's worth of social events.

Finally, the city itself was a great arena for learning. I spent a good deal of my fieldwork period simply roaming the streets with my various cohorts from the punk scene, hanging out in markets, plazas, and parks. Weekends were usually my busiest periods of fieldwork, beginning at the Chopo and then continuing through Sunday activities. On weekdays, I might meet up with individuals and small groups of friends to go to a lecture, a meeting, a film, or just to wander and chat a bit. I gave sporadic violin lessons to a few people who hung out to greater or lesser degrees in the punk scene, and received classes in other skills in turn, from learning how to operate a sewing machine to attending at least three different self-defense trainings. And so the big, chaotic city itself was key to my participation in the punk scene, as together my new friends and I perambulated its unruly maze of streets, plazas, and parks. Various subgenres of punk might be clamoring at the heart of these events or at the margins, but they were almost always present.

To examine scene participants' relationships with the city, with me, and with one another, I turn in the next chapter to an affect that punk-scene participants discuss as central to their experience. I link discourse about rage to equally prevalent conversations about violence that occur both within the scene and beyond it, as local "punks" have frequently been labeled as violent and angry within the national and even international media. While the process of befriending scene participants was challenging in the beginning, it was even harder for me to truly experience the stimulation of rage, a process that I also recount in this chapter as essential to my own participation in the scene, one that is particularly illustrative of the gender dynamics of my fieldwork experience.

Chapter 3: Dissent, provides detailed information about a local punk poetics of oppositionality, giving further background on the histories of punk and anarchism in Mexico City simultaneously, while demonstrating that dissent has been key to the establishment of sociability in these overlapping networks. This ordering, from "Rage" to "Dissent" also mirrors my fieldwork process, in which I engaged initially with more overt, even stereotyped, elements of punk-scene practices before learning more deeply about local histories, refining my community of collaborators, and taking on less obvious topics, such as how love can be understood to function affectively in such a contentious space.

In chapter 4: Love, I explore how participants in the punk scene attempt to rise above the violence and insecurity that impact their daily existence, using the rage they experience to create strong bonds of friendship and solidarity among themselves and, ideally, among others. Here, I consider more deeply the relevance of affective labor within the punk scene, as well as explore broad labor conditions that complicate attempts to mediate older ideas about work and how it relates to masculine belonging in Mexican society. In addition to providing a discussion of how punk performance stimulates love and rage, I unpack the concept of autogestión, detailing some ways that its processes are enacted in the context of the punk scene. Despite my focus on affective labor and how it intersects with prominent ideas about masculinity in an overwhelmingly male-dominated punk scene, in that chapter I recount key experiences with female punk-scene participants, who invited me to take part in rather than observe the activities of their collective organization, a perspective that was particularly helpful for thinking about the challenges of directly democratic practices.

In chapter 5: Autonomy, I consider the implications of the sounds, images, and practices bound up with the love and rage of Mexico City's punk scene to further address participants' politics, particularly with regard to shifts in thinking as people look to new models of organizing and social justice work, including the shaping of autonomous spaces. Throughout, I describe my own entanglements in the intensely affective practices within the scene, describing it as a noisy and conflictive but oddly nurturing space, a site of overlapping social networks, where people can be inspired to engage with various big feelings and big ideas—anarchism, autogestión, rage, solidarity, dissent, friendship, love, and autonomy—and to act on them in equally various ways.

TWO

Rage

SEED: POLICE BRUTALITY

The show at El Clandestino, a club out in the northern municipality of Ecatepec, had been a marathon event, with several bands playing loud, noisy sets. Between bands, the roar of the crowd surged forth, dense layers of screamed conversations juxtaposed with the distortions of guitars, voice, and drums. The *tocada* began in the late afternoon and its intense energy was still animating surging bodies "slamming" in the tightly cramped space close to midnight, when I decided that I had better begin my fairly long journey back to the city center.[1] Throughout the walk from the club to the metro station, the stench of so-called *aguas negras* ("black waters" from intensely polluted nearby canals) hung in the air.

At first, the metro station appeared tranquil, deserted. But as I descended the stairs to the platform, a different kind of shouting assaulted my ears. Just in front of the turnstiles, a handful of police were beating up on two teenage boys and a girl, all dressed in the style of old-school 1980s punk rock, with ripped black fabric, spikes studding and chains dangling from their clothes. One boy was taking the brunt of the beating as a particularly aggressive policeman kicked him and dug his plastic armor into the boy's ribs. The girl clung to him as best she could, trying to act as a human shield while yelling at the cop and to her friend in support. Several bystanders witnessed the beating, as no one could pass through the turnstiles to the platform. The police were evidently unconcerned about who saw it.

Finally, the aggressive policeman shoved the boy away, sending him scrambling. Regaining his balance, he clutched his ribs as the trio limped back up the stairs. I followed. As they seated themselves wearily, both boys were on the verge of tears, big dark eyes wet and lips trembling. The girl was cool and collected, however, giving me a shrewd glance. I had the impression that she was sizing me up, trying to decide of what use a concerned white foreigner could be to them.

But they didn't need my help. All at once, about ten older men from the show swept in, claiming the space with deep, loud, resonant voices and broad, confident gestures. The three teenagers ran over to tell their story, and without breaking stride the whole group charged down to the platform. This time, no one attempted to stop them.

A SPECTRUM OF VIOLENCE

The figure of the *puerco* (police officer, though literally "pig") is everywhere in Mexican punk imagery and song lyrics. In fact, it's such a ubiquitous cliché that some find it boring. I've spoken to vocalists struggling to write new songs without any invective against the police. Certainly, a widespread, targeted desconfianza, a mistrust of all police, is commonplace. Mexicans of various backgrounds share stories about their corruption and abuses of power. But for many in the punk scene, that desconfianza is a dramatic, visceral matter of physical force and power in numbers. It hinges not only on experiences of the infamous mordida—the bite, or, more literally, the bribe that some police officers expect as tributes to their power to invent or ignore small offenses like traffic violations—but also on multiple instances of police brutality. The arbitrary beating I witnessed in the metro is a shockingly common scene, and it illuminates one reason why song lyrics are not enough, why punk-scene participants also build participatory practices that stoke, rather than simply evoke, the heat of rage.

The teenagers in the metro were evidently vulnerable, not just physically but also emotionally. They had not yet learned how to avoid externalizing their feelings in the face of violence inflicted directly upon them. But also, they had made a tactical error: traveling through the city as a small, at-risk group. One of my friends, a strong and capable man in his forties who was nursing a bruised jaw after an attack in his neighborhood, informed me that not only must a man in Mexico City show that he can defend himself but that he also needs to keep tough friends close at hand, ready to help him when faced with such situations. In telling the tale, he repeatedly reported a phrase uttered by one of his aggressors, when he apparently decided it was futile to attack him: "Tiene huevos" (He has balls). Despite the fact that this phrase originated with his attacker, my friend employed the quote several times in the course of our conversation, underscoring his masculine preparedness in the face of such an assault. However, he also emphasized the fact that he had similarly prepared male friends and family nearby, at the ready to come and help him if need be. While he was able to hold off an attack in the moment, he explained, his ability to defend himself in the long run—since he had to live among the neighbors who were menacing him—was predicated on the aggressors realizing that, despite their unusual appearance and behaviors, he and his friends were ready to defend not only themselves but each other.[2]

The experience in the metro station was a "seed" that prompted me to keep my ear keenly attuned to conversations about insecurity, violence, and self-defense, and one that ultimately germinated into an understanding of how rage-inducing punk-scene practices help participants train for their difficult environment. It also helped me understand how "violence"—a term that I use with caution, given its closely contested nature among punk-scene participants, as well as its history as an unjust indictment against Mexico City's young people and young men in particular—could be perceived as a form of self-defense. Such an experience of witnessing was also key to counteracting many negative stereotypes that I encountered when I began to turn my attention to the local punk scene. During my early field research in particular, media representations depicted a monolithic punk youth culture in the city and metropolitan zone as a wild, ungovernable force fueled by the impotent rage of a lumpen proletarian class (see chapter 3).

But though local punk-scene participants valorize feelings of rage, do moments of rage necessarily end in violence? To put the stereotype of the angry, violent "punk" into ethnographic perspective, I explore rage in Mexico City's punk scene, providing context on the types of violence and insecurity that impact participants in their everyday lives before unpacking a common phrase that people use when they talk about experiencing intense anger in the context of a punk show. As people told me again and again, punk shows are opportunities to *sacar la rabia*, to "take out the rage" in the context of a musical performance. I link the intensity of sound and feeling sparked by live punk performance, detailing how the various subgenres of punk played in Mexico City's scene create dynamic, affectively charged spaces where harsh musical sounds aggressively touch and ultimately condition bodies to perform an enhanced resilience through practices like the slam dance. In the process, I consider how experiencing rage helps punk-scene participants carry out the training of autogestión, preparing them for their challenging environments and encouraging further engagement with self-defense training—a goal that was urged on me explicitly.

Ideally, stoking rage awakens social consciousness and enhances feelings of individual and collective security in the face of various forms of direct and structural violence that scene participants experience, though it can also be weaponized internally, causing disruptions to the good feeling of a show. The threshold of a punk show also provides a challenging liminal zone, the place where some people enact another, more controversial tradition in the punk scene: a storming of the doors to a venue, an action called a *portazo*. Are people who participate in the portazo performing an appropriate rage? And how can the rage stimulated in a punk show be used to motivate scene participants to continue embracing elements of autogestión once the show is over?

While Mexico City's "punks" have had a long and fearsome reputation for being a destructive lot, drunk and disorderly, and prone to fighting to get what they want, my own experience revealed something different, if not entirely divorced, from the fighting and aggression at the heart of stereotypes about them. Certainly, I learned that the social organization of the punk scene was much more fluid, loose, and diverse than media or even many sociological descriptions would suggest. Ideas about the appropriateness of aggressive or violent practices were equally diverse and dispersed among a large network of individuals. I could not dispute the fact that most people who participated in the punk scene had an affinity for loud, harsh aesthetics—sonically, visually, linguistically—nor that they also had a high tolerance for argument and brusque, even rude, interpersonal interactions. Feuding and disloyalty within the punk scene is common, something that, in calmer moments, participants themselves joke and gossip about. Less amusingly, arguments turn into physical fights at times. Several practices, however—especially those around music making, such as the slam dance and the portazo—serve to highlight the aggression of punk-scene sociability even as they may also emphasize positive affective ties.

Nevertheless, at a time when it was difficult to avoid a bombardment of images and anecdotes of extreme violence happening in Mexico City and especially in other states of the republic impacted by narco-trafficking, even the "violence" of which punk-scene participants were accused seemed like something else altogether, something far milder along a broad spectrum of aggressive acts. Some scholars have concluded that violence is actually constitutive of democracy in Mexico, baked into its political structures (Arias and Goldstein 2010). Others point out that problems of violence and criminality long predate the existence of today's young people, opposing a continued scapegoating of the young as a dangerous source of violence and criminality in some scholarship and journalistic work (Nateras 2008; Magaña 2020).[3]

In fact, while they may be accused of violence themselves, punk-scene participants see and experience a great deal of violence happening all around them. They experience it in their neighborhoods, where the lack of stable employment and a scarcity of basic resources makes life difficult even for the most talented or ambitious. Many friends recount experiencing a great deal of violence in the schools as they grew up, encountering bullies and having to learn to fight physically to repel other children's aggression. Some alluded to domestic violence in their homes or communities. Women in Mexico City contend with high rates of sexual harassment and assault, and in recent years Ecatepec has been identified as being among the worst places in the nation for its high rate of feminicidios (González Rodríguez 2012). Plenty of men—and not just my male friends in the punk scene, but among all my Mexico City acquaintances—had stories about being attacked by strangers in the city's streets. Still others had worked for periods in the United States, experiencing the everyday, political, and structural violence that all too commonly affect migrants.

In addition to interpersonal experiences of violence, many punk-scene participants are also acutely aware of state violence that occurs in Mexico, having encountered it when attending protests or other activist events in public spaces. When discussing a perceived dip in activity in the punk scene for roughly a decade—which extended through the entirety of my initial fieldwork period from 2008 to 2011—people have frequently pointed to the political violence that they themselves experienced at or in the aftermath of demonstrations, especially in police custody. Personal experiences of state violence, from police brutality to abuse at the hands of the hated *granaderos* (riot police), prompt feelings of solidarity with other oppressed people in Mexico, from Indigenous groups to striking workers (see chapter 3).[4] They also have been impacted by the rise of the "drug war," which during my most recent periods of fieldwork seemed to be reaching its tentacles even into the heart of Mexico City, briefly thought to be a haven from narco violence. Like many Mexicans, they speculate about

FIGURE 2.1. The largest of several protests against femicide in August 2019 in Mexico City. Photo by Yaz "Punk" Núñez.

exactly what happened to the forty-three *normalistas* who disappeared from the Guerrero countryside in 2014 and mourn the loss of reporters who strive to cover politically sensitive topics, paying for that commitment with their lives in the nation that has for years ranked as the most dangerous country in which to practice journalism.[5]

For these and other reasons, many in the punk scene feel responsible for commenting upon this broad, multifaceted spectrum of violence, and at times offering ideas for how to confront its sources. As participants navigate lives impacted by various forms of violence, they attempt to frame an affectively appropriate, ethical response (Cassaniti and Hickman 2014). This prompts discussion of when and how aggressive or violent acts may be understood as self-defense, influenced by contemporary and historical social justice groups who have had to defend themselves from state violence, from the Zapatistas to the Black Panthers. However, because punk-scene participants in Mexico City have long been understood as violent subjects, I contend that the stereotype continues to shape the ways that they move through city spaces, either encouraging them to play it safe to avoid police and other aggressors or to exploit the notion of punk "violence," embracing it for the protection that the reputation may confer. The characterization of "punks" as violent individuals also shapes some subjects' self-identity and their relationships with various people in their broad social networks, privileging a certain toughness perceived among themselves and their like-minded friends, while viewing others as weak, uninformed, or both.

Another important aspect of local debates about violence in the context of Mexico City's punk scene is that participants emphasize the significance of rage as a key affect that stimulates not only social consciousness among individuals but also their collective bonding. As in many places, expressing rage in Mexico is generally considered more culturally appropriate for men than for women, a topic that writers on women in Mexico City's punk scene have addressed specifically (Urteaga Castro-Pozo 1998; Estrada and Palacios 2004). The link between punk, rage, and masculinity is both explicit in scholarship on punk and gender but also implicit in ideas that

circulate in the scene. On my first visit in August 2017 to a new Mexico City club called El Mundano, which had opened recently to accommodate many types of cultural events, a friend who participates in the punk scene enumerated the kinds of shows that happen there, including "happy punk," a kind of highly pop-infused post-punk that he described as appealing to "muchas chavillas" (lots of young girls), his use of the diminutive form suggesting both youth and superficiality.

But what represents an even greater difficulty than the gendered division of affective experience is the way that rage and violence are conflated in the minds of many, including some punk-scene participants themselves. Certain practices in the scene are said to stoke rage, perhaps in order to purge it, allowing for the love of solidarity

FIGURE 2.2. Newspaper headlines from *Metro* and *El Gráfico* on October 3, 2009. Photo by Zack Sievers.

and friendship to flow. These practices, like the slam dance, are widely valorized, seen as central to the traditions of the punk scene and useful to building good feeling there. Other practices, such as the portazo, also appear to be based on rage but are not similarly understood as being directed toward collective good feeling. And certainly, even though actions like the portazo can happen among other groups, people beyond the punk scene continue to imagine "punks" as especially prone to violence, labeling protestors who engage in property damage as such, for example, whether or not they have direct evidence that they identify that way themselves.

SEED: *ANARCO FURIOSOS*

On October 2, 2009, Mexico City residents once again carried out a march, an annual event to memorialize the people who were massacred, imprisoned, or disappeared on October 2, 1968, the event that signaled the demise of the so-called student movement, which had burgeoned over the course of that year.[6] Several friends from the punk scene told me that they would be participating with specific groups or as individuals. Despite several hundred people in attendance, the packed crowds snaking through the downtown streets on their way to a rally in the Zócalo, I saw a fair number of familiar faces dispersed broadly throughout the crowd.

From the sidelines of the march near the Palacio de Bellas Artes, a majestic art deco building in the city center bordered by white marble pavement, the demonstration looked lively. Despite being a somber remembrance of collective trauma, groups of varying ages marched energetically under banners proclaiming their identities, representing preparatory high schools, groups from the autonomous national university, the electrician's union, and more. One group chanted "Chingue su madre" (Fuck your mother) to then-president Felipe Calderón, ironically using the polite, formal address while shouting their rude insult.

The parade stopped its advance for a moment, a pause occurring as another large group of marchers joined the main group, two parades merging into one while the demonstrators began moving through the final blocks of the route, filing into the giant public plaza at the heart of the city. But during the pause, disturbances began to happen. My tall friend, who could see above the crowd, reported that someone had thrown something at the riot police, the hated granaderos lining the parade route, and all hell was breaking loose. A couple of people then climbed onto the stone buildings opposite us, spray-painting something onto their colonial facades. Meanwhile, more people began throwing bottles and stones at the granaderos, multiple projectiles thudding and crashing against their plastic armor.

After a few moments of pandemonium, a line of riot police moved, spreading across the parade route, blocking in marchers and onlookers alike. People around us began to panic, running, pushing, and shoving, trying desperately to leave the scene. Glass bottles broke around us as we jogged against our will, powerless to resist a stampeding crowd. Police launched tear gas into the throng of demonstrators ahead of us. We continued walking to our destination but took a detour to buy yogurt drinks to cool the sting in our noses and throats, encountering some punk-scene friends doing the same. Once in the Zócalo, we witnessed a small group of protestors attacking the riot police surrounding government buildings. Well-heeled onlookers watched us from balconies, seemingly in a festive mood.

The next morning, a newspaper seller helpfully appeared under my own first-floor balcony, selling issues of *Metro*.[7] One headline read, "Dominan anarcopunks marcha del 2 de octubre!" (Anarcopunks dominate the October 2 march)

FIGURE 2.3. Riot police confronting protestors near la Alameda Central at a march commemorating the first of May, International Workers' Day. Photo by Yaz "Punk" Núñez.

RAGE INTO VIOLENCE?

This splashy post-protest news coverage, with its provocative headlines, underscores a common tendency to link intense affects like anger and rage with violence. However, appreciating the intensity of rage does not necessarily mean endorsing violent actions (Arendt 1970; Das et al. 2000; Bourgois and Scheper-Hughes 2004; Whitehead 2004; Lawrence and Karim 2007). As cultural anthropologist Neil Whitehead cautioned, the term "violence," often used to describe physical actions, more properly refers to quality than to type of action. In practice, "violence" alludes to a vehemence present in actions or ideas believed to be unusually intense. There is not necessarily any one particular emotional state, rage or otherwise, that prompts vehement behaviors or attitudes, and, indeed, seemingly passionless, premeditated violent acts are among those that may provoke the greatest sense of horror. As anthropologists have argued, violence has its own cultural logic, specific to its context, an idea that many people try to reject, calling violence "senseless" in order to distance it from properly human expression (Whitehead 2004, 61).

Additionally, in considering the relationship between music and violence—a discourse that has been entangled with youth culture studies—that link has often been overly simplified. Music has been represented as something that soothes rage and discourages antisocial behavior, decreasing the potential for violent acts. Or it has been represented as something that can promote or even incite violence (Ochoa 2006; Fast and Pegley 2012). Recent scholarship complicates this dichotomy, identifying the many ways that music saturates power relations, becoming inseparable from certain kinds of interpersonal and institutional forms of violence, while also being instrumentalized as a tool of war in some cases (Cusick 2006; Pieslak 2007; McDonald 2009; Daughtry 2015).

Separating truly violent acts from vehement attitudes and behaviors makes sense in the context of Mexico City's punk scene, in which punk shows encompassing various musical and social practices are described as events at which participants equally generate intense energy and feeling. While outsiders to the punk scene may see such energy, embodied in high-intensity practices at the punk show, as violent, scene participants typically reserve their discussions of violence for the people who break with the unwritten rules of appropriate behavior to engage in individualistic aggressions, or for scenarios completely separate from the practices that take place in the context of a punk show.

Ideally, aggression is mediated in the context of a punk show, not allowed to become something that might be experienced as violence. People try to de-escalate arguments or physical fights. Some may try to support a woman if she is repelling aggressive attention from a man. Judging from talk within the scene, violence is a key topic of concern. Heated debates about violence and its desirability or political efficacy have the power to generate arguments and even to disrupt long-standing friendships. After the embers had cooled following a very public rift in a prominent punk-scene collective, I questioned people on both sides. Though this had not been evident in online debates among members that I'd followed from afar, in person they all indicated that differences of opinion over what constitutes violence and how to talk about it appropriately was among the reasons for the argument.

Rage, on the other hand, is almost universally praised as a particularly vehement, intense, motivating feeling. While other terms for anger and rage show up in punk song lyrics, and as the names for collectives and bands, on the whole punk-scene participants prefer the term *rabia*. Like the overlapping valences of "mad" in English, which can mean angry, insane, or both simultaneously, the Spanish-language term *rabia* preserves a centuries-old link to viral rabies phonetically, as the term for rage is identical to the term for hydrophobia, the disease that afflicts mad dogs. In Spanish, rabia encodes an extreme form of anger with a veneer of madness, a hint of being infuriated to the brink of insanity, an intense feeling-state expressed through great physical and verbal vehemence.[8] Punk shows are frequently referred to as opportunities to sacar la rabia (take out the rage).

Though this positive valuation of "rage" among punk-scene participants is striking, it shares some features with the valuation of other terms for intense, moral anger among peoples around the world. The extremity of rabia, seemingly an especially strong form of *enojo* (anger), makes for an interesting comparison with similar emotional or affective states described in ethnographies that account for the powerful role that such feelings play in social life, such as Michelle Rosaldo's (1980) and Renato Rosaldo's (2007) ethnographic accounts of *liget* among the Ilongot of the Philippines, or Louise Meintjes's more recent explication of *ulaka* among contemporary Zulu-identified South African men (2017).

Liget and ulaka both are understood among their speakers to refer to feeling-states that are useful, powerful, but potentially dangerous should they be allowed to increase beyond control. In the Philippines, the term *liget* is one that has been used to describe a broad spectrum of feeling-states, from the admirably intense energy of women at work in their households, to the excitement of men hunting game, to the potentially murderous anger that drove Ilongot men into a traditional (and, by the 1970s, dwindling) practice of decapitating male victims from beyond their social groups. Following this violent act of "taking heads," motivated by liget, the men would throw them away, thereby casting off a depth of liget that would be harmful to their bodies and communities. Michelle Rosaldo, a pioneering anthropologist of the emotions, wrote about liget in various Ilongot practices before her tragic, accidental death. Decades later, her husband, Renato Rosaldo, evoked the rage that he experienced while grieving for her, suggesting that his own feeling of intense anger gave him the emotional intelligence that he needed to better understand the ways that Ilongot men talked about liget and their desire to "take heads" in the decade just before the practice was outlawed by Philippino authorities.

In a contemporary South African context, Louise Meintjes describes ulaka as being "in control at the edge" (2017, 65), a positive form of masculine moral anger that impresses onlookers with its depth, its harnessed potential for violence. Ulaka may be an intense anger, but it must be leashed, directed by a higher moral code in order to be understood as such. It's heard in the strained timbres of the voice and seen in physical exertions such as taking part in *ngoma* dance, embodying dancers' complex links to a storied Zulu warrior figure. Ultimately, to express ulaka means to behave with manly propriety, displaying the maturity of men who recognize their anger, explore its limits, but ultimately keep it in check to guide powerful, positive, collective purpose.

Like liget or ulaka, rabia in Mexico City's punk scene is a highly motivating feeling, one that ideally prompts strong, appropriate (and often appropriately masculine) action. However, the term *rabia*, with its valence of raving or madness, also suggests something just beyond the bounds of propriety, a limit already crossed. Negotiating that limit becomes a key discursive task for those who spend time in the local punk scene, a negotiation that also involves the relationship between rage and other key affective states, variously referred to as amor (love), amistad (friendship), or solidaridad (solidarity).[9] What is also interesting about how participants in Mexico City's punk scene talk about rage is that they speak of it not only as an individual emotion locked within a single subjectivity but also as a feeling with public muscularity, an affective potential to join large groups of participants together (Massumi 1995; Brennan 2004; Mazzarella 2009; Gregg and Seigworth 2010; Wetherell 2012; Hofman 2015, 2020; White 2017; Gray 2021).

For some, this process is akin to a personal and collective catharsis. In discussing rage with some regulars of punk shows, I found that my own use of the word

FIGURE 2.4. Meeting place at the Monumento a la Revolución
before the May 1 march. Photo by Yaz "Punk" Núñez.

cartarsis resonated with my interlocutors, who would eagerly nod and agree that
what they experienced was exactly that: a stimulation and then a purging of rage.
This suggests that some participants in the scene believe in a hydraulic theory of
emotions, imagining them to be like fluid in the body, able to swell and recede.[10]
In fact, in August 2009 I attended a festival in Ecatepec named for this process:
Festival Katartico. The *propa* for the show claimed that this was the nineteenth
iteration of the event, opining that "catharsis continues to be relevant; liberating
it is our way of life." (The flier reads, "19th aniversario porque la catarsis sigue
vigente liberarla [*sic*] es nuestra forma de vida.")

Other friends emphasized the stimulation of rage more than its purging, talking of the ways that punk songs and shows helped spur scene participants' social
consciousness and political activity, ideally beyond the show itself. In that sense,
the notion of "taking out the rage" described the prompting or acknowledging
of feelings of rage, letting them emerge as a way to motivate further action. But
for many who emphasize the existence of a catharsis involved in attending punk
shows, the purging of rage was also imagined as a means of ensuring the flow
of positive feelings like the love of friendship and solidarity. This is also key to
fostering appropriate action both within and beyond the punk show, actions that
are stimulated by a diverse array of harsh, loud, distorted sounds.

SEED: CREATING COMPELLING PUNK SOUNDS

There were many odd things about the show featuring visiting Spanish-Portuguese crust-punk band Etacarinae. For starters, it was in an odd space for a punk show, loaned by local Hare Krishnas, smack in the heart of the historic district. The central location was unusual, given that most shows at that time happened out in the metropolitan zone. Further, the Hare Krishnas had apparently stipulated that it was to be a substance-free event, and so there was no smoking or drinking. The show's organizers were doing their utmost to ensure that people followed the rules, at least inside the building. The interior of the space was a low-ceilinged, long and narrow room with extremely muddy acoustics. At some shows, it's possible that few people would notice the sound qualities of the space. But on this occasion, the musicians were thoughtful, checking the sound equipment with greater care than I'd seen before.

The first band, called Masacre—not to be confused with famous band Masacre 68—played a quick set of grindcore, a roar of distorted instrumentals accompanied by harsh, guttural vocals, all disappearing into a wall of sound in the challenging acoustic space. Billing itself as "epic crust," the second band, named simply K, presented something else entirely, a more melodious sound cut through with interesting pedal effects, five distinct parts rather than one blended sound. The third band, Strangulation, was also a grindcore band, but with a sound quite different from the first one, a propulsive drummer and vocalist skillfully punctuating phrases of intense noise. However, just moments into their performance, the guitar player broke a string. Worse, he had no spare. One of the other guitarists present lent his instrument, and for a moment it seemed that the show could go on. The teetotaling crowd was remarkably quiet as the guitarist bent over the loaner, attempting to tune it up to his satisfaction.

But the minutes passed and the tuning went on and on. Teasing commentary began to ripple through the crowd. "He doesn't want to play!" shouted one person from the audience, just a few feet from the band. Another suggested that the tuning was in fact the performance, prompting mocking chants of "Otra! Otra!" when the guitarist finally paused. But instead of resuming the performance, he indicated that he couldn't get comfortable with the guitar, and so the band just quit.

Etacarinae was fabulous, providing just the right balance between a tight envelope of distortion and variation within it, including bursts of rhythmic intensity and melodic riffs—an exciting, physically impactful sound that, for the first time that evening, "called" listeners to dance, hurling their bodies at one another in the *eslam*.

Despite all the excitement, the show was done well before midnight.

HARD, HEAVY, THICK: INTENSE SOUND AND FEELING IN THE TOCADA

When discussing how punk shows—or tocadas—encourage them to sacar la rabia, experiencing, acknowledging, and sharing intense feeling, many punk-scene participants pinpoint lyrics on social justice themes as key to the process of stoking rage and social consciousness. "For me," says an influential musician within the scene, as we chat in the shade of his vendor's booth one afternoon, "the words are the most important aspect of punk." Another long-term scene participant, lounging in the Biblioteca Social Reconstruir before a meeting of the Revuelta Anarco Punk (RAP) collective, proudly proclaims that he's "old-fashioned," preferring punk in which the message is most central. When hardcore punk spread across a globalizing punk scene in the late 1970s and into the 1980s, nudging aside if not entirely displacing local punk rock styles, it precipitated an aesthetic shift in Mexico City. But equally importantly, it also coincided with a real engagement with anarchism and local anarchist role models on the part of punk-scene participants. Hardcore punk therefore remains central to people who see themselves as punk or otherwise participate in Mexico City's punk scene today. In fact, not many people still use the term "anarcopunk" with much frequency after its apparent heyday in the 1990s, but when they do, it is often primarily to the sounds and political messages of hardcore punk that they refer.

Though local scene participants often lean heavily on the lyrics as a marker of punk's authenticity and its potential to raise listeners' consciousness about infuriating political realities, the sound of punk live in performance is also necessary to fully experience its power (Frith 1989). I argue that appreciating the power of punk as sound is also key to its training potential as a tool of autogestión. Punk shows are "thick events," as Nina Eidsheim has described them, experiences that make it especially clear that "not only aurality but also tactile, spatial, physical, material, and vibrational sensations are at the core of all music" (2015, 8). The tactile, vibrational sensations of the music are particularly germane to the experience of punk's sounds. The volume, resonance, and distortion of the music cause vibrations within and on the body, making the air feel close, viscous, tangible, connecting bodies to the space and to each other.

As Tomie Hahn has written of monster truck rallies, extreme sounds can also give bodies the sensation of being moved from within.[11] It's no accident, then, that people in Mexico City's punk scene speak of being "called" (from the verb *llamar*) to participate in the slam dance, their bodies compelled into frenetic action by the sound beckoning through its physical presence. Despite the notion that punk is by and for amateurs, the tradition of being called to slam may sometimes refute the idea that all performances of punk are equal. In my observation, punk performances that called people to slam were typically tight, executed by musicians who could stay together even at breakneck tempos rather than give sloppy performances at an uncertain pace. Bands that called people to participate in the slam also tended to have a loud, powerful, resonant-while-distorted sound, an achievement that they could sustain even in acoustically challenging spaces.

Jeremy Wallach et al. have described the way that such a powerful sonic presence can blot out other awareness, writing, "it becomes impossible to think about or feel anything else, an experience of *affective overdrive*" (2011, 13), a physical-emotional sensation that can be intensely empowering.[12] And though they emphasize that the meaning of this intensely affective experience shifts across various metal and punk scenes, they also underscore a broadly observed importance of the awakening of energy in such contexts as an "antidote to apathy" (15). Indeed, one of the slam's monikers in Mexico City is *el baile de energía* (the dance of energy).

Ideally, the awakening of energy provided by local punk shows is not only an individualistic experience but a collective one. Beyond the intense, multisensory individual experience, the collective experience of the thick event emphasizes the bonds between all participants. The insistently audible and vibrational presence of the sound levels them, making everyone equally susceptible to its encroaching, tactile power. As the intense sound beats upon musicians' and listeners' bodies alike, discourse in the local scene frames activities at the show as more or less appropriate ways to experience its intense affect in response to others. Through valorized practices like the slam, the punk show should be a multifaceted experience that constitutes scene participants as hardened, tough subjects who take out their rage in response to its intensities. Within the context of the tocada,

FIGURE 2.5. "Tenochtitlán Hardcore": Punk show
in El Mundano. Photo by Yaz "Punk" Núñez.

the lyrics ideally help keep that rage directed outward, beyond the punk show, toward noxious, repressive political authorities.

For this reason, also, hardcore punk remains key to many local punk shows. The tempo of hardcore punk songs is usually rapid, often in a simple duple meter or maybe a quick common time. The harmonies are also simple, as are any melodic features, and the vocals are likely screamed rather than sung, bringing an especially acute awareness of vocalists' bodies into play.[13] At shows where hardcore punk dominates, screaming along with the performers is a key form of participation available to everyone. To do so, scene participants engage in intertextual practices, learning song lyrics via the packaging of recordings or in fanzines, where printed song lyrics are often featured.

The radical simplicity of some hardcore punk sound also emphasizes its availability to musicians who don't need to reach virtuosic heights in order to create effective performances.[14] But while some musicians and listeners are content with this simplicity, others grow bored with its constraints. "Es puro *tu-pa tu-pa*," one friend said to me, describing the type of punk I would hear at a performance of hardcore bands. His use of onomatopoeia is a common way of referring to the simple march rhythms of much hardcore punk. In addition to that allusion to the music's simplicity, this particular friend—fairly unusually—criticized the musicians in the bands, several of whom had been playing for many years, accusing them of "auto-marginalization." Why couldn't they learn new skills in ten years?

Rage **61**

he wondered, pointing out their longevity and accusing them of creative stasis. He believed that they were content not to develop their musical talents. This was his attempt to persuade me to check out the Etacarinae show I described earlier instead of the hardcore line-up happening at a tocada on the same Sunday out beyond the city center in the metropolitan zone.

In fact, while many people prefer and create a distinctly old-school hardcore punk—fast, pared down, and screamed—many others have long since embraced the influence of extreme metal subgenres on local punk sounds, combining them with a hardcore ethic. In this, Mexico City's punk scene is not unusual. Despite their seeming differences, metal and punk have been influencing one another on a global scale since they were both codified as distinctive rock subgenres decades ago (Kahn-Harris 2007; Waksman 2009).

Rhythmic and metric simplicity were among the first things to go when musicians around the world began to tinker with the sounds of hardcore punk. The British band Discharge is widely credited with introducing a distinctive drumbeat, the "d-beat," into the context of hardcore punk, something that would push its sound further toward a harsh, propulsive style. A common-time pattern, the d-beat typically articulates the first and third beats with the kick drum, but within a constellation of accents on rhythmic subdivisions created by both kick and snare drums, plus crash cymbal and sometimes the hi-hat as well. The effect is to draw attention to the smaller rhythmic units, creating a more sustained and noisier sound through increased percussion while also refusing the stability of a more typical metric emphasis that alerts listeners to the arrival of each bar. The d-beat creates a sense of faster forward motion, a galloping sound that frequently trips against an off-beat accent or a fill between vocal lines. It also moves hardcore punk away from the regularity of a march to a more disorienting wash of noise. During my time, Antimaster was one prominent local punk band well liked for their use of a d-beat style in Mexico City, though they incorporated several other elements of metal into their sound too.

In addition to rhythmic play, with the influence of thrash metal from bands like Metallica in their ears, punk musicians in the late 1980s and 1990s also began to experiment a bit more with tempo, mashing together sections of a song played at vastly different speeds to produce "cycles of energy" (Pillsbury 2006). High speeds got higher and low speeds got lower, enhancing the contrast. Mexico City punk band Kagada de Perro frequently makes use of such play with tempo, such as in one song titled "Antisocial." Lasting roughly three minutes, the song begins in a slow four-four meter, with a clear common-time feel. But suddenly, roughly a minute into the song, there is a second's worth of silence, and the bass steps forward with some low trembling. The vocalist breaks into a scream, cuing the band to switch to a faster duple meter. This kind of metric play is particularly compelling for slam participants at live performances, who throw their bodies at one another more slowly, and then switch to frenetic movements when the tempo quickens.

In addition to fast tempos, lots of percussive noise, and cycles of energy, other musical elements in both punk and metal that contribute to an intense physical and affective response from participants are the use of distortion, high volume, and an emphasis on lower-pitched sounds. Through the influence of extreme metal subgenres, punk became more bass-oriented, a shift that impacted not only its pitch but also the power of its sound. Much punk in Mexico City today has a certain "heaviness," a distinctive melding of distorted timbre and frequency characteristics that is better associated with heavy metal (Walser 1993; Fales 2002; Fales and Berger 2005). But arguably, a preference for a more bass-oriented sound has always been a hallmark of Mexican punk, since even some of the first hardcore bands, like Masacre 68, incorporated a less trebly sound and featured a vocalist who screamed in a lower, more guttural register than much high-pitched hardcore punk screaming. Bands that incorporate a mixture of punk and metal influences often feature a more powerful sustain in the guitars, underscoring that heavy sound and its impact on bodies in live performance.

Mexico City band Rhuckuss, which was active during my extended stay in the city, called its music "metal-punk," suggesting its adherence to such a crossover aesthetic. Rhuckuss's song "Retribución" emphasizes a particular metal-inflected heaviness of sound, and slight changes of tempo are overshadowed by more complex rhythmic play that occurs within the larger time structure. The drummer opens the song, for example, in the common time that defines it, but, unusually, delineating two measures' worth of triplets rather than a duple rhythm. Meanwhile, the overall sound of the band is defined by a greater proximity of the bass and lead guitars, playing in similar registers and with high levels of distortion, achieving a richer and more resonant sustain. This infuses the musical texture with some of the iconic "power and strength" of metal, while the introduction of the crash cymbal does a great deal to emphasize a more brittle, higher-pitched noise layered on top of it. Rhuckuss's vocalist also adds to this more treble register, employing the more strained, screaming timbres of hardcore punk.

Because of the ways that the melding of punk with extreme metal subgenres has complicated certain subgenres of punk, musicians who play in these styles tend to be more overtly aware of sonic details like the proper tuning of a guitar or the lack of good sound equipment in many club spaces. For this, they may sustain charges of elitism by other local punk-scene participants; in fact, a preference for hardcore punk may help burnish a reputation as an activist within the scene. Metal influences are often more present in punk bands that have something of a global reach, bands like Antimaster and Rhuckuss, who are profiled in international publications like *Maximumrocknroll*. These bands more likely curate performances by international, visiting bands and may organize their own Canadian, European, and Latin American tours through their friendship networks as well.[15] Local bands that draw from metal sounds usually continue to privilege lyrics on political topics in their music, however, leading some of them to refer to themselves as hardcore, even if their music is that and more, complex rather than purposively simple.

Meanwhile, the popularity of the grindcore subgenre within Mexico City's punk scene may signal a slow shift away from the emphasis on the audibility of political lyrics, which has kept hardcore punk prominent in the mix for so many years. Of all the different punk-metal crossover styles that were popular in Mexico City at this time, from punk rock and hardcore to thrash, d-beat, and crust, grindcore was the one that eschewed lyrics altogether, favoring non-linguistic shrieks and guttural wails. These cries and shouts accompany a barrage of noise, from high levels of instrumental distortion and down-tuned guitars (like the one with the broken string during the show featuring Etacarinae), to extremely high tempos accentuated by the use of blast beats.[16] The visual logos of grindcore bands are often virtually unreadable, created through a shaky, spidery aesthetic, their names a central mass of white surrounded by skittering lines etching their way into an inky black background. With no lyrics to decipher, the physical impact of grindcore bands dominates the especially powerful, layered experience of their sound.

The impressive sounds achieved in live punk performance of all kinds impact different parts of the body differently, as vibrations travel through denser or lighter types of flesh. At punk shows, I love feeling the variations in how differently intense, tactile sound impacts my body. The kick drum thumps in my abdomen, which also vibrates in a sustained way to low bass frequencies, while other percussive sounds batter my chest and limbs.[17] Meanwhile, higher-pitched distorted sounds cause a certain congestion around my head and ears, a sensation that can be mildly pleasant or downright painful. Though as a careful musician I usually carry ear plugs with me everywhere, many people who frequent shows in Mexico City's punk scene choose not to wear them. For some, to protect the ears by dampening the sound would be to muffle its physical power, dulling its ability to alter their moods while perhaps calling into question their ability to withstand discomfort.

As the intense sound batters bodies in the performance space, it ideally sparks the intense feeling that scene participants valorize. Beyond screaming along with lyrics at some shows, there are two further, highly visible collective practices that people talk about as key to experiencing the affects of punk shows. The portazo, which I'll discuss in detail later, happens at the outer limits of a punk show, at its doors. It's a controversial practice, the subject of a great deal of disagreement about its value in the scene. Another way to experience rage—and perhaps the love of friendship and solidarity simultaneously—is widely encouraged: participation in el eslam.

THE SLAM: CATHARSIS AND TRANSFORMATION

While a discourse of rage is applied to the punk show writ large, specific practices like the slam are also referred to as opportunities to sacar la rabia. The experience is described variously as not only a "dance of energy" but also a "dance of friendship" and a "dance of solidarity." For those who see the slam as a means of achieving catharsis, it's important to note that this particular understanding of catharsis contrasts with the classic Aristotelian understanding of the term, stipulating that the experience should leave participants feeling stimulated by their experience of rage, not enervated. Certainly, the exercise is a wearying one, and people do leave the dance with clear signs of physical fatigue. However, they also tend to look as though lit from within through its incandescent energy and excitement, and perhaps demonstrate a feeling of camaraderie by throwing their arms around friends while they catch their breath. This is the kind of transformation that the dance and its stimulation of rage is meant to prompt, whether or not the dancer believes in the necessity of purging rabia.

Ideally, participants "take out" their rage in ways that allow them to remain engaged in the social justice questions raised in song lyrics, while also feeling a redoubled sense of community with others present. However, this is not always what occurs, as the stimulation of rage can cause participants to act out in ways that injure or upset other people. Certainly, for those who view the slam from an outsider's perspective—including people who participate in other global punk scenes, where the slam may have gone out of fashion—the dance appears to be an expression of aggression, if not to say violence.

The very idea that the slam is considered a dance may puzzle observers who fail to see patterns or skill in movement that characterize other dance forms, such as popular Latin American staples like the salsa and cumbia. There are no steps to perform, and no particular prescriptions for how to feel or move with the music's beat. Specific performers or performances are never held up as exemplars of the form. The fact that technical skill is unnecessary for participation in the slam is one of its more important characteristics, further evidence of punk's rejection of performative excellence or virtuosity. In turn, this rejection of notions like talent or mastery ostensibly makes participation available for everyone.

However, there is a key difference between the accessible slam and other kinds of easily performed dances that people use to move to other styles of popular music. The slam dance provides opportunities for participants to enact their hardness in response to hard music. Other dance styles, even those performed to other kinds of rock music, may be seen as *fresa*, reflecting soft, middle-class tastes and constitutions.[18] At a show in August 2015, a large number of friends from the punk scene gathered in an unusual space for local punk performance, a bar near the city center. There, U.K. hardcore band the Mob was scheduled to appear, following a handful of local punk bands and also Juanita y Los Feos, a self-described "punk/new wave" band from Spain, which was in town to play at the Viva Glam festival, but was opening our show on that night.

At first, we paid them scant attention, ignoring their melodic sung vocals, their moderate tempos, and the clearer, less distorted quality of their instrumental sound. But later, that undesirable sound demanded notice from members of our group. Two of them began to dance with exaggerated gestures and theatrically vapid expressions. "Es música por una tardeada!" (It's music for an afternoon party), exclaimed one friend, referring to the tame gatherings where rock 'n' roll was performed in middle-class households in the early 1960s, executing some Twist-like rock moves to illustrate (Zolov 1999). His spirit caught on, and soon I found myself moving among a number of friends who twisted and swayed with a mocking little gleam in their eyes. Dancing to more mainstream rock music was silly and uninspiring, their response suggested, a kind of individualistic dance style that privileged teenagers enjoy in their parents' comfortable homes.

Initially, however, a dance like the Twist was not all that unlike the ways that people moved to punk rock. In Mexico, as elsewhere, the slam dance was preceded in punk rock scenes by a dance called the pogo, in which dancers jumped around in a fairly circumscribed space, bobbing more or less with the rhythm, but in a far more exaggerated, individualistic manner than audience members who move rhythmically in place at a rock show. I occasionally glimpsed the pogo at more punk rock–oriented shows even during my time in Mexico City, though the slam was far more common. Among global punk scenes, the switch from the relatively mild and introspective pogo to the slam appears to have occurred first in the hardcore punk scene in Southern California in the early 1980s. Participants in that scene, looking back, recall that the slam was a dance of aggression, a kind of free-for-all among "pissed-off" teenagers who entered into a dense crowd of their peers with elbows and fists flying. They recount that visitors to the scene or their own visits to other scenes prompted startled reactions, as teenage boys used to performing the pogo had to accustom themselves to the more aggressive practice of the slam, which was spreading rapidly from the scenes of the West Coast to major East Coast scenes like Washington, DC, and New York, as well as south of the U.S.-Mexico border.[19]

Watching punk-scene participants in modern-day Mexico City perform el eslam, it can be difficult to imagine that it has changed much since its inception in California's Orange County of the 1980s. At least in terms of form, it's the same—though if the dancers have a small amount of space in which to move, and if the excitement of the crowd is especially intense, the results of the practice may look a bit different. The dancers launch their bodies at each other as they cycle through the space, colliding and then spinning off again into their individual circuits, perhaps crashing less purposively into others as they regain their balance and momentum. In tightly packed spaces, there may be less obvious or quick circular motion, and the circle of dancers may appear to bounce largely in place, slowly moving through space, though maintaining a high incidence of collision among themselves. At large events where the feeling runs particularly high, the majority of the dancers might use their arms to push and shove others in addition to colliding with the full force of their bodies, in an apparent attempt to increase their participation through forceful, fast, and regular contact with others. In loosely packed spaces, the effort involved in jumping at the other dancers is more apparent, as is individual variation in the manner of performing it. Some participants may target the same friends among the group again and again; others might appear not to willingly collide with others at all, but rather to bounce off them randomly. One friend was unusual in this sense because, while he seemed to collide with people haphazardly, he appeared not to experience intense feeling while doing it, his face beatific and his large frame surprisingly light and graceful, drifting among the surging bodies like an autumn leaf on a breeze.

In general, however, such frenetic energy and movement dominate that it's interesting how few people lose their balance and fall. But if anyone should tumble during the course of the dance, several others move quickly to hoist that person back to his or her feet. To a greater or lesser extent depending on the venue and the character of the crowd, a kind of protective wall of people may also form behind the dancers, as those who don't care to participate directly nevertheless absorb and repel some of the dancers' force. Standing securely rooted to the ground, they allow the dancers to bump up against them, marking the limit of the dancing space and perhaps pushing back slightly to let dancers know they've reached its edge. I was always particularly glad when this happened, as it lessened the chances that I would once again be hit by a random, flailing body or limb, as had happened to me on several occasions, once causing me a lingering backache.

Despite appearing like a rough, lawless activity, then, the pure expression of dancers' aggression, the dance is rule governed. Observation of the dancers may sometimes support their commentary that the dance is about energy and friendship rather than about venting rage. However, there are many occasions in which the dance becomes too frenetic, or someone behaves inappropriately within the circle of dancers, touching female participants against their will or using the dance to aggressively target a particular dancer with the force of his body. Then some kind of response occurs, spearheaded either by the band or by others in the audience. On occasion, individual men have been physically restrained or ridiculed by their peers. Or there may be a judgment that the crowd in general has become excessive in its behavior, prompting a pause or change in the music. A fight or some other disturbance certainly is a failure of the ideal experience of the dance.

Thus far, this characterization of the slam dance in Mexico City's punk scene does not differ greatly from other descriptions in the scant literature on the topic, written by observers of various historical and contemporary punk scenes, primarily in the United States and the United Kingdom (Roman 1988; Simon 1997; Tsitsos 1999; Palmer 2005; Waksman 2009). Several of these accounts describe the slam dance as a rule-governed practice, despite its seemingly violent and chaotic appearance, and they also discuss the activity as one prompted by feelings of anger. Some authors admit, however, that the rules are not always carried out in everyday practice (Roman 1988; Simon 1997). Furthermore, some participants of different gender and class backgrounds in these punk scenes appear more comfortable with the rules, and the extent to which they're followed, than others.[20]

Though I was a woman with no previous experience of punk-scene participation, I had no desire to join the slam dance. Shorter than most of the men who participated in it, I tended to experience flying limbs coming directly at my face and head rather than at my torso. But, said one of my earliest punk-scene interlocutors when I first started going to punk shows, "You must learn to dance with the people." Female punk-scene participants do join in the slam on occasion, though because there are so few women who regularly attend shows, their participation is a far rarer occurrence. When women did participate, I often had the sense that they tried to show that they could be just as tough as the male participants, seeking out regular, forceful contact with the other dancers in an attitude of determination. Ultimately, I did not make the choice to join the slam, but was propelled into it. One day, a male friend simply collared me, clamping an arm tightly around my neck and shoulder from behind, steering me into the whirling circle of dancers. The experience was likely more difficult for being in his grip, something that made me feel off-balance, hardly able to stay on my feet as my body crashed both into other dancers' and into his. Fortunately, punk songs are usually short, and the experience was soon over. Finally able to disentangle myself, I found that I was a bit light-headed. I had barely breathed throughout the experience.

Among those who choose to take part in the slam dance, the experience is far more pleasurable. They report feeling a rush of adrenaline, quickening the heartbeat and prompting the body to a greater sense of power and liveliness. Whether the dance has been faster or slower, and more or less full of rapid bodily collisions, dancers tend to limp away from the circle at the end of the song wet with their sweat and that of the other dancers, perhaps having sustained minor injuries like bruises or lips cut open with self-inflicted bites. Friends throw their arms around one another both during and after the dance, intensifying their expression of friendship. No matter how worn out or beaten up they may be, dancers tend to come away from the slam weary but bright-eyed, the excitement and energy of the activity still radiating from them.

At one show, I stood off to the side of the crowd, towered over by an exceptionally tall friend who was watching the proceedings with some impatience, waiting for the slam to begin. Once it did, I found it easy to follow his motion through the dense cluster of dancers, until suddenly he zigged and zagged, seeming to stumble, his body briefly eluding my sight. Afterward, he limped back, having twisted an ankle. While he winced each time he put his weight on the affected leg and announced to me the nature of his injury, he also waved it off and never stopped smiling as he wiped the sweat from his face. He rejoined the dance again a bit later in the day.

When it comes to accidental injuries sustained during the slam dance, no one talks much about them. They are par for the course, an unavoidable consequence of entering into the wild mass of slamming bodies. Encouraging participants to take minor blows with equanimity, the slam dance reveals itself as a means of conditioning what I, following one among several descriptors for good music within the scene, call "hardness": an unflappable, tough reaction, of a piece with the loud, harsh aesthetics of the music and the physical demands of moving appropriately to it.[21] Many of those who participate in the slam dance bear their wounds with no small pride, making it clear that they have been injured but refusing to dwell on their pain. Intentional injury or violence that may arise during the course of the dance is not so blithely tolerated, however.

In fact, I contend that the slam provides plenty of opportunities to witness a revealing negotiation between the real and ideal practice, particularly when it comes to the level of aggression and the desired sense of solidarity that may or may not emerge in the dance. While dancers may perform a certain kind of violence through their participation, they do so under the charge of protecting one another, manifesting appropriate attitudes about pleasure, pain, and collective feeling.

This channeling of an appropriate rage happens most easily within the context of a tocada itself, but there are several reasons that people may choose to remain outside of one. Just as in the extremely repressive 1970s and 1980s, it has often been difficult to find spaces for punk performance, and when people beyond the local DIY networks organize shows of interest, they are frequently too expensive for punk-scene participants. Especially during my early fieldwork from 2008 to 2011, people often chose to remain outside of shows rather than pay to enter them. On one memorable occasion, large groups of punk-scene participants trekked down to El Circo Volador after the Chopo market wound down on a Saturday evening, hoping that they would be able to secure reduced-price tickets to a show featuring Brazilian metal band Ratos de Porão. But the venue would not bargain over ticket prices, and so we simply remained outside, socializing late into a mild July evening.[22]

At El Circo Volador, it was not possible to hear the band outside the performance venue, but the festive atmosphere of anticipation among those who did pay for the show was enough to stimulate an impromptu street party, though of course with the usual problems. This includes the potential for police action, ostensibly in response to public drinking. Despite its illegality, drinking more or less surreptitiously is one of the main entertainments in the street. Publicly consuming large quantities of beer, often in shared caguamas, creates problems beyond its prohibition, however. There is also the lack of access to toilets, which is particularly detrimental to female participation in the scene. While many men simply engage in flagrant public urination—though, of course, looking over their shoulders in case of a patrol car rolling up—women typically felt forced to be more creative, if they stayed for the street party at all. But on other occasions, people might choose not to enter into the space of the show not only because they preferred to save their money but also because of the extremely crowded and uncomfortable conditions inside, as I experienced at multiple shows at El Clandestino, a club in Ecatepec where it was always possible to hear the band while remaining on the street outside.

So, I spent a number of shows on the sidewalk rather than indoors because my friends chose not to enter. The atmosphere outside of the shows was frequently even more rowdy than the atmosphere within them, however, as people focused more on socializing, paying little to no attention to the music. Certainly, there was no circle of slam dancers, with fights and other disturbances often more likely to happen outside of the space than within, despite the fact that crowds of young men gathered on a sidewalk often drew police attention, even in the less closely monitored metropolitan zone.

The different behaviors within and outside the show demonstrate that the interior of the tocada functions like a liminal space of ritual, a space in which to engage in prized affective practices like the slam, but only for those with the means and inclination to go inside (Turner 1986). Its discipline is therefore unevenly experienced. And the liminal space surrounding the show can also become a target for another kind of aggressive, rage-prompted behavior: el portazo.

MY FIRST PORTAZO

It was a cold February day out in the Estado de México, where we gathered for a show featuring a long list of local bands. People began congregating outside of the concert venue early, hopping in place to keep the cold at bay, chatting, sharing caguamas, and smoking. The vibe was sociable and even relaxed, though in hindsight I realized that there were signs of impending conflict. Security personnel were grouped around the venue's ticket window, broad-chested scowling men in red shirts. A sign posted above the window read: "Price: 130 pesos. With discount: 130 pesos," effectively shutting down the possibility for fans to bargain for a collective entrance fee that would allow them to pool their money.

As it became clear that the music would soon start, people who had paid for tickets began to move indoors. Others approached the ticket window and, ignoring the sign, attempted to bargain over the price. Each group was turned away. Soon, the sound of smashing glass shattered the low hum of the pre-show buzz. The ticket-window area formed a narrow funnel leading up to the venue's doors, and scene participants had converged on it, surrounding the security guards while throwing empty bottles and rocks, yelling insults and demands to be admitted to the building for free. A short standoff ensued, which encouraged the fans to increase their noise and their threat level, menacing the security guards with shouted warnings of what would happen if they remained. More empty bottles were smashed and people began chanting, "Por-ta-zo! Por-ta-zo!," calling for a full-blown storming of the doors.

At that point, an audience had gathered on a nearby highway overpass as pedestrians waited with interest to see what would happen. The police also arrived but were chased away. Bottlenecked in their tight space, the security guards had little option but to give way as the crowd increased its raucous sound and energy. People at the front of the crowd yelled as they surged toward the doors, with the people at the back continuing to shout and hurl objects. It did not take long for them to gain entrance, and calm and quiet was soon renewed outside of the concert venue. To my knowledge, no actual physical fighting had occurred, despite a large amount of intimidation directed to the security personnel. As one of the audience members who had waited to see what would transpire, I paid 30 (rather than 130) pesos for entrance a few moments later.

THE PORTAZO: INAPPROPRIATE RAGE?

While shouting along with song texts or entering into the slam dance can provide prime opportunities to engage in sanctioned performances of hardness, ideally provoking rage and good feeling, the portazo is a controversial tradition that some people believe damages the cohesiveness of the scene. A portazo in the context of the punk scene often occurs when fans claim that a ticket price for a tocada is unfair, beyond the means of the average person or so excessive as to raise suspicions that the concert organizers' only aim is to turn a profit. Adding insult to the injury of a high ticket price, concert organizers may also deny people the right to engage in the time-honored practice of *hacer la vaca*, the negotiation of a collective entrance fee for a group of friends.

Like equations of soft middle-class values with a more mainstream rock-music aesthetic, the portazo and its traditions have a substantial local history. In this case, the heyday of the portazo appears to have been in the tumultuous 1970s, the mythical "lost decade," when the Mexican government attempted to crack down on youth culture and particularly rock-music performance, as historian Abraham Ríos Manzano (1999, 29) has described it. He also evokes the rarity of rock music available in any form during that decade, whether in imported recordings, local recordings, via the media, or in public performance. What few public rock concerts occurred were typically offered for a select public, moneyed guests in upscale hotels or at large venues with exorbitant ticket prices. Ríos Manzano mentions three memorable portazos that occurred at the Auditorio Nacional, apparently the angry reaction of young fans who were prevented from accessing the scarce opportunities to witness live rock music performance. As an underground rock scene developed in the 1970s, these performances became frequent targets for police abuse.

The repression of that long moment became legendary. When finally in the early 1980s, restrictions began to ease and rock music fans had one place where they could gather in relative peace—at the market that would become the Tianguis Cultural del Chopo—Ríos Manzano waxes poetic about the diversity and tolerance of the people who met there, before commenting on their reminiscences: "In the street, the anecdotes, the story of the portazo, of the repression, of the suspension of shows" (1999, 30). Despite knowing relatively few people who witnessed the 1970s as young adult rock music fans, I heard many such stories myself.

Today, police repression of youth culture is still all too prevalent, though less overtly tolerated by city authorities—during my time, affiliated with the Partido de la Revolución Democrática (Democratic Revolution Party, or PRD), which wanted to appear more liberal and friendly to young people than its PRI predecessors. Certainly, rock music performance has long been acceptable to the government, which now sponsors popular music concerts in accessible places like the Zócalo. Accordingly, while the portazo might continue to be performed, its meanings and its justifications have shifted. Contemporary punk-scene participants often frame their practice of the portazo in terms of a somewhat vague opposition to capitalism rather than to police or governmental repression, denouncing high costs or the guarding of the doors to a venue, but without the same context of a general prohibition.

Nevertheless, something of the mythical "lost decade" still clings to portazos, even modern-day ones, which are frequently filmed and put up on YouTube, aestheticized in an era of cheap digital recording. The most successful videos are those whose sound and images replicate something of the visual and aural chaos of the live event, as well as those that capture an especially audacious act of property destruction, the efficacy of property destruction and whether it can be counted as true violence being another heated topic of punk-scene discourse. For example, even years after the event, it is still possible to find video imagery of a portazo that occurred at an event that I attended in 2011, in which Gatillazo, a descendant of the popular Spanish punk band LaPolla Records, performed.[23]

In choosing performance sites, the band had actually passed over Mexico City. It was rumored that Mexico City's punk scene had developed too forbidding a reputation, precisely for its propensity to stage portazos and its especially intense behavior at shows. Supposedly, Gatillazo would not perform in the capital because they were unwilling to deal with such a crowd. Not to be deterred, several busloads of Mexico City fans made the six-hour trip out to Guadalajara to see the performance, where a few beloved bands from the capital were also slated to play. While relatively high ticket prices and security at the large-scale event may have angered fans, those who ultimately staged a portazo at the show had not been put off by the prospect of paying for transportation and other incidental costs to get there. The move seemed inspired more by the opportunity to confirm the rumors that Mexico City's "punks" were formidable, and perhaps was an attempt to strike back at the band for its supposed snub as well. In this case, as in others I witnessed, money was the justification for an action that actually seemed to be prompted by more multifaceted motivations.

It bears mentioning that the portazo is performed by a relatively small portion of any audience, and typically by those deemed "rockers" as opposed to "radicals." Generally, it's a tiny handful of people who begin to shout and throw things in order to threaten security personnel. Then there is a small cohort of people around them who assist by raising the noise level and perhaps by clustering around the disturbance, fostering the image of an angry and potentially violent mob. But the portazo is a spectator sport for many more. The vast majority of the audience waits and watches, perhaps cheering the instigators on, perhaps shaking their heads with dismay. Though the portazo may come with risks, such as enticing heavy-handed police response, it may also create rewards that are shared throughout the entire audience, whether they disapprove or not. I never heard of anyone refusing on principle to take advantage of a lower ticket price than initially demanded, for example. At the Gatillazo event, people also responded with outright glee when, after the portazo overwhelmed security, a few audience members continued the disturbance by looting the bars that lined the audience space, distributing beer freely into the crowd.

To people unfamiliar with punk and its history in Mexico City particularly, both the slam dance and the portazo may seem disturbingly aggressive, if not actually violent. So why is the slam lauded as key to the maintenance of a proper attitude and collective unity while the portazo, though a tradition in its own right, is often condemned as actually threatening to a proper punk spirit? The slam dance plays a valued role in the constitution of punk subjects, who perform their readiness for conflict through engagement with hard musical sound, inspiring forceful contact with others' bodies. In addition to providing a concrete experience in which to sacar la rabia, the slam gives punk-scene participants a chance to practice their hardness, enjoying that quality in company with friends who affirm it through their own aggression. Valorized also through a discourse of friendship and solidarity, the slam fits with the broad consensus in the scene about the necessity of self-defense.

The responsibility to watch out for others while behaving aggressively is one element of a moral conditioning that links the dance to a pervasive discourse about the importance of self-defense in the punk scene, imagined as not just an individual's self-protection but a community's. The slam-as-training-ground encourages participants to exhibit a hardened body that can not only withstand but also enjoy the impact of others' bodies upon it, feeling energized, elevated, and reassured from that intense or aggressive contact. Marked by meta-discourse about its purpose as a dance of friendship and solidarity, the slam allows punk-scene participants to practice the hardness that they value in themselves and their friends in a fairly safe, rule-governed space, albeit a rough and rowdy one.

The portazo is not similarly supported by a meta-discourse of love, friendship, and solidarity. Though the portazo may be another means to take out rage and practice hardness among friends, its outcomes are uncertain and may create problems for punk-scene participants who have not involved themselves in the storming of the doors. Additionally, scene participants may argue about who the proper targets of a portazo are, and whether a boycott wouldn't be a better tactic for opposing high ticket prices or obnoxious security practices.

Still, the spontaneous, unpredictable portazo plays an interesting role in Mexico City's punk scene exactly by denying the staging and framing of the slam and by refuting the idea that musicians or concert organizers can dictate proper behavior to fans, implicitly questioning the supposed parity of these groups. In other words, it reinforces punk-scene participants' sense of their anti-authoritarianism, even among one another. Discourse about the slam and the portazo also mirrors a contentious dialogue within the punk scene about the nature and effectiveness of violence as a tool for political protest and change, even as both practices foster a sense of self-protection in some way.

In fact, the portazo challenges punk-scene participants to decide where the line should be drawn between defense and offense, between self-defense and violence. This is a controversial theme that plays out in various ways among the broad network of people who identify as punk and anarchist. However, despite the different valorization of the two practices, I contend that they are in fact symbiotic, drawing strength from one another. While not everyone will participate in both activities regularly, they are two frequent occurrences in the scene that characterize it, both to people within and beyond it, helping "punks" maintain their sense of self-sufficiency and a broad reputation for a toughness that seems poised to escape the containment of punk-scene events. Though the slam dance gives punk-scene participants the chance to practice their hardness, the portazo enacts a threat of violence that spills beyond the punk scene and into the broader community, suggesting participants' willingness to take their rage outside. When traveling with punk-scene participants through the city—particularly when they're in groups—the anxiety that they provoke can be visceral.

I argue that self-protection lies at the heart of both the slam and the portazo as together they fulfill the training and outreach proscribed by a belief in auto-gestión: the slam as a training ground for hard "punk" bodies and minds, and the portazo as a kind of outreach, a notice and warning to authorities and other outsiders of punk-scene participants' corporeal and mental hardness. Just as all punk-scene participants may benefit by lower ticket prices in the wake of a successful portazo, they may also benefit from the notion among Mexico City residents at large that "punks" are not only hardened physically and emotionally, ready to defend themselves from attack, but unpredictable and potentially violent. The slam and the portazo together provide scene participants with the opportunity to test their camaraderie, their readiness for the difficult metropolis, and their edgy ideals, but they may also help prevent the need to test their skills, as some adversaries may think twice before tangling with such apparently hardened opponents. The harsh, loud, noisy sounds of punk, along with the tough, informative, consciousness-raising lyrics ideally create punk-scene subjects who can move with a degree of ease through difficult environments and even create difficulties for others when need be. While this reputation can confer problems, it also has its rewards.

SEED: PRACTICING PREPAREDNESS

Twice already, my friend had launched herself into me, slam style, laughing as I careened forward a few paces each time. Again, I looked at her in puzzlement. No one else was feeling it. That night's band, in a small, acoustically dead space with a poor turnout, had not inspired anyone to instigate the slam. So, what was she up to?

"You look as though you might break!" she responded to my questioning glance, preparing to launch herself at me again.

I steeled myself. I had taken yoga, tai chi, and numerous self-defense classes, both in the U.S. and locally. In fact, I'd been told numerous times by friends in the punk scene that I looked vulnerable and needed more self-defense training. I had dutifully attended the classes they recommended, some run by scene participants themselves. Surely, if I readied myself, I thought, I could stay firmly grounded enough to avoid being knocked down by a woman of my own size.

As she lunged at me, I staggered forward a bit less. But still she was able to move me.

SEED: LEARNING RAGE

One night, I was invited to a friend's home way out in Ecatepec, part of Mexico City's densely populous metropolitan zone. The gathering was like many house parties in the punk scene, a low-key affair with people chatting and drinking, listening to more punk and—very late—even dancing to a few salsa tracks in the wee small hours. My friend and I spent a good bit of time talking intently in spite of the noise. But around five in the morning, we had a minor misunderstanding. He immediately, incorrectly, assumed that I had failed to understand his point because of a weakness in my Spanish-language abilities, when in fact I simply didn't agree with him. Exhausted and annoyed, but trying to avoid an argument, I found a chair and attempted to doze off for a bit, planning to head for the metro when it opened at seven that Sunday.

As the hour approached, I made my way for the door, but my friend intercepted me. He claimed that it was unsafe for me to walk to the metro alone because gangs operated in the neighborhood. I continued to advance on the door as we debated, my irritation renewed. Finally, he stepped in front of the door, blocking my path, and began to grab at my angrily gesticulating hands in an effort to keep me inside.

Now furious, I threw my arms at his belly, attempting to shove him away. As our eyes met in mutual astonishment, I darted past him into the street. Children played with a soccer ball in the early morning light. He sent someone to tail me, to "protect me" on my walk to the train. Rage now blazing, I argued sarcastically with the tail, too, almost all the way to the metro station before I relented, my ire spent.

RABIA AND SELF-DEFENSE

In fact, many people warned me not to travel alone in Mexico City's tough metropolitan zones, believing that as an evident foreigner I would be especially susceptible to assault or abduction. While less dire in their warnings, and seldom inclined to impinge upon my freedom of movement, several punk-scene friends repeatedly urged me to take action to protect myself. This was an admonition that I did not take lightly, even if their ideas about self-defense were different—louder, more aggressive—than my own. For my friends in the punk scene, learning self-defense tactics is important as a means to confront daily challenges in the overstretched, overcrowded megalopolis of Mexico City, where many earn their living informally, some in the streets themselves. This often means knowing not just how to avoid problems, but how to deal with them head-on when they arise.

Anticipating the problems I might have while living alone in the "monster city," I had indeed completed a six-month self-defense course in Durham, North Carolina, before heading to Mexico. But the weekly hands-on training classes designed expressly for women emphasized escape techniques, which I and my fellow trainees practiced in an air-conditioned gym, wearing a class uniform of branded T-shirts and *gi* martial arts pants. In Durham, we learned that flight was always preferable to fight, but self-defense classes in Mexico City—whether or not they were created by and for women—focused more on offensive techniques. I was frequently called upon to learn how to strike an opponent, something that I found physically and emotionally difficult. As a musician, I also worried about breaking my wrists or otherwise hurting my hands. While the mostly male teachers attempted to talk women through the process of using our stronger lower bodies to propel force through our comparatively weaker arms, I once watched a woman struggle because she had long, talon-like fingernails and could not even close her hand into a fist. On the other hand, there were impressive female role models within the punk scene, from women who had trained extensively in the martial arts to those who had developed admirable physical strength and prowess generally. Nevertheless, the style of self-defense propagated at several of the classes I attended in Mexico City did not make me feel empowered, but rather helped to reinforce my feelings of vulnerability.

Additionally, while the logic of flight that I encountered in my Durham class resonated better with me, the setting and focus of that training was way off the mark in terms of preparing me for my life in Mexico City. In contrast to the spacious, cool, orderly gym setting in Durham, exclusively catering to women, even attending a punk show in Mexico City—whether it was one that achieved scene ideals of intensified camaraderie or not—required navigating rough, crowded, sweaty, male-dominated spaces. There, I was impacted by various kinds of aggression happening around or literally on my body, some of which threatened me physically, whether or not they were just part of the action. Escaping from a chokehold—choking being a notorious tactic among domestic abusers and therefore highlighted in my class in Durham—was a skill that quickly receded from my embodied memory in such a completely different environment requiring completely different self-defense strategies. When my friend clamped an arm across my neck and upper torso, steering me into the slam dance, for example, not only was this an unfamiliar hold, but I was also hampered in my effort to disengage myself by the fact that we were jumping around, our bodies colliding together and with other dancers'.

But as I had feared, the city also provided plenty of hard knocks. On one occasion, I was robbed at gunpoint. On another, I was grabbed from behind while unlocking the door to my building. I was sexually harassed by men I knew and by police, by strangers in the street, in the metro, in the market, in public buildings—too many times to remember. Though I certainly experienced sexual harassment in the u.s., I was more visible on the streets of the neighborhoods I frequented in Mexico City because of my differences from the local population, and I often traveled alone. Early on, I cut off all of my hair in the misplaced hope that greater androgyny might protect me, but to no avail.

Most disturbingly, men from the punk scene who I increasingly trusted might suddenly behave in aggressive or sexually suggestive ways. One wrangled an invitation to visit me at home and then refused to leave for hours, repeatedly hinting that he wanted to stay the night. Another man unexpectedly folded his arms around me when we found ourselves alone together in a room. Bizarrely, one friend bit my shoulder in full view of many others at a party, where, unbeknownst to me, he had been drunkenly insinuating all evening that we were having a sexual relationship. Most of these incidents caused rifts that were later healed but left me thinking hard about the line between intimacy and violence.

Throughout my fieldwork period, I was also haunted by the memory of Marcella Grace Eiler (known as "Sali"), a fiercely independent North American artist and activist I never met but whose travels in Mexico inspired me just as much as her brutal rape and murder in Oaxaca in 2008 frightened me, all while I weighed the risks of my decisions to trust new friends and move freely with them or alone, in the city and in the country broadly. Many women were rattled by Sali's horrific death, including her own friends in Mexico City's punk scene. In one of my earliest interactions, I listened to two women and a man speculate furtively about the assault as we had a beer following a punk show. They spoke softly and didn't name her, darting quick glances in my direction as they exchanged opinions about the man believed to have murdered her. I guessed that they didn't want to tell me about her or thought that, as a relative newcomer, I wouldn't have heard. But in fact I knew exactly who they were talking about, having first learned about Sali from a fellow North American woman, a traveler I met through a local hostel who was feeling anxious about leaving for social justice work in the southern part of the country.[24]

In the "seeds" I've recounted, being encouraged to practice a certain physical toughness or simply feeling and acting upon rage with punk-scene friends enabled me to cross my limits, surpassing an intensely embodied resistance to engage in—let alone initiate—physical aggression, even in self-defense. Perhaps like many women, I had not previously experienced the arousal of a "fight or flight" reaction naturally, but I had learned over time to prompt something like it.[25] Incensed at and also slightly fearful of the friend who obstructed my path, I reacted not only with a loud, enraged voice but also with my own strategic and forceful action. Among the complex range of emotions, including humiliation, that I experience when reflecting on the incident, relief also stems from having been tested in a tough situation.[26] It was a lesson I learned not in self-defense classes but from the intimate contact I had with punk-scene friends, who believed both in the power of rage to stimulate necessary action and in the place of physical confrontation as part of a plan for self-defense. Like Renato Rosaldo trying to understand head hunters' rage, I better understood the affective practices and the discourse on rabia that happened around me with punk-scene friends when I was able to fully experience and express my own sense of rage among them.

As a result of my fieldwork in Mexico City's punk scene, I also began to notice how often I reacted with sadness rather than anger when observing structural inequities in the world around me. Women friends in the punk scene did not report feeling similarly but described feeling anger, which motivated rather than enervated them. This, too, was a powerful lesson that helped me better understand how I had likely been conditioned by my gender and race, as well as what was happening around me with punk-scene friends.[27]

Though I was never able to experience the adrenaline-soaked joy of full participation in the slam, the playfulness of the moment with my female friend recounted earlier stuck with me, as she suggested my laughable physical vulnerability with a bit of affection, attempting to teach me. Ideally, the slam itself should have an element of play, even if it helps toughen its participants. A sense of play is harder to discern in the context of the portazo, as those who create its noise and its threat want to appear aggressive, menacing, and, above all, purposeful.

Physical aggression occupies an uneasy place in local punk-scene discourse. Many of the most universally respected figures in the scene are actually quite pacific in their interpersonal relations, or at least do not engage in bodily violence with any regularity. Others have a strong history and reputation for their prowess in street fighting. While some punk-scene participants insist that their fearful public image as violence-prone is an unfair stereotype, motivated by hostility to their politics, others insist on the necessity of being prepared for attack. Moreover, punk-scene participants' reputation for physical violence actually seems to help them achieve certain group goals, particularly when relating to individuals and groups outside of the scene. The Espacio Anarcopunk within the Chopo market, for example, owes its existence in part to the threat of violence that thwarted punk participation might incur.

That same threat of violence means that the portazo is almost always a successful endeavor, despite the fact that the scene itself sustains the collateral damage of detentions and police brutality, sometimes unleashed on innocent bystanders. Since everyone present outside the event benefits from the lowered ticket price, there are many people in the scene who welcome the practice nevertheless. The portazo also creates quite a spectacle, which passersby frequently stop to watch, just as fistfights among scene participants generate large, enthusiastic audiences of peers, as well as disinterested onlookers. These displays of hardness help spread the word that people who associate with the city's punk scene are tough and potentially aggressive. The public display of hardness also extends to the appearance that some participants adhere to, which may incorporate items such as military boots, army fatigues, brass knuckles, spiked jackets, and chains, in addition to the multiple piercings and tattoos that broadcast their toughness. On at least two occasions, I saw men wearing protective cups on the outsides of their trousers, a humorous play on the theme of defense-inspired attire. But while irony may lurk at the edges, protecting oneself continues to be serious business.

Due to the difficult environment of el DeFectuoso, rage may be prompted by the chaos, noise, and dysfunction of one of the biggest cities on earth, but punk-scene participants know that its intensity can be harnessed. What some might term violence—from aggressive interpersonal behaviors to edgy song lyrics that seem to promote violence against state authorities—many would likely term self-defense against the myriad ways in which they must encounter the violence of everyday life. The vehemence of rage promotes a necessary mental and physical toughness, an acute awareness of political and social ills, and motivates a quest for self-protection through various kinds of self-defense training, from the overt participation in training classes to the more subtle ways in which bodies are conditioned through intense sound and participation in affective practices like the slam dance.

While there is a great deal of conversation about feeling and channeling rage, scene participants spend far less energy on defining what solidarity entails in such a climate. In fact, a practice like the portazo reveals the challenges and instabilities of friendship and solidarity among punk-scene participants. And of course, participants in Mexico City's punk scene engage in many activities beyond tocadas. The challenge, then, is not just to ignite rage in the context of the punk show but, ideally, to keep it alight while creating and distributing fanzines, organizing shows and events, cohering in bands and collective organizations, attending meetings and protests, and participating in other kinds of political activities. Attention to these activities reveal multiple forms of agency among punk-scene participants, who are not simply impacted by musical feelings contained within specific configurations of sound or affective practices built through decades of socializing in the context of Mexico City's punk scene, but actively refashion them with a great deal of debate and even conflict. For many participants in Mexico City's punk scene, conflict, opposition, and dissent are pleasurable. A taste for these pleasures extends from punk shows to many other events in the scene, prompting heated debates about how to tell the story of punk and anarchism in Mexico City and who has the right to do so, the subject of the next chapter.

THREE

Dissent

SEED: PROTEST IN SOUND

¡A luchar, a luchar, por la libertad!
¡A luchar, a luchar, por la libertad!
¡A luchar, a luchar, por la libertad!
¡A luchar, a luchar, por la libertad!

Masacre 68, "No estamos conformes," from their album
No estamos conformes *(We are not satisfied), 1990.*

"Let's fight, let's fight, for freedom!" This repeated phrase, from the title track of the 1990 album by Mexican hardcore punk band Masacre 68, is voiced so many times that it begins to sound like a chant and possibly even a mantra. On the fuzzy, lo-fi recording, featuring raspy, guttural vocals, the song "No estamos conformes" opens with a brief instrumental introduction by a distorted guitar and drums at a fairly slow tempo, establishing the foundation for the opening verse. This describes the situation that the band stands in opposition to: "Human rights; they violate them everywhere . . . in Mexico, it's our destiny."[1] The rest of band joins the lead vocalist to shout, "Hambre, miseria, y represión," citing problems such as "hunger," "misery," and "repression," though in different repetitions of the chorus, the vocalists substitute "depression" for "repression." After the four iterations of the exhortation to fight, the band switches meter to a quick march, picking up the pace, with the vocalist yelling "Nooooo!" above the instrumental distortion while the intensity of the song grows.

With the much faster tempo, the gravelly lead voice frames a response to the inhumane conditions he described briefly in the opening verse: "We must free ourselves; from exploitative dominance; of capitalist pigs; we initiate a protest."[2] Here, the song structure creates a slight pause for clarity if not for cool. Who is the "we" that initiates this protest? The answer, intoned in a second up-tempo chorus, featuring the whole band shouting together, expresses a broad solidarity: "punks y gente reprimida" (punks and repressed peoples). Still at the faster tempo, the band again repeats the threat they face: "Hambre, miseria, y represión!"

But suddenly the pace slows, and there's a tiny bit of an interlude before the vocalist begins a long, nonverbal, seemingly tortured shout, a string of vocables: "Aaaaaaah, ya, ya, ya, ya, yaaaaaaa!" Now the final chorus begins, with the band calling "A luchar!" as the lead vocalist responds, "por la libertad!" After four iterations of this call-and-response, the entire song repeats with minimal differences. This time, when the final chorus arrives, the band again repeats the lyric four times but then shortens and repeats it several times more: "por la libertad, por la libertad!" The effect is like phasing, hypnotic in its repetition, the words losing their precise meaning and becoming reminiscent of the moment in a protest when a slogan becomes purely participatory, the words' meaning largely succumbing to the feeling of being affectively in sync within a group of chanting, shouting protestors. To me, this performance simulates a rally in the context of a punk song. Stuck on repeat, the phrase "A luchar, a luchar, por la libertad!" frames action for social justice within the context of a protest, urging listeners to direct their rage into fighting against the government, the perpetrator of human rights abuses.

THE PLEASURES OF DISSENT

Participating in certain affectively charged protests and rallies may stimulate the same feelings of rage as a good punk show does. Certainly, some of my friends looked forward to protests with the same excitement that gripped them when well-liked punk bands traveled through town. Confirming my own observations that demonstrations were well-anticipated events, a grinning older scene participant at the Biblioteca Social Reconstruir validated my sense of the readiness with which many greet the prospect. "Punks just love a protest!" he exclaimed.

FIGURE 3.1. Punk show featuring the band Ak47 at the Foro Alicia
in 2017. Photo by Yaz "Punk" Núñez.

Among a substantial number of punk-scene participants who attended protests
with some regularity, demonstrations were like tocadas, marking a key part of
their sense of punk identification. Because demonstrations were important to
friends in the scene, I attended many of them over the years, from an Antifa
march, to annual October 2 commemorations and May Day rallies, to protests
outside of prisons where people were being unfairly detained, to demonstrations
in front of the U.S. embassy, and more.

The intensity of rabia is not only useful in the context of the tocada but also
pleasurable. In fact, a taste for rabia animates encounters and events beyond
the punk show, with protests being one clear parallel in which feeling a motivating rage can be a stimulant to individual and collective enjoyment. In both
cases, rabia is figured as something that surges against some perceived wrong
or obstacle. In the tocada, rabia is stimulated by lyrics that detail opposition to
political failings as well as by intense, physically impactful sound and the impact
of other people's bodies reacting to it. In the protest, there is a clear target of
opposition. While Kevin Dunn (2016) claims that oppositionality forms a key
part of a global punk identity, something that prompts an awakening to action or
"disalienation," I take that a step further. I assert that assuming an oppositional
stance is in fact a source of pleasure, at least for people who participate in the

scene that I know best. The pleasant charge of punk shows and protests are both created through a kind of oppositionality, a pleasure in dissent—something that forms a key part of a local punk poetics.

Moreover, it's important to note that the pleasures of dissent animate more than the ritual-like events of tocadas and demonstrations. It also animates everyday interpersonal dynamics and conversations, particularly those in which people seek to define what punk is, what anarchism is, and what their histories are. This is hotly contested material, inspiring dissent among friends, bandmates, and collectives who value different authors, different definitions of key terms, and different versions of histories that themselves include many stories about dissent, from the contested arrival of rock music in Mexico to the 1968 student movement to the burgeoning interest in anarchism as a tool for activism globally.

FIGURE 3.2. Preparing for a march from the Monumento a la Revolución on May Day 2018. Photo by Yaz "Punk" Núñez.

I learned quickly that dissenting over the accuracy of histories was important to my new friends in the punk scene, as many began to educate me about their favored versions of events, recommending books and telling me not to read others, debating about whether someone who had participated in the local scene decades ago still had the credibility to write a history of punk in Mexico today. They also invited me to pertinent exhibitions, to attend lectures or talks by respected local scholars or journalists, and so on. Beyond the contested histories of rock and punk music, friends in the punk scene also got into debates about other historical conflicts, particularly the Mexican Revolution, the 1968 student movement, the Spanish Civil War, and the Zapatista rebellion, as well as many more contemporary political movements. I found I needed to brush up on my knowledge of Mexican history if I wanted to enter into the fray of debate. The debates made these histories feel more alive, personal, and tangible as they animated everyday exchanges, forming the stuff of ordinary conversation.

As it happened, my first personal encounters with local rock music histories happened even before I began to spend time in Mexico City's punk scene, so I had some little experiential preparation to begin. Rock music is still widely beloved in Mexico City, and listening to older bands is not just for older people (Meyers 2015). I learned this at big arena shows by still-touring bands like German heavy metal band the Scorpions, who I witnessed playing to an enthusiastic, generationally mixed crowd in the Foro Sol during September 2008. However, even that enthusiasm was nothing like the adulation I later experienced for homegrown heroes of the Mexican rock music scene a few weeks later.

SEED: A BIRTHDAY PARTY FOR MEXICAN ROCK

At the vast Palacio de los Deportes stadium in October 2008, a band originally called Three Souls in My Mind celebrated forty years since their first concert in October 1968, just days after a horrifying massacre of protestors perpetrated by the Mexican government. At the birthday concert, there were twenty special musical guests, a light show, a giant cake shaped like a guitar, video projections, and a packed audience of diehard fans who screamed and danced through a five-hour concert presentation, the 40th anniversary of El Tri (as the band was renamed early in its history)—arguably, Mexico's most famous rock band.

I was in a special box for the press, invited by some new friends who worked in the local newspaper industry. Free tickets to musical events in town were mundane perks for them, but this time their excitement was palpable as they gathered to witness the concert. Not only was El Tri performing, but luminaries like Celso Piña and popular bands such as Molotov and Tex-Tex also appeared among a long parade of invited artists.

El Tri's vocalist, Alex Lora, presided over the ceremonies, looking and sounding the old-school rocker with long hair, sunglasses, and a black leather jacket, shouting into the microphone with his distinctively pressed, raspy voice. After hours as ebullient emcee, he closed the concert with his famous hoarse yell, "Viva México y qué viva el rock 'n' roooooooll!" (Long live Mexico and long live rock 'n' roll).

ROCK IN MEXICO: FROM CENSORSHIP TO THE UNDERGROUND

As I was finishing this manuscript in late 2020, the international streaming platform Netflix released a documentary series called *Rompan todo* (Break it all), a history of rock in Latin America from the 1950s through the present day, produced and partly narrated by Argentine composer Gustavo Santaolalla, who played with the band Arco Iris during his youth in Buenos Aires. Within a day of its release, I began to see howls of protest and derision cropping up on Mexico City friends' social media posts. Some of this centered on the lack of proper representation for punk in Mexico, including protests about one specific "punk" who was name-checked in a brief interview segment. But many of the commentators panned the series generally, suggesting it to be the work of an out-of-touch bourgeois.

According to my friends in Mexico City, this documentary is going to teach you not what you should know about rock in Latin America, but only one privileged perspective on the topic. They have a point. The musicians who represent rock music in the series are not people who continued struggling in an underground scene, but those who ultimately achieved mainstream success. Though some lived and performed through earlier periods when the music was repressed and criminalized by hostile governments, they later became national and international stars, many forming part of a global music industry elite.

Though his books were by no means immune from criticism in the scene, several people recommended that I read the work of José Agustín as I delved deeper into the history of rock in Mexico to understand the conflict-filled backstory of Mexican punk. Agustín (2008) is a cultural critic who lived through the turbulent sixties and seventies, including a stint in prison on charges of drug possession, one experience that would lead him to write a book titled *El rock de la carcel* (Prison rock, 2007), as well as other, more historical narratives about what he and others refer to as *la contracultura* in Mexico.

Like others I would later read on my own steam, Agustín recounted that—as in various Latin American nations grappling with the outcomes of revolutions in their recent histories—rock music was taken as a menace in Mexico (Zolov 1999; Pacini Hernandez et al. 2004; Avant-Mier 2010). While leftists perceived the music to be a product of a neo-imperialist culture industry in the United States, conservative Mexican critics began to view it as a threat to the established moral order, undermining the *buenas costumbres*, the sanctioned forms of good behavior that maintained church and state hierarchies (Zolov 1999, 27). Increasingly, governmental and other cultural authorities attempted to restrict and repress the performance and consumption of rock music, moves that were also symptomatic of a growing intergenerational disconnect between Mexican youth and their elders.

Though the enthusiastic reception of early rock 'n' roll imported from the u.s. was short lived, initially it had been a success among a small body of cosmopolitan listeners, they themselves the product of a so-called "miracle" of political stability, economic development, and global integration, which allowed for some small growth in the number of people enjoying a comfortable, urbane, middle-class lifestyle. That brief, midcentury moment of seeming prosperity followed decades of difficult post-revolutionary transition, but ultimately generated further inequities among Mexicans of various backgrounds.

The first years following the Mexican Revolution had been bloody, turbulent ones, after its first objective, the toppling of dictator Porfirio Díaz, was accomplished by 1911. In the ensuing decade, different political factions vied for power, creating a civil war–like situation, in which many more people were killed. By the early 1920s, a modicum of stability had been achieved, stimulating not only a period of political consolidations but also a focus on populist goals that could unite vast portions of the population after years of divisions. This period also produced a cultural flowering, as Mexico's artists, particularly famous muralists like Diego Rivera, David Siqueiros, and José Clemente Orozco, worked together with the nascent federal government to legitimize the new "revolutionary" state (O'Malley 1986; Gonzales 2002; Coffey 2012; Joseph and Buchenau 2013). Over the course of the 1930s, the state continued to gain power, welding itself to the emerging Partido Revolucionario Institucional (Institutional Revolutionary Party, or the PRI for short).[3] The last stages of PRI consolidation occurred simultaneously with the state's accomplishment of savvy, popular objectives, such as the expropriation of lands and the nationalization of the oil industry, events that took place during the administration of President Lázaro Cárdenas, which lasted until 1940. Over the next several decades, however, the PRI would continue to maintain a stranglehold on Mexican political power, becoming what some have called a "soft dictatorship" of one-party rule that would last for over seventy years.

By the mid-1950s, when rock 'n' roll first appeared in Mexico, the by-then well-established PRI government had moved away from populist programs toward a focus on large-scale development, aspiring for integration into the global economy and instituting policies that, while creating a small and prosperous middle class in urban areas, also left many rural and Indigenous populations in poverty. Mexico City was the heart of the country, the seat of the federal government, and the nation's economic engine. It grew exponentially at midcentury, drawing migrants in from the countryside, particularly those who sought to leave behind increasingly poor conditions in agricultural areas.

While at first the middle-class Mexican audience happily accepted rock 'n' roll as one choice among a cornucopia of sophisticated musical options to consume, the music imported from the U.S. came to be linked in public opinion to youth delinquency at home and abroad—though not through happenstance. Governmental and private-sector forces rallied against it, instituting various legal and economic measures to stall its popularity, including restrictions on radio play, high import tariffs that drove up the price of foreign recordings, and, increasingly into the 1960s, police raids on the *cafés cantantes*, the coffeehouses where live, local rock music performance occurred in Mexico City. This occurred despite the fact that by the end of the 1950s, Mexico's music industry had taken advantage of the restrictive climate for foreign rock 'n' roll by creating a tame but successful version of the music that was reconceived as *rocanrol*: covers of English-language hits translated into Spanish and scoured clean of offensive words or ideas.

The PRI government was not just showing an increasingly authoritarian force in the cultural realm, however. Over the course of the late 1950s, many people became disillusioned with the so-called "revolutionary state," which—among other issues—was suppressing labor rights, co-opting unions, and imprisoning political dissidents. Perhaps most ironically, the state also refused full-throated support for the Cuban Revolution, though the Cuban revolutionaries themselves had been inspired in part by Mexico's 1910 revolution. Initially, PRI leaders had attempted to capitalize on this link, hoping that it would reinvigorate faith in the Mexican Revolution's aftermath. But when thousands marched in Mexico City to express solidarity with the Cuban people during the Bay of Pigs Invasion in 1961, the state responded with violent repression (Hodges 1995, 111). Slowly, unrest had been coalescing from the late 1950s onward, during what some historians refer to as the "long 1960s," a period of incremental but growing cultural and political upheaval that would come to a head in 1968, just as youth movements did in many other nations around the world (Hodges 1995; Joseph and Buchenau 2013; Pensado 2013; Draper 2018).

Meanwhile, by the mid-1960s, bands outside of the sanctioned national music-industry orbit had achieved success in u.s. border-town nightclubs, not by creating clean-cut, Spanish-language rocanrol, but by performing rock songs by the Beatles, the Rolling Stones, and other British acts, creating close copies of the English-language originals. These bands began to travel to Mexico City to perform, fueling the transformation of rocanrol to Mexican rock. Authorities across the political spectrum were again united in their condemnation of this turn of events, especially since further changing behaviors among youth—from desires to dress with greater informality, to increased alcohol or marijuana use, to a homegrown version of hippies (dubbed *jipitecas*) roaming the Mexican countryside—were once again attributed to the impact of rock music (Marroquín 1975; Zolov 1999; Agustín 2008).[4]

For a long while, rock music was better linked to rejecting the cultural status quo than to outright political rebellion. Like their counterparts in other Latin American nations, more politically engaged young people in Mexico tended to prefer the genre "new song" (*nueva canción* or *nueva trova*) because it utilized native folk instruments and fostered close listening to politically conscious lyrics instead of encouraging dancing as early rock 'n' roll did (Pacini Hernandez et al. 2004). But by late 1968, as a growing youth movement gathered steam, young Mexicans increasingly began to share a "grammar of youth rebellion that incorporated discourses of Latin American folk revival, rock music, and revolutionary struggle" (Zolov 1999, 118). Over the course of 1968, rock music would be incorporated into the soundtrack of the burgeoning student movement, which ultimately became a broader coalition of students and other young people, educators, political leftists, and workers. As dissent expanded among social groups in the summer of 1968, attracting participants beyond students and educators, this palette of musical choices fostered a broad solidarity and cultural exchange among the various groups that formed the growing movement (Agustín 2008, 82).

Many participants in the student movement were reformists who believed in the principles of the post-revolutionary 1917 Constitution and lamented the state's subsequent move away from its ideals. But there was also a more radical current within it, something that appealed to people I know in the punk scene. Informed not only by Marxism, movement leaders and participants also began to look again at anarchism, a well-rooted, if marginalized, political tradition in Mexico that had been largely ignored by leftists since the Revolution.[5] In this, they were inspired by well-known figures like José Revueltas, a member of Mexico's Communist Party who helped revive interest in the legacy of Mexican anarchist Ricardo Flores Magón.[6] The movement marked a moment when many young people in Mexico not only became politicized but also first experimented with organizing in a grassroots manner, across class and other differences.

Over the summer of 1968, students and others in the movement staged strikes and demonstrations, attempted to attract working people to their cause by creating flash meetings in poor neighborhoods, and responded to increasing repression by police, military, and riot troops. Small groups of radical *brigadistas* modeled their tactics on the May Revolution in Paris. Many protestors recalled the importance of equitable participation in the movement, despite the fact that several historical narratives would later create a vision at odds with its heterogeneity, reinscribing a hierarchical image of the movement and its seeming majority of middle-class male protagonists (Poniatowska 1971; Carey 2005; Draper 2018).

But bringing this narrative of inclusive, hopeful civil disobedience almost to a halt, on October 2, 1968, the movement suffered a devastating event: the massacre at the Plaza de las Tres Culturas, part of the Tlatelolco housing complex in Mexico City. With thousands of people massed for a peaceful rally in the confined plaza of the apartment complex, government agents opened fire, beginning an indiscriminate shoot-out that lasted for hours, killing and wounding a large number of people, from movement participants to innocent bystanders.[7] For decades, the government claimed that the protestors themselves had begun firing weapons and denied public efforts to obtain official information on the events.

Despite evidence of the government's culpability surfacing over the years, there has never has been a formal investigation or judicial reckoning with those responsible for the massacre over fifty years later, and the number of fatalities remains unknown, though it has been estimated at about 325 people.[8] In addition to the many deaths in the plaza, many more people were beaten and taken into police custody, with several tortured in prison, some remaining incarcerated for years with the state refusing to acknowledge them as political prisoners. Some people simply vanished after October 2, either "disappeared" or gone into exile. The violence of the massacre stunned people—not only for its extremity but also for the fact that an attack of such magnitude had not been foreseen, despite escalating repression against demonstrators in previous months and weeks. It became one of an increasing number of shocks and scares that would undermine public confidence in the PRI over the next decades, leading to its ultimate loss of federal power in the year 2000.[9]

Directly after October 2, 1968, many young people believed that overt political dissent had been closed off to them, leaving them to voice their outrage through cultural channels instead. This attitude had an impact not only on social movement organizing but also on the development of rock music in Mexico. A broad coalition of Mexican youth was dubbed "La Onda" (the wave or groove), signaling a sense of being in tune with a new vibe, a new way of living. Gradually turning away from rock music imports and covers of Anglo-American hits, the music of La Onda increasingly included original rock music created by Mexican bands, though initially the language of choice was still mostly English. In part, this reflected young people's continued interest in forming part of a politically progressive, global youth culture that consumed rock music.

La Onda's signature moment was the Avándaro rock music festival in September 1971, an event frequently compared to Woodstock in upstate New York in 1969. Despite the violent repression of 1968—and the more recent Corpus Christi Mas-

FIGURE 3.3. Protestor at the march in 2018 in remembrance of the massacre of October 2, 1968. Some people believe the government's repression was so harsh because the movement was seen as an embarrassment on the international stage as Mexico prepared to hold its first Olympic Games later in October 1968. Photo by Yaz "Punk" Núñez.

sacre just three months before, in June 1971—thousands of young people traveled to the Valle de Bravo outside of Mexico City to listen to homegrown Mexican rock bands.[10] Like Woodstock, the event drew thousands more participants than anyone had anticipated, but it also happened peacefully in spite of its mix of young people from various places and social classes.

Nevertheless, participants' freewheeling behavior, including drug consumption, public nudity, and some display of the American flag, shocked many (Urteaga Castro-Pozo 1998; Zolov 1999; Agustín 2008). Rock musicians who participated in the festival recall that it was being broadcast live, but that the radio connection and electrical power were cut when one of the performers swore.[11] Examples from media headlines give a sense of the moral outrage that colored much subsequent newspaper coverage: "The Hell of Avándaro: A disgusting hippie orgy" and "Nudity, Marijuana, Degenerate Sexuality, Filth, Hair, Blood, and Death" (Urteaga Castro-Pozo 1998, 95). Following Avándaro, cultural authorities across the political spectrum attacked La Onda. Leftists, who had always rejected rock music as a neo-colonialist cultural infiltration, joined governmental officials and conservative cultural critics, doubling down with their disapproval. Rock musicians, distributors, and concert organizers were increasingly repressed by police and attacked in the press. Large-scale concerts, regular rock music venues, and the distribution of rock music records were virtually abolished for much of the ensuing ten-year period, with the occasional public rock music performance available only for wealthy guests in upscale establishments (Ríos Manzano 1999; Pacini Hernandez et al. 2004).

Many aspects of the student movement and the youth culture that had intertwined with it, including much rock music performance, went underground as young people suffered further low-level repression by police forces and condemnation by diverse cultural authorities. Some of the militants from the student movement created urban guerrilla groups that carried out assaults, robberies, and other aggressive actions in Mexico City and other cities across Mexico during the 1970s. The state fought back through a "dirty war," in which further activists were killed or disappeared. Other people chose to focus on community organizing in the aftermath of the massacres, often opting to leave the city for more rural areas (Hodges 1995; Agustín 2008).

In the face of police repression and media scorn, most middle-class young people abandoned their public interest in rock music. While many musicians of the late 1960s and early 1970s also abandoned the genre, a few took on the substantial challenges of performing in a nascent underground rock music scene

(Estrada and Palacios 2004, 150). This much-appreciated steadfastness is one reason why El Tri was still around to celebrate its fiftieth anniversary in October 2018, in a style just as splashy as the fortieth birthday bash I attended.

Providing me with another favored local voice, a punk musician friend loaned me a slim volume published in the late 1990s by Abraham Ríos Manzano, another local man who had participated in the events he describes. In his book, he refers to the 1970s as "la mítica década perdida," the mythical lost decade, a lost time for rock music and youth culture generally (Ríos Manzano 1999, 29). However, local rock music performance did survive, mostly in "hoyos fonquis," "funky holes," so called because of the dirty, smelly, and even somewhat dangerous conditions that prevailed in many spaces available for such activity, though there were some locations in wealthier parts of the city that continued to present rock performance with impunity (Urteaga Castro-Pozo 1998, 159). Some hoyos fonquis were derelict clubs with unscrupulous organizers willing to undertake the risk of holding public rock concerts in exchange for the chance to make quick cash, providing little in the way of proper sound equipment, hygienic conditions, or security. Many others were organized by musicians and fans, held in whatever spaces they could find— empty warehouses, parking lots, gyms, corner stores, or abandoned properties that were quickly and temporarily taken over for one-off concerts.

The atmosphere at these performances was notoriously rough and rowdy, another factor that dissuaded middle-class audiences and even many rock music performers from attending them. Women in particular recount the sexual harassment they experienced while performing in the hoyos fonquis, where alcohol and drug abuse were also openly tolerated (Estrada 2008). These concerts were frequent targets of the police, their tactics including everything from beating and detaining musicians and fans to the confiscation of equipment. People I met who had been rock music fans in the 1970s recounted that even family or neighborhood parties might be raided on the excuse that rock music performance was happening within them. It was in these scrappy circumstances that rock music survived the lost decade, driven increasingly to the economically marginalized neighborhoods of the city. Here, punk rock would also make its home a little while later.

Writing about Mexican youth culture following the repressions of the late 1960s and early 1970s, former ondero José Agustín commented:

Towards 1974, there was a lot of talk, with an insistence that resembled a campaign, of the death of rock. Naturally, this was "wishful thinking" or the old trick of saying something to see if it will come true. What was clear was that a phase of the counterculture had been left behind, the romantic, peace-and-love of the '60s. The new phase was coming on particularly dark.[12]

SEED: "HEY, BANDA!"

So shouted my new, smiling acquaintance late Saturday afternoon at the Chopo market. He was coming toward me, or so I thought. I checked, throwing a quick glance over my shoulder to see if he might be speaking to someone just behind me. With mystified pleasure, I awkwardly took his hand and then bumped his fist with my own, returning the banda handshake he extended.

A few people always greeted me this way, offering me a sense of belonging despite our differences. But many others kept to the more formal handshake-and-air-kiss greeting common among Mexico City residents broadly. As a foreigner, I was harder to characterize. People often demurred when I asked them to classify me. But in the minds of many, I always assumed, I was definitely more fresa—a slang term akin to "bougie"—than banda.

LA BANDA AND PUNK ROCK'S SURVIVAL IN MEXICO CITY

If an affinity for rock music briefly helped unite young people across class differences during La Onda, the subsequent repression of people who championed it fractured that sense of solidarity, heightening class divisions and encouraging the coining of the term *la banda*, which I'll unpack further later in this chapter. While there was dissent and disagreement about long-past histories that nevertheless meant something to people in the punk scene, the ability and the right to recount history became especially contested when it began to touch upon people's own lived experiences. Meanwhile, the history of punk rock's arrival in Mexico City is itself one of strife. Héctor Castillo Berthier (2004), a well-respected local sociologist, published a chapter about the subject whose title says it all: "My Generation: Rock and *La Banda*'s Forced Survival Opposite the Mexican State." In it, he details the late 1970s into the 1980s, when punk rock began making an impact, particularly in the city's metropolitan zone.

In fact, by that time the state was shifting tactics in its campaign against youth culture, not only repressing rock music performance but later co-opting rock and punk music as a method of gaining young people's trust. Some people who participated in the early punk scene actually collaborated with government programs during that time (Urteaga Castro-Pozo 1998; Detor Escobar and Hernández Sánchez n.d.). Some of these people have sustained their participation in the scene since its earliest days, while others occasionally surface to represent it despite having become far less active in the scene decades later. People who have participated in the punk scene since its early days have curated its history in various ways, amassing archives of recordings, collaborating with artists and cultural institutions, doing podcasts and interviews, and publishing books and fanzines about the history of punk in Mexico. Some of these projects were recommended to me as worthy study guides, while others generated a good deal of controversy as people debated the merits of the authors, their information, and their methods.

People who attempted to catalogue the events of the mid-1970s to the late 1980s had a tumultuous period to portray. As José Agustín wrote, the new generation of rock music lovers in the 1970s were living dark days. In addition to the great shock, frustration, and disillusionment that accompanied the death of the student movement in the late 1960s and the repression that followed in the 1970s, Mexico weathered a series of economic crises from 1973 to 1982 and afterward that intensified poverty and income inequality, creating *cinturones de miseria* (belts of misery) throughout the capital city. Crime rates began climbing, and with young people especially having little hope to work their way toward a better life, *bandas* (street gangs) began proliferating in more economically marginalized neighborhoods. The press highlighted the violence of the gangs, which not only warred with each other but also created havoc in their communities and in battles with the police. Various sociologists and cultural critics also weighed in on the confounding problem believed to exist among less economically privileged young men in particular (Gomezjara 1987, 1988; García-Robles 2013).

Interestingly, like rock 'n' roll in the 1950s, one route for punk rock's initial entrance into Mexico City had been through middle-class fans, young people who had better access to high-priced goods from foreign markets, including records. As punk rock took off in the mid-1970s, a handful of privileged Mexican young people began listening to bands like the Sex Pistols, sporting the latest fashions from London, and performing in early punk rock bands, making use of the economic and cultural capital available to them to buy records and instruments while also making use of their previous music education. Their interest in punk lasted only a little while. But in that brief moment of middle-class punk performance, some economically marginalized young people recount that they caught wind of the new, edgier subgenre of rock music happening in other parts of the city. Though punk rock was not to be found on Mexican radio or television at the time, lower-class young people took some of their cues from live, local performances by short-lived middle-class punk bands like Dangerous Rhythm and Size, as well as from a couple of publications that were produced by more privileged participants in the city's musical vanguard, little magazines titled *Conecte* and *Sonido*.[13]

Perhaps more importantly, however, my own friends in the contemporary punk scene have asserted that migration to the United States also helped fuel a new interest in punk rock, especially in Mexico City's tough suburbs. People who went to work for a time in "Gringolandia" brought back recordings that they most likely could not have afforded to buy directly in Mexico City, bringing in a mixture of "hard" rock, punk, and metal over the course of the 1970s and 1980s. Certainly, during that same time, Tijuana would become a recognized hotspot in the national Mexican punk scene, as a border town in proximity to active and innovative punk scenes in Southern California with substantial Latinx participation (Valenzuela 1988; Urteaga Castro-Pozo 1998; Berríos-Miranda et al. 2018; Rapport 2020). This happened before the intensive militarization of the border in the later 1990s, when people could still move back and forth between the two countries—not exactly with ease, but not with the same high risk of violence and death that undocumented border-crossing came to entail.

Among the less economically privileged punk-rockers in Mexico City, the concept of DIY—"do-it-yourself," which became key to punk communities in the Global North in the 1980s—was unavoidable from the start.[14] Lower-resourced fans had no choice but to attempt to create their own punk sounds and fashions, with access to records and other foreign goods remaining difficult, even if a family member or neighbor back from the States did have a small record collection. Punk rock fans from the early days of the local scene recount how they imitated the looks of bands from the United Kingdom and the United States, beginning to sell items with a punk rock aesthetic in the city's tianguis. Others scrounged for instruments and began to form bands, buoyed by the relative simplicity of the music. In the city's marginalized neighborhoods, the *chavos banda*—the gang kids, as they came to be known—were particularly enamored with the new rock subgenre (Valenzuela 1988; Urteaga Castro-Pozo 1998; Castillo Berthier 2004; Agustín 2008). Large, prominent gangs even took names associated with punk rock, labeling themselves with titles redolent of a punk aesthetic: Mierdas

Punk (Punk Shits), Apestosos (Stinkies), Ratas Punks (Punk Rats), and Vagos (Vagrants), among others (Castillo Berthier 2004, 246).

As these chavos banda reached a critical mass in the city's "popular neighbor-hoods" in the late 1970s, government officials looked to academic and journalistic research to understand what was believed to be a growing crisis among urban youth. Amid this attention, some chavos banda described the difficulties of their lives for academics, artists, and cultural critics, resulting in well-known works that documented a nascent punk scene in the city's outer zone, particularly in Nezahualcóyotl, where the docudrama *Nadie es inocente* (Nobody is innocent, directed by Sarah Minter) was filmed in 1986, young local men performing the key roles. Despite the acknowledged violence of gang members, who did not have frequent access to firearms and so largely fought with fists, knives, and other homemade weapons, sociologists and anthropologists, as well as newspaper columnists, published work that highlighted the good, cooperative qualities of the young people who participated in gangs. This tendency created what Héc-tor Castillo Berthier describes as a "mythology" of the chavos banda, painting them in a romantic light as a new kind of socially engaged actor. This notion of a potentially untapped body of politically engaged young people awakened the interest of an increasingly anemic PRI (Castillo Berthier 2004, 247).

Seeing its political stranglehold loosening in the later decades of the twentieth century following its political repression and economic failures, the PRI was compelled by positive accounts of the chavos banda. Officials began to imagine ways to co-opt their perceived social awareness for the project of shoring up party power. Changing its stance on enforcing cultural norms somewhat, the government created a new institution to engage with young people's expression, the Consejo Nacional de Recursos para la Atención de la Juventud (CREA). An innovative government initiative, CREA fostered cultural programming designed to appeal to marginalized urban youth, which included rock music performance. While many people, including the youth that the institution attempted to target, regarded CREA with well-deserved cynicism, its existence from 1977 to 1987 did help in opening up new spaces and opportunities for youth culture. Some early punk-scene participants collaborated with CREA to create visual art exhibitions and punk shows, though by the time of my own residence in the city, most of the people who could remember back to the organization regarded it as a program of naked exploitation.[15]

At the same time as the government began tinkering with its stance toward young people's free association and expression, the city's more privileged music fans also created a new outlet for musical and cultural exchange: the Chopo market. Created in 1980, the Chopo originally was a place where connoisseurs of all types of rare, expensive, or out-of-print music could meet to exchange information and goods. Demand for the market was high, and so it became a weekly event, held in the Museo del Chopo, a museum in the Santa María de la Ribera neighborhood, not far from the city center. By 1982, the market's success was becoming a bother for the museum, however, attracting large crowds that the indoor space could not accommodate. The market moved outdoors and, like many tianguis in Mexico City, it soon dominated the street.

Once outside, the tianguis also attracted the attention of people beyond the more middle-class connoisseurs that had founded it, as youth from all over the city and metropolitan zone began to attend, including large numbers of the chavos banda in search of rock and, increasingly, punk music. At the centrally located tianguis, punk fans converged from across the city, the metropolitan zone, and, finally, from other locations in the country as it became a destination for Mexicans broadly. Over the years, the Chopo became a key meeting place where punk fans swapped cassette recordings, collaborated on forming bands and writing fanzines, and otherwise began to create a sense of community and social solidarity (Gaytán Santiago 2001). This was important, some claim, one of many interventions that appeared to help address the problem of violence among young men in the barrios. As one theory goes, once the Chopo became a meeting place, gangs of chavos banda became less attached to any one particular neighborhood, prompting new networks of young people to form through their shared interest in punk and through regular attendance at the tianguis (Urteaga Castro-Pozo 1998, 167).

Others write that initiatives from within the gangs themselves were also underway in the 1980s to curb the problem of violence between the chavos banda. Recognizing the heavy toll that repeated encounters with the police had on gang members and their neighborhoods, in addition to the problem of the gang feuds themselves, the chavos banda reportedly began to form councils in the first half of the 1980s, crossing into one another's territories in order to "join forces and coordinate a defense against the police offensive, the insults of the press, and the incomprehension of society" (Agustín 2008, 110). Drawing on testimony from ex-members of gangs like the Mierdas Punk, youth-culture scholar Maritza Urteaga Castro-Pozo has described the reorganization of the gang into sectors. Apparently, this organizational tactic greatly reduced the number of violent fights among that notorious gang (1998, 201).

Another push toward this shift in self-image among the young men forming Mexico City's nascent punk scene appears to have come in the aftermath of the great earthquake that devastated Mexico City in 1985. Many thousands of people died in the powerful earthquake, which hit the city in the morning as people were leaving their homes for the day's activities. Thousands more were trapped in scores of damaged buildings, mostly in and around the centro histórico. In another blow to PRI authority, the fallout of the catastrophic earthquake again disillusioned Mexicans, who watched the shocking mismanagement of the crisis with disbelief and mounting anger. Ultimately, the government's horrifyingly inadequate response meant that city residents themselves were the ones to take charge of urgent rescue and cleanup operations. Citizens formed brigades to dig out the trapped and injured, to find and catalogue the dead, and to clear away the rubble, all while providing food and other services to the suddenly homeless.

During this traumatic series of events, the chavos banda won some approbation from the public at large, due to the perception that they selflessly assisted in these efforts and participated in the brigades with great courage and industry, though many lived far enough in the city's outskirts that they didn't experience the same level of impact from the tragedy. Author Elena Poniatowska, who already had earned a great deal of respect for her reporting on the Tlatelolco massacre, joined the brigades as a means of investigating the earthquake's aftermath. Writing about her experiences, she praised the chavos banda for their bravery while lamenting their marginality and the low esteem in which many continued to hold them.[16] Maritza Urteaga Castro-Pozo, too, recounts that the participation in the brigades created further self-reflection among members of the Mierdas and other gangs, an opinion confirmed by chavos banda and early punk-scene participants, remembering the moment decades later (1998; Detor Escobar and Hernández Sánchez n.d.).

For these and perhaps other reasons in a constellation of causes over time, various authors recount that many bandas became la banda. José Agustín, for example, writes, "By whatever means, little by little the gangs decreased the violence a bit, and without losing their contentious character, began converting themselves into 'la banda,' something much wider that included all the 'lumpen' kids that listened to rock and grouped themselves together to feel more powerful" (2008, 110). As the generalized concept of la banda cemented itself over time, it has accreted a range of meanings that encode a sense of solidarity among less economically privileged young people, a sense of solidarity that continues to rest upon signifiers of class, including musical taste and style.

However, despite the prevalence of the term *la banda* in daily Mexico City life, few people have seriously attempted to define the slippery concept. Héctor Castillo Berthier is among that handful, one who has tried to suggest its wide range of significance. His lengthy description goes on for almost an entire page of text, but I share just a key bit of it here, in which he emphasizes the intertwining of three important aspects of la banda—its contentious nature, its sense of solidarity, and banda individuals' affinity for rock music:

> *banda* is also a space of social contention; it empowers youth who have very limited economic, social, or even moral resources, who do daily battle just to stay alive. *Banda* implies not being alone. *Banda* allows for unity within the marginalized urban zones . . . that continue to proliferate throughout the Mexican capital—as well as a defense from the world outside. . . . Above all, *la banda* implies rock. (2004, 243)

However, as Castillo Berthier also notes, over the course of the 1980s, rock music in Mexico experienced a "slow but steady return toward the middle classes" (2004, 248). By the mid-1980s, middle-class young people began consuming rock music imports from Argentina and Spain, fueling an eventual boom in *rock en español* in Mexico, which finally gave Mexican rock bands the opportunity to record original music on national labels. Still, a class-informed split would remain among fans of different rock subgenres. As Castillo Berthier emphasized in his definition of la banda, a love of rock music often distinguished people from the more economically marginalized parts of the city, beginning in the 1970s.

But by the late 1980s, rock music in Spanish informed by a pop aesthetic, with references to Latin American folk and commercial music styles, was often perceived by la banda as fresa. Literally translated as "strawberry," the term *fresa* suggests the soft, fruity delicacy of middle-class values and aesthetics, constituting a fragile, out-of-touch sensibility. Among my friends in Mexico City, the descriptor *fresa* continues to be borderline slanderous, something damning to say about someone, a pejorative label. Though no one ever called me a fresa to my face, as a white North American who didn't claim a punk identity, I believed that I was probably perceived as one, at least by those who didn't know me well. This was why it was always a surprise and a pleasure when friends in the punk scene lent me honorary banda status.

Despite the fact that punk informed some prevalent rock en español bands across Latin America, many employing a post-punk aesthetic, in Mexico City the unmediated sound of punk continued to be associated with less-privileged youth, particularly young men from parts of the metropolitan zone like Ecatepec, which earned the nickname "Ecatepunk" for the many punk fans who came from that municipality.[17] Ironically, the Chopo market not only provided a central meeting place for the far-flung banda, but it also helped make rock acceptable to Mexican cultural authorities once more as other marketgoers shared rock en español recordings there.

Nevertheless, the tianguis itself had experienced a rocky journey over the course of the early 1980s. When the market moved to the street, with an increase in the quantity of economically marginalized young people attending, problems arose between the market and its neighbors, who soon began to complain to the authorities. Starting in 1985, the tianguis was repeatedly threatened with dissolution, forced to relocate several times. Despite various interventions—including the notable backing of *La Jornada*, a fairly new, left-leaning national newspaper based in Mexico City—the Chopo remained without a permanent home for the next few years, bouncing between locations across the city that presented greater or lesser challenges for its continued existence.

Finally, the market found its current home in the Colonia Guerrero, where it remains to this day, taking place every Saturday afternoon. Problems between the market and its neighbors subsided somewhat in the later 1980s but were not fully resolved. Accordingly, some of the founders created the Asociación Civil, a group organized to defend the tianguis from legal problems, and El Tianguis Cultural del Chopo was reborn under its current name. But with organization came changes (Meneses Reyes 2003). Intricate rules were established regarding the ownership and use of puestos, the booths where vendors display merchandise, and an internal committee attempted to quash the consumption of alcohol and drugs within the market. Perhaps most importantly, the organization began to favor certain vendors active within its membership, thereby lessening the voice of those who believed in trading and exchange as a key part of market sociability (Ríos Manzano 1999, 38). Divisions apparent among rock music fans were ultimately knit into the structure and customs of the market itself.

Sonically and ideologically, these divisions became even more apparent over the latter course of the decade. As fresas listened to a more pop-infused rock en español, hardcore punk, with its loud, pared-down aesthetics, was also making its way into the metropolitan zone, transforming what punk rock sounded like and what it meant for *la banda punk*, who became increasingly invested in learning about anarchism and its histories (Poma and Gravante 2016).

FIGURE 3.4. Punk show featuring the band Atoxxxico at the Foro Libélula (formerly El Clandestino) in 2019. Photo by Yaz "Punk" Núñez.

SEED: DESCONFIANZA AMONG THE HISTORIANS

While getting to know the local punk scene, I regularly went to one of its fixtures, the Biblioteca Social Reconstruir, a personal library amassed and shared by Ricardo Mestre Ventura, who had immigrated to Mexico as a Spanish Civil War exile decades before. This was when the library was located in rented quarters downtown near the Palacio de Bellas Artes, just weeks before it would be forced to close for a period of nearly six years. In the library, I sorted through old newspapers from the Spanish Civil War, browsed and borrowed from its shelves of books, attended a few collectives' meetings, and chatted with its caretakers and visitors. After the library closed one afternoon, I was invited to tag along with a group of men of varying ages who were going to a showing of Republican propaganda films from the Spanish Civil War.

The curator of the films was visiting from Spain, where she taught in a high school, giving her spare time to do independent research on the Spanish Civil War era. After the lights came up, she spoke about her investigations to an oddly aggressive audience in the context of a free, public museum event. One persistent questioner, an older man, belittled her by using the familiar form of address—choosing *tú* (you) instead of the formal and polite *usted*—as he excoriated her conclusions, the interaction clouded with gendered as well as nationalistic implications. Later, outside with my punk-scene friends, no one echoed my outrage. I found that the majority of them also resented her. They claimed that she was a bourgeois intellectual, interested only in exploring revolutionary political history because it would enhance her career, giving me significant looks as they framed this verdict.

HARDCORE PUNK AND ANARCHISMS

As hardcore punk began to overshadow punk rock on a broad scale, with people in various global scenes experimenting in the creation of their own DIY shows, recordings, and distribution networks, a significant number of punk-scene participants around the world were also investigating anarchism with greater seriousness.[18] Though a well-known punk rock song like the Sex Pistols' "Anarchy in the U.K." refers in its fairly nonsensical lyrics to anarchy, the word use was an uninformed, stereotypical one, presuming a vague equivalence of anarchy with destruction and chaos. Another U.K. punk band, Crass, provided a better model, not just for the punk scene in Mexico but for many around the world. Despite their higher-class, art school origins, Crass members promoted DIY production and the practice of squatting, and championed causes from environmentalism and animal rights to anti-fascism and anti-authoritarianism. When enumerating their favorite bands, many of my friends still placed Crass among them decades later, despite the fact that, by and large, most preferred Spanish-language punk.[19]

As participants in Mexico City's punk scene began to investigate more complex meanings of anarchy, they uncovered a rich national tradition of anarchism and its expansive global history, its rhizomes spread out over a variety of international origins. Unlike a tradition like Marxism, anarchism does not have one central author or text that its proponents may respond to, challenge, and re-create. Peter Marshall, a historian of anarchism, compares its history to a river with many tributaries, flowing from ideas that predate the coalescence of anarchism proper, including Taoist and early Christian philosophy, through to "classical" anarchists of the eighteenth and nineteenth centuries, such as Godwin and Tolstoy. If that river appeared to have mostly petered out in many places in the early twentieth century, it sprang forth again at midcentury among the New Left and in 1960s counterculture more broadly.[20] More recently, anti-globalization networks of the late 1990s and early twenty-first century—as well as protest movements from anti-austerity protestors in Greece to "Los Indignados" in Spain to Occupy encampments and Black Lives Matter initiatives—have also demonstrated an awareness of anarchist thought and practice.

As historians themselves detail, many historical accounts of anarchism as a political philosophy begin with stereotypical images of the anarchist as violent provocateur, if only to put that imagery into tension with another image of the anarchist as utopian (Jun 2012, 109). Many accounts also proceed quickly to the etymology of the word "anarchy," as interpretations of it still create controversy. Looking at the ancient Greek origin of the word, Marshall translates it as "without a leader or ruler."[21] Again, various commentators voice disagreement as to how that phrase might be interpreted. Nevertheless, most anarchists agree on two basic ethical principles upon which the political philosophy has always been based: freedom from authority, and the fundamental equality of all people.

Dissent arrives again in consideration of what constitutes "authority" as well as "freedom." Discussing the anti-authoritarian basis for anarchism, some theorists adhere to the notion that "authority" refers to states or to government more broadly, while others draw on a post-structuralist understanding of power to frame a more encompassing perspective (Kuhn 2009). While many classical anarchists like Proudhon were blind to forms of authority like the sexist authority of men over women, more contemporary understandings of anarchism confront the diverse hierarchies that multiple forms of authority create. Dismantling these hierarchies becomes part of the anti-authoritarian ethics of anarchism, as well as its promotion of total equality. In seeking to disturb all hierarchies, however, many anarchists are quick to point out that they do not seek the chaos of absolute freedom, in which all people may do exactly as they see fit. The definition of "freedom" and how it may be applied to individuals, in contrast to social groups, is another bone of contention among anarchists, some of whom embrace a more individualistic notion of freedom than others.

In fact, if anarchism provokes fears of destruction and even violence through its oppositional politics, the "anti" of its anti-authoritarianism, anarchist conceptions of freedom often ground the contrasting charges of utopianism. Some anarchists see coercive, hierarchical relationships as the evil that perverts a fundamentally good and cooperative human nature. Others reject this idealized view of human behavior.[22] Not all anarchists would wish to disavow utopianism, however. Some willingly embrace it, pointing out that models of utopia allow anarchists to imagine what alternative realities they work for. Increasingly, people engaged in autonomous organizing, whether overtly anarchist or not, model the kind of society they would like to see in the world rather than waiting for large-scale revolution (Polletta 2002; Juris 2008; Graeber 2009).

Certainly, many of my friends in Mexico City's punk scene dissent with one another over proper anarchist terminology and goals. Some are committed to social and political experimentation to foster good practices. However, they also have been influenced by long-standing anarchist ideas that have been circulating in Mexico specifically for many decades. Anarchism has a deep and diverse history in Mexico in particular, stretching back more than a century. Over the course of the late 1980s and 1990s, many of Mexico City's punk-scene participants—and participants in other scenes in Mexico—informed themselves about these histories, as their sense of identification with anarchist political philosophy intensified (Poma and Gravante 2016; Magaña 2020).

Conditions in Mexico had provided fertile ground for anarchists even before the revolutionary period, in the second half of the nineteenth century. In addition to the country's increasing industrialization, which impacted workers flowing into the cities to take manufacturing jobs, Mexico also experienced a great deal of turmoil in the countryside, prompted by land redistribution laws enacted in the 1850s, when the Catholic Church lost some of its power. According to some political historians, Mexican anarchism developed along two parallel trajectories during the final decades of the nineteenth century, becoming an anarco-communist tradition in rural areas and an anarco-syndicalist tradition in the cities. In rural areas, this tradition was founded on some Indigenous peoples' communalist practices. A good number of the anarchists active in urban contexts also came from an influx of European expatriates from across the Continent, who settled both in Mexico and the United States (Hart 1978; Lida and Illades 2001). Both of these strains of influence would impact the growth of Ricardo Flores Magón's political philosophy (Viñas 2004; Bufe and Verter 2005; Magaña 2020).

Despite adherence to some different ideological roots and tactics, over time there was increased coordination between anarcho-syndicalist urban labor organizers and anarco-communist agrarian communities, in addition to more sophisticated communication between anarchists in Europe, Mexico, and the United States.[23] While there were agrarian uprisings in rural areas, anarco-syndicalists led worker strikes and boycotts in the urban environment in the last decades of the nineteenth century, especially in Mexico City.

Regarding the Mexican Revolution, historians G. M. Joseph and Jürgen Buchenau (2013, 44) call anarchism the "road not taken" when surveying its outcomes. They note that, being allied with the international anarchist movement, Ricardo Flores Magón and his associates were so intensely persecuted by both Mexican and U.S. forces that they played less of a role in the Mexican Revolution than they might otherwise have done. However, despite this marginalization, the authors emphasize that a few of the intellectuals of the Magonista movement resurfaced and managed to inject their ideas into the Constitution of 1917. After the consolidation of the Mexican state, overt adherents of anarchism became scarce, though anarchist thought began to simmer below the surface of Mexican political organizations once again during midcentury struggles with the PRI government.

As participants in Mexico City's punk scene began to think more seriously about anarchism in the 1980s, not only did they enjoy discovering a rich national and global history, but they also, importantly, encountered older local people who served as role models for them during a time of intense autogestión. Among them was the small group of elderly people who had come to Mexico in their own youth, Republican exiles from the Spanish Civil War. From late 1939 until 1945, Mexico, under the populist Cárdenas administration, provided refuge for those who had to flee Franco's Spain. Roughly twenty-five thousand refugees arrived in Mexico during that period, and most remained in Mexico City. Despite their small numbers, the Spanish exiles made an impact on the city around them because they were largely skilled tradespeople, professionals, intellectuals, and artists who represented an influx of a great range of cultural capital (Pla Brugat 1999, 20).

By the late 1980s, this population of Spanish exiles had shrunk, due not only to their advancing age but also to the death of the dictator Franco in 1975, which allowed those who had dreamed of returning home to do so. Among those who chose to stay was Ricardo Mestre Ventura, who, as a member of the anarcosyndicalist Confederación Nacional de Trabajo in his youth in Spain, had witnessed the importance of lending libraries and informed debate on the creation of a vital working class. Due to his wartime experiences, he was also a vocal pacifist. In Mexico, he worked as a bookseller and editor, amassing a large and impressive personal library of materials, including works on Latin American history and literature, anarchism and other political theory, and a large collection of newspapers from the Spanish Civil War era. Mestre and a small circle of aging Spanish exiles held *tertulias*, regular talks on social and political themes.

In the 1980s, they befriended some young punk-scene participants, and Mestre's library, known since 1978 as the Biblioteca Social Reconstruir, became an important resource and meeting place for the punk scene (Detor Escobar and Hernández Sánchez n.d., 202). In fact, when Mestre died in 1997, the library went into the care of punk-scene participants who had known and loved him. Despite some periods of disuse—such as the six-year period that began just months after my initial arrival in Mexico City—the library remains a key space for punk-scene sociability today. Currently, the library has an understanding with the Frente Auténtico de Trabajo (FAT), a confederation of labor unions created in 1960 to counter the disappearance of independent labor unions in midcentury Mexico.[24] In exchange for help with maintenance and utility bills, the library is allowed to occupy a portion of the union's building.

Beyond the Spanish exiles, others in Mexico City noted the growing interest in anarchism among young punk-scene participants and tried to help them access key materials for their learning. In May 1992, the Museo del Chopo, the first home of the Chopo tianguis, collaborated with punk-scene participants and others to create an event series on "alternative culture," with one event dedicated to the theme "Anarchismo [*sic*] y movimiento punk" (Anarchism and the punk movement). The event included an exhibition and a roundtable, with the participation of the publishers at Ediciones Antorcha, who had participated in the 1960s counterculture. A small independent operation that created translations of anarchist texts, Ediciones Antorcha put out a series of works written by key classical anarchists: Kropotkin, Bakunin, Pelloutier, Armand, and Proudhon, mounting them in the visual exhibition while also putting together a compilation for distribution in periodical form.[25]

Both the Biblioteca Social Reconstruir and Ediciones Antorcha provided an invaluable service for punk-scene participants, as books on anarchism were not only scarce but costly. Mexico City's public library system is not robust, with few public libraries and even fewer that lend books. (The Biblioteca Vasconcelos, which fully opened in 2008 right next to the place where the Chopo market convenes weekly, is one library in the city that does lend books to the public. However, the process of getting a borrower's permit was a time-consuming bureaucratic tangle, as I discovered when making my own application for one.) In later years, Ediciones Antorcha turned to internet publishing, amassing a large collection of texts and audiovisual materials in a database online. By my time in the city, beginning in 2008, punk-scene participants themselves had developed anarchist literature publication projects. One example was an independent publishing venture called the Hormiga Libertaria, which used the Chopo market as a distribution point.[26]

As young punk-scene participants in the 1980s set out on their independent, largely self-motivated education about anarchism, some of them collaborated with their older friends and acquaintances in the Biblioteca Social Reconstruir and other organizations. As time passed, local punk-scene participants gained further perspectives beyond the key support and examples of Spanish exiles and other knowledgeable activists in Mexico City. The Zapatista uprising in the southern state of Chiapas in 1994 provided inspiration to punk-scene participants, just as it had inspired leftists of various stripes around the world (Olesen 2005; Khasnabish 2010; Poma and Gravante 2016). While rejecting any one particular doctrine, spokespeople for the Ejército Zapatista de Liberación Nacional (EZLN) were clear about their deep respect for Mexican anarchist figures like Ricardo Flores Magón. The Zapatistas' grassroots practices of decision-making, with power in communal hands rather than in those of a political or military elite, also aligned with historical anarco-communist traditions that had long been practiced in parts of rural Mexico.

Moreover, the EZLN was media savvy, and its message resonated not only with many in the Mexican public but also with activists and social justice organizations around the world (Vodovnik 2004; Khasnabish 2010; Léger and Tomas 2017). Invigorated by the Zapatistas' example, participants in Mexico City's punk scene became more interested in Indigenous life and also attempted to reorganize their own social networks, creating new collectives and contacts with other anarchist groups within the city and the surrounding metropolitan area. Even at this time, the punk scene was politically diverse, with certain collectives supporting one cause more than another. In an attempt to create a modicum of unity, different collectives came together under the umbrella of an organization that they called la Juventud Antiautoritaria Revolucionaria, or the JAR for short.[27] Ties to punk scenes in other parts of Latin America also intensified at this time, leading to exchanges at international meetings to encourage communication and solidarity.

At the very end of the 1990s, the strike at Mexico's national university was another influential moment. In 1999, the university's rector imposed tuition and service fees in a move to privatize education at the oldest and largest university in the Americas, which had long been a free, public institution.[28] In a show of mass outrage against this neoliberal move, students occupied the university's schools, forcing the cessation of classes. Some faculty and staff were intensely involved in the strike, particularly those affiliated with unions linked to the university, which acted in solidarity with the strikers. Other groups from beyond the university also acted in solidarity with the strike, from the national electricians' union (the Sindicato Mexicano de Electricistas, which itself would strike during my time in the city ten years later) to the EZLN itself, which also provided an important inspiration and model, prompting the strikers to try to organize themselves in a more horizontal manner.

While the strike is often referred to as the "university strike," some emphasize its popular character because of its links to actors from beyond the university. Some punk-scene participants were involved in the many activities that helped support the strike. Underscoring the importance of this student-popular movement, a friend in the punk scene gave me a book about the university strike while we were in the Chopo market because he felt that if I was investigating the punk scene, then I should know more about it (Sotelo 2009). Up to the present day, the Auditorio Che Guevara on the Ciudad Universitaria campus has continued to be an important site for punk-scene sociability. This is despite the violent termination of the strike in the year 2000, when, after nine months of protest, federal troops were allowed onto the campus of the supposedly autonomous university to break up the strike, detaining hundreds.

It was during this long, heady moment of increased political awareness and action over the course of the 1990s, both in Mexico City and throughout the nation broadly, that another key location for local punk-scene sociability originated, in a space carved out of the Chopo market. The market had become ever more regulated over the course of the late 1980s and into the 1990s, leaving little room for the inclusion of those who did not have express permission and the funds to erect booths for the sale of merchandise. Feeling marginalized at the Chopo market, punk-scene participants were emboldened to make their own organizational moves, protesting the hegemony of the market's rule-making body, the Asociación Civil. Their insistence on using their own space within the market created serial conflicts, including physical clashes with the Asociación Civil security detail and police. Finally, market authorities agreed to a compromise in which various individuals and collectives in the punk scene could make use of a space at the back of the tianguis, thereafter dubbed the Espacio Anarcopunk. There, members of the punk scene share, distribute, and sell materials ranging from books and fanzines to recordings to clothing and accessories to vegan food. The space also continues to serve as a meeting location for some punk-scene participants, who still live all over the city and metropolitan area and make the trip to the city center to experience that sociability on a Saturday afternoon.

Into the first decade of the new millennium, people in Mexico City's punk scene continued to accrete new frames of reference regarding anarchism and its practices. These include anti-globalization actions that happened in Mexico and around the world, resistance in Atenco, and the uprising in Oaxaca City in 2006 (O'Connor 2003, 2004; Poma and Gravante 2016; Magaña 2020). The repression that occurred against participants in the anti-globalization protests in Guadalajara and in Atenco had particularly dire consequences for Mexico City's punk scene, however, which descended into a period of lesser activity that lasted into my own early days of fieldwork. My friends in the scene told me about repression that they or their friends had suffered after their engagement in these conflicts, citing them as one reason why they believed the punk scene was then a shadow of its former self. While it's not uncommon for scene participants to express nostalgia for some imagined heyday, this was a common story that I also encountered in fanzine literature and other materials. However, over the course of many years of returning to engage with Mexico City's punk scene, it seemed to grow stronger, with more bands, venues, collectives, social projects, and intersections with anarchist and other social movement groups in subsequent years. While the global coronavirus pandemic has been a major blow to the scene, there are some causes for optimism as people weather that additional crisis (see chapter 5).

Despite various stylistic and political differences, as well as various historical influences embraced by participants in Mexico City's punk scene, many people continued to see punk as a monolithic and violent "subculture." While I've recounted that some commentators have employed the notion of la banda to recuperate economically marginalized young men in the public eye, plenty of others continue to fear these men, still believing them to be prone to criminality. During my initial years in Mexico City, sociologist Michel Maffesoli's concept of the "urban tribe" had caught hold of the imaginations of journalists and academics alike, with media stories penned about the fractious nature of young, primarily male lower-class youth and their tendency to create problems with other urban tribes and the population at large (Maffesoli 1996; Feixa 2006; Castillo Berthier 2008; Nateras 2008). Not infrequently, "punks" were singled out as the aggressors in this kind of coverage. As my new friends voiced their outrage to me and to one another about this all-too-familiar discourse, I had the opportunity to learn more about how people who participated in the punk scene saw themselves and their politics.

FIGURE 3.5. Graffiti as dissent at the Garibaldi Underpass.
Photo by Yaz "Punk" Núñez.

SEED: PUNKS VERSUS EMOS?

Music-based subcultures have permeated Mexico's major cities for decades, fueled by constant migration from rural cities. But only in the past year have emos begun to make their presence felt in the streets. In response, many of the established so-called *tribus urbanas* like punks and metalheads are responding with violence. The emo-punk battles are reminiscent of earlier subculture fights among various factions, like the Hell's Angels fighting hippies at the Altamont Music Festival or the Mods taking on the Rockers.

Alexis Madrigal, writing for Wired, *March 27, 2008*[29]

URBAN TRIBES

Just before I began spending significant time in Mexico City's punk scene, "punks" and members of other "urban tribes" stood accused of violence against a group of young people imagined to be particularly vulnerable—the so-called "emos." The story began in the main plaza in the capital city of the state of Querétaro, not far from Mexico City. It appeared that some people, primarily young men, were attempting to mark that public space as their territory, using physical threats to keep a group of younger teens from congregating there. Word of the incident quickly spread on social media and in the press, and before long a similar dynamic between groups variously designated as punks, "darks" (goths), *metaleros* (metalheads), rockers, or a mixture of all of these were reported to have pitted themselves against a group again called emos, but now in Mexico City.

To introduce the public to this novel "subculture," several news stories appeared, attempting to educate the reader on what an emo was. In this coverage, the term "emo" was affixed to very young teenagers who embraced a certain style—tight, pegged trousers, lots of pink and glitter, dramatic makeup on both girls and boys, long, lank bangs—and, supposedly, behaviors that suggest a morose, depressive character. Notably, in addition to rejecting traditional gender norms for men in particular, these young people were also identified as middle class, allegedly pursuing the trappings of emo style with ready cash and a conspicuous consumerism. In the newspaper *La Jornada*, sociologists and psychologists denied emos tribu urbana status and put forward some rather incredible statistics, such as that 40 percent of emos display suicidal tendencies.[30]

Initially, the anti-emo story grabbed headlines only in Mexico. But it soon garnered international attention.[31] This was in part due to high-profile, pro-tolerance events organized in Mexico City, including a march from the Glorieta de Insurgentes—a large public space and popular hangout spot encircling a metro station, where local aggression was reported to have been centered—to the Chopo market. Despite the novelty of a new identity among young people, this public discourse about youth sociability was the latest in a decades-long line of similar conversations about the problems that young people pose to Mexican society. But if youth culture has long been a site of attention in Mexico City, the concern was especially acute during my first years there, due to contextual factors that enhanced anxiety. Expert opinions on young people and the dangers they could pose were not only confined to questions of their identity and sociability but were also fueled by their numbers, as an enormous generation of young people grew to face the nation's especially bleak job prospects, having been worsened again by the global economic crisis of 2008.

Many people I knew in less well-off parts of the city and metropolitan zone greeted dire predictions about the global financial crisis with a shrug. Born largely in the late 1970s, 1980s, and into the 1990s, my closest collaborators in Mexico City grew up in an environment where economic crisis was normal, in which real wages had been drastically reduced over time as the cost of essential goods rose, and yet a few, like telecommunications magnate Carlos Slim, became immensely wealthy, among the wealthiest men in the world. Over the course of the latter half of the twentieth century, from the "miracle" of the midcentury through the end of the millennium, wealth disparity continued increasing. In fact, the process accelerated, along with the rate of neoliberalization, especially following the inauguration of Carlos Salinas de Gortari as president in 1988.

Under Salinas, state employment was halved, the banks were privatized, and the government sought to revoke Indigenous rights to collectively owned *ejido* territory.[32] Meanwhile, the lowering of import barriers on key agricultural products caused their severe devaluation, forcing even more people out of farmwork into the cities or out of the country. In 1994, the Tequila Crisis further weakened the peso, precipitating a multimillion-dollar bailout by the International Monetary Fund. In the early 2000s, many manufacturing jobs were outsourced to China. During my years in Mexico, informal employment had soared, with at least six out of every ten Mexicans relying on informal work to get by, including many of my friends in Mexico City's punk scene.[33]

All of these circumstances spurred public debate about so-called *ninis*, young people who neither work nor study (*ni trabajan ni estudian*). The age range and number of *ninis* varied according to different reports, but generally they were thought to be between 12 and 29 years of age, and totaled between 7 and 10 million people in an overall population of roughly 113,500,000 Mexicans. They were imagined as easy pickings for criminal organizations that exploit youth labor. One commentator concluded that the rise in violence on public transportation routes in the metropolitan zone surrounding the Distrito Federal was to a large extent because of the problem with ninis, for example.[34] To many, ninis presented a new face on the old problem of young people's delinquency in Mexico City, threatening the public with prolonging and extending the extreme violence and insecurity of the "war on drugs" in addition to a general weakening of public security and Mexican cultural values.

In exploring their fears about ninis, various cultural authorities drew on the concept of the urban tribe during my early fieldwork. Maffesoli had proposed a fluid, postmodern model of sociability in small groups, where people play multiple roles and associate with various cohorts according to shifting affective ties. But while the scholar's larger aim was not lost on academics (Arce Cortés 2008), many journalists focused on the tribal terminology that he and his academic colleagues used to emphasize the affective relationships involved in building these more fluid social groups. In fact, the concept of tribalism encouraged various writers to exoticize networks of young people, identifying them only as members of one particular social group, such as "punks" or "*reggaetoneros*" (people who listen to *reggaetón*). Ultimately, this conversation permeated popular culture, with the topic of urban tribes becoming the material for entertainment as well as for academic and journalistic debate. One example was a documentary series titled *Esquizofrenia*, which aired on Canal 22, Mexico City's "cultural channel," featuring an episode on "punks."[35]

Certainly, the high-profile *fracas* over "punks," urban tribes, and emos made an impact on my friends in Mexico City's punk scene. My early fieldwork was marked by this public discourse, as punk-scene friends attempted to teach me what punk was not, trying explicitly to contradict the stereotypes then being reemphasized by the media. Rehashing these events from the recent past during our early acquaintance, my new companions found it suspicious that emos should have received police support during the tolerance march and so much sympathetic media coverage. They attributed this perceived deference to class bias. They bandied around the notion that perhaps *porros*, or government stooges, had been the ones to beat up on the emos to discredit urban tribes and "punks" in particular.[36] Some admitted that members of la banda had participated in anti-emo attacks. But these were not really punks. Rockers, perhaps, but not punks.

However, while "punks" were represented as violent and clannish in academic and media representations, they were also somewhat redeemed in the comparison with emos by depictions of their virile masculinity and lower-class origins, described in many accounts as more naturally resistant, something that props up the continued romanticization of la banda that Castillo Berthier noted in the 1980s context.[37] But if some people romanticize la banda, and "punks" in particular, others continue to see them as angry and scary, targets ripe for discipline at the hands of the police. While in the next chapter, I turn to "love," exploring how bonds of friendship and solidarity are created and maintained, I have previously emphasized the pleasure that many take in displaying their oppositionality and engaging in dissent. I have also argued that a fierce public image formed by the association between "punks" and rage may at times prevent punk-scene participants from experiencing violence (see chapter 2) as they encounter the difficulties of everyday city life. And so, a "punk" reputation for alarming rage, violence, and oppositionality has had a lasting impact. I would later learn what a far-reaching geographical one it has had as well.

SEED: A FEARSOME REPUTATION LIVES ON

In September 2017, I sat on a folding chair in the Lozano branch of the Chicago Public Library system in Pilsen, a strongly Mexican American neighborhood. Martín Sorrondeguy, the Chicago-based vocalist for well-known punk bands Los Crudos and Limp Wrist—someone who is as famous in global punk networks as a person can get without (frequently) being labeled a sellout—was doing a presentation on Latinx punk history in Chicago, largely through reminiscences about Los Crudos. During his presentation, there was a technical glitch, right after Sorrondeguy showed images from the 1990s of punk shows in Mexico City, where Los Crudos had played as part of their first Mexican tour. The lights partially up as people fiddled with the audiovisual equipment, I listened to a conversation between two young guys sitting next to me.

"The punk scene in Mexico City is totally crazy," said one. "Did you hear about how a bunch of punks beat the crap out of some emos a few years back?"

"Seriously, man? Wow, that's insane."

FOUR

Love

If participants in Mexico City's punk scene take pleasure in oppositionality and dissent, reveling in the intensity of rage stoked at punk shows, at protests, in contestations over accurate histories, and sometimes in combative interpersonal exchanges, then how do they also stimulate the love that ideally helps the scene cohere and spurs people to act according to their anarchist principles—hopefully, beyond the context of punk shows as well as within them? In addition to witnessing many moments of conflict and strife, I saw plenty of camaraderie and commiseration. I listened to a great deal of talk about the positive, respectful relationships that people valued. I heard love and rage paired, the two affects tangled together as a way of suggesting how to actively, consciously respond to injustice—a pairing not uncommon in leftist circles in Mexico and elsewhere (San Filippo 2003; Owens 2020).

Although I heard a great deal about how to experience rage properly in the context of the punk show, I witnessed comparatively little consensus about the love side of the equation in any context. People spoke a lot about friendship in telling me about their histories in the scene, who they admired, and who they time with, but also in discussing specific practices like the slam, one of whose monikers is *un baile de amistad* (a dance of friendship). Noting the importance of friendship in another global punk scene, Ingo Rohrer (2014) has extensively analyzed it as a key relationship undergirding the local and translocal punk scene in Buenos Aires, his observations extending to both the utility of friendship as a method of social cohesion and its capacity to break down, causing dissolution.[1] Additionally, Francesca Polletta (2002) has written about the benefits and drawbacks of friendship as a foundation for social movement organizing since the mid-twentieth century, something that helped me think about the interactions unfolding around me, especially in the context of punk collectives trying to accomplish projects in the scene or with groups beyond it.

Though a key practice like the slam may occasionally be referred to as a dance of friendship, it's also referred to as *un baile de solidaridad* (a dance of solidarity).[2] Even more frequently and in a more pointed manner than that with which they mentioned friendship in conversation, people emphasized the importance of solidarity, which clearly was a goal for many who saw themselves as taking part in a politically active punk scene. Scene participants used the term *solidaridad* a great deal when speaking about the way that punk and an anarchist politics aligned, particularly through the practices of autogestión. Solidarity was sometimes employed to explain a sense of unity among la banda as a class-based relation that many people in the punk scene and beyond it share. It was also invoked to name a sense of commonality with people in other punk scenes internationally. But as often as not, the concept of solidarity was discussed as an ideal, conjured to lament failures of good feeling such as fighting or feuds, contrasted with a sense of lack that scene participants experienced in their relationships both within the scene and with others in their broader networks.

A shifting concept of solidarity itself may contribute to a sense of its illusiveness among participants in Mexico City's punk scene. While the use of solidaridad to indicate banda unity accords with a deep, class-based history of both terms, scholars and activists have been questioning the definition of solidarity for some time. In the early theorizing of solidarity, from Hegel to Durkheim, issues around class and wage labor were central to it.[3] In this historical view, solidarity occurs as workers unite to denounce the disproportionate rewards they experience, being producers rather than owners of capital, receiving relatively low wages in exchange for their labor while owners reap large profits. In recent decades, some scholars have shifted away from considering waged labor as central to solidary relationships, however, not only because of the lessening power of labor unions and the rise of informal employment in deregulated neoliberal contexts, but also because of a greater recognition that other affective ties can ground solidary relationships in a globally networked world.[4]

In this chapter, I pay attention to those affective ties in Mexico City's punk scene, heeding the discourse of friendship and solidarity and grouping the two concepts together under the idea of "love."[5] I ask, what does love entail in a scene built largely among men and a small number of women who are knit together through deep, long-standing friendship ties? And how do you go from the love of friendship within the punk scene to a relational politics that can extend not only throughout but beyond it, fostering solidarity with people who have different ways of relating, different beliefs, and different backgrounds?

To get at these questions, I'm compelled by recent voices on the importance of friendship and romantic love in activist contexts. For example, in *The Radicality of Love*, philosopher Srećko Horvat values solidarity but ultimately privileges love over it in the work of revolutionary movements. He identifies an impressive act of solidarity from the recent past, when Coptic Christians formed a human chain to protect Muslim worshippers during protests in Tahrir Square, commenting, "This was—and still is—one of the most remarkable scenes from the so-called 'Arab Spring'; this moment of unity, courage and . . . *discipline*."[6] Naming other spectacular moments of solidarity like this one, Horvat nevertheless continues to privilege love as an even more effective relation for changing political systems:

> solidarity already contains love . . . but to arrive at love one must go a step further. To love would mean to do it even when there is no event, no special occasion, or level of consciousness. That would be the true event: when love is not (only) provoked by extraordinary cracks in the world, but can be found in the seemingly boring daily activities, even repetitions, or—reinventions. (2016, 8)

In Mexico City's punk scene, there is a name and a whole constellation of practices through which to enact a discipline of boring, everyday actions in the pursuit of a kind of revolution: autogestión. To achieve autogestión, energy must be spent in consistent activities—training, outreach, mutual aid, direct action, and direct democracy—practices that, ideally, prepare individuals and groups to bond together in ensuring their own needs. Learned from local anarchists, the term *autogestión* suggests the dogged commitment and effort it takes to change social and political life. In the punk scene, this emphasis on political commitment expresses itself not only in the embrace of the practices of autogestión but also in a prominent split that participants perceive between what is most frequently called "destroy punk" versus a more conscientious, socially engaged way of participating in the scene.[7]

While there is some controversy regarding the acceptability of what might be termed a "lifestyle politics," in which an individual's personal choices—such as not consuming animal products—are understood to represent that person's political engagement, some people validate that as a productive political stance as people model behaviors they'd like to see more of in the world.[8] The "destroy punk" (or, less often, "rocker") is the figure far more consistently singled out for derision among local punk-scene participants for having an inappropriate politics and work ethic. Allegedly, the destroy punk sees the punk scene solely as a series of opportunities to *hacer desmadre* (create mess or chaos), often in spectacularly destructive ways like binge drinking, certain forms of drug consumption, provoking fights, or perhaps even instigating a portazo.[9] Certainly, destroy punks aren't judged to have the knowledge or commitment to carry out the practices of autogestión, especially when they happen beyond the confines of pleasurable punk shows.

While I have argued that taking a dissenting stance and feeling rage are pleasurable for participants in the punk scene, negative discourse around the more hedonistic destroy punk reveals that this pleasure exists in tension with a strongly positive valuation of effort and work. This is striking in the context of Mexico City, where many scene participants struggle to make a living. Though I heard a few people talk about their interest in "work refusal"—with some attempting to link their work in the informal economy to that politicized rejection of waged labor and the central value accorded to work in modern life (Weeks 2011)—there is still a strong, traditional work ethic that pervades the scene.[10] Not only did the majority of punk-scene participants identify as banda, having grown up in more economically marginalized neighborhoods in Mexico City, but several participants I knew had been migrants to the u.s. or Europe. Many more had relatives, friends, and neighbors who had migrated in search of better work opportunities. For many of my male friends in the scene especially, their work appeared to weigh heavily in their sense of self-worth and status, despite the difficulty of finding the sort of regular, waged labor that might have marked a sense of masculine social belonging in earlier periods.[11]

Getting by is a potentially all-encompassing endeavor, requiring ingenuity and grit as people navigate the daunting economic landscape of Mexico City. My friends repeatedly drew my attention to issues of work during my time in the monster city, inviting me to visit them in their workplaces, seeking out my company when they were without work, and talking about the kinds of nonpaid work they did within the scene and in support of causes they championed. The pervasiveness of talk about work and identities centered on industriousness led me to see the punk scene as a site of affective labor, where various practices—including the practices encoded in autogestión and the rigors of punk performance itself—build relationships, whether or not those relationships lead to the accumulation of capital (Hardt 1999).[12] While no one of my acquaintance is free from the hustle to make ends meet, some participants' activities to earn money clash with their anti-capitalist beliefs, as well as with more meaningful forms of work experienced as autogestión. Other friends attempted to knit their work-for-sustenance with their autogestive work when they could.

All this focus on work took place against a backdrop of high-profile problems with labor in Mexico City during my fieldwork period. These events compelled me to further investigate labor conditions for punk-scene participants and how their work to get by accorded—or didn't—with the affective labor encoded in autogestión. In this chapter, I'll further describe the work involved in punk performance while detailing the various practices of autogestión and how they are enacted within and sometimes beyond the punk scene.

SEED: SIDEWALK SCENE

Out of the blue, my friend called, inviting me to tag along with him as he worked on a rainy summer evening. He sold books and DVDs in a makeshift booth near a large, popular park during the week, and then in the Chopo market on Saturdays. In the past, I had accompanied him as he sourced books. Tonight, my task was simply to provide company as he watched over his puesto, one of a long row of metal rods and thin wooden slabs, protected by a blue plastic tarp. We stood around on the pavement chatting as passersby wove their paths along the busy sidewalk.

It was not unusual for this mischievous friend to press me to borrow out-there pornographic videos, enjoying my marked lack of appreciation for such offers. But specializing in that little niche had its benefits, he informed me. He had developed a clientele. He familiarized himself with his regular customers' preferences, and they would repeatedly come back for his personalized attention. There wasn't much traffic on this gloomy evening, however, and the vendors began to thin out. He piled his books and the elements of the booth into a shopping cart, and we walked slowly through the drizzle as he leaned his back into the heavy, creaking vehicle, pushing it through a long, unwieldy maze of streets, sidewalks, and empty lots.

LOVE'S LABORS

During my initial fieldwork period in Mexico City, several high-profile events served to draw attention to labor issues across the country and especially in the Federal District, including disputes with organized labor and continued action by the city government to contain the street vendors who crowd public space. A few punk-scene participants had a personal interest in the outcome of these demonstrations, as they also worked in traditional working-class sectors like manufacturing, often encountering on-site dangers and job insecurity as they labored in factories large and small. One day in the Chopo market, I winced as I saw a punk-scene friend approaching with deep, purpling blisters covering most of his face and hands. He explained that he had got a bit of work at a soap factory, but that the temperature on the factory floor was so high that no one wanted to wear the protective gear they were given by the management and so preferred to risk getting chemical burns instead. Another friend recounted a similar story at his factory job, where he handled sharp blades all day but refused the equipment to protect his hands because it would slow him down and decrease his wages. Having found a factory job that was boring but not hazardous, yet another friend was laid off periodically, unpredictably, and for long stretches.

The precarity of labor in Mexico City was a familiar situation for almost all my friends both within the punk scene and beyond it, and certainly not only for those who labored in traditional working-class jobs. In Mexico, few people have the opportunity to work with one another in salaried workplaces. Economists calculate that as many as 60 percent or more of the working population labors in the informal economy, receiving payment *bajo el agua* (literally "under the water," but better aligned semantically with "under the table") for jobs like restaurant service, taxi driving, construction work, domestic labor, and, for many, street vending. A traditional practice in Mexico, street vending has become more common and more difficult to contain in recent decades, though John C. Cross has argued that despite the fact that Mexico City's government has condemned the practice of informal street vending as being beyond the reach of state regulation and incompatible with the modern, cosmopolitan image of the capital the state wants to project, it has tacitly approved the development of informal labor since the middle of the twentieth century (Cross 1998; Alarcón 2008; Bustamante Lemus 2012).

Despite all of the obstacles to secure, waged work that most of my friends in the punk scene experienced, I was interested to find that many, if not most, still demonstrated a strong work ethic, taking pride in whatever type of work they were able to accomplish.[13] But in the face of changing ideas about labor, solidarity, and informality over the course of the past couple of decades, much anarchist ideology of the local punk scene in Mexico City remains tied to anarcho-syndicalism. This is a tradition of anarchism tied to labor union activism (Saño 1977; Hart 1978; Arvon 1980). Imagery of the proud, dignified manual laborer who exchanges his labor for a decent, if hard-won, salary continues to circulate. The Biblioteca Social Reconstruir—an independent library that forms one of the punk scene's most respected institutions—is now located in the headquarters of the Frente Auténtico del Trabajo (Authentic Labor Front) a prominent labor organization.[14] Among many of Mexico City's punk-scene participants, hard physical work is nothing to be ashamed of. On the contrary, physical labor like factory and construction work continues to be valorized, despite its scarcity, precarity, and the idealism of scene participants who would like to avoid working for employers with objectionable politics or ties to the state.

Clearly, this traditional working-class labor still has its benefits, even if those have been drastically reduced. One friend with intermittent factory work told me that the wages were still good, if sporadic. If he was careful with his money, and continued to live in his family's home, he didn't suffer too much in the periods when he had to go without work. This fortunate friend welcomed his time laid-off as periods of freedom, though he did worry what would happen to him after his parents' deaths, when the family home might be claimed by multiple brothers' and sisters' families.

In the hardscrabble economic conditions in which most of my punk-scene friends operate, people recognize the precarity of informal work, but some also attempt to reconsider its benefits, such as the possibility of self-employment, evading the exchange of labor for a wage entailed under the Fordist economic system. As a sort of cold consolation for its insecurities, some of my friends who labor informally choose to count their blessings, seeing in its embrace something akin to work refusal, one way of escaping both wage slavery and the authority of a boss. This dovetails nicely with the punk slogan "ni dios ni amo" (neither god nor master).

Making a living as a street vendor—either in an established market, with a booth, or as an ambulatory vendor—also necessitates a tough, can-do stance, one that benefits from the hardening of the body and spirit made possible in part through punk shows (Cross 1998, 2011; Goldstein 2016). If the responsible, manly, blue-collar breadwinner continues to be a model of a local work ethic, another may be found in the punk-scene participants who are evidently successful at gaming the informal economic system, earning a decent, if hard-won, living for themselves and their families through their selling of goods and services in various kinds of markets, such as a man who runs a booth in one of the city's most notoriously large and crime-ridden tianguis, where various kinds of black-market sales flourish.

The coexistence of these two models—the self-employed or work-refusing subject versus the blue-collar worker—mirrors local images of labor in the punk scene. Conversations, too, presented a dynamic, if uneasy, balance between an interest in the kinds of "post-work imaginaries" (Weeks 2011) that can be found in global punk scenes and a sense of nostalgia for the Fordist economic system, particularly regarding the idealized masculinity it entailed, promoting hard work for not only the security of a wage but, through it, social status and belonging. This coexistence is not unusual. Writing about the rise of state-sponsored volunteerism in Italy as part of its transformation to a post-Fordist economy, Andrea Muehlebach imagines Fordism as "a ghostly presence, even as its absence is proclaimed" (2011, 62). Having formed the backbone to a particular view of masculine labor for decades, that image of working-class masculinity continues to haunt the present day, even if the labor market no longer supports many traditional working-class men.[15]

Still, within this duality, many attempt to reimagine their working lives, recognizing a distinction between the labor they do to make a living and the more clearly voluntary labor that they undertake in the processes of autogestión. Sometimes there is some overlap, as with street vendors who sell informative goods at various city markets during the week and then perhaps for marginally higher prices at the Chopo on Saturdays. Though they make much-needed cash from this activity, they may also feel that they are doing something meaningful if they are curating a body of documentaries to sell that inform people about important contemporary issues, for example. In addition to selling or trading books, music, and videos that fuel others' acquisition of knowledge, the work of creating and maintaining autogestive projects may be encountered through a variety of other activities, such as living in collective organizations or squats; playing in bands; planning workshops and festivals; taking part in anarchist or social movement organizations; writing and designing fanzines; creating and distributing cheap "clones" of recordings; and participating in skill swapping.

Through such projects, punk-scene participants perform an affective labor that attempts to encourage rage and love to circulate not only within but also beyond the punk show and, hopefully, beyond the punk scene.

SEED: THE HARD WORK OF SCREAMING

Punk vocalists are not infrequently hoarse after performance. One musician friend confided that his head and back also hurt after extended bouts of vocalization. After his performances, I could hear his discomfort, his voice reduced to a croaking whisper though his eyes sparkled with the excitement of performing. Out of curiosity, I acquired a teaching video by a singer who claimed to have created exercises for vocalists working in extreme styles, to help them avoid damage to their vocal folds.[16]

To my surprise, my friend wanted to borrow it. But over the course of the next several months, it became a running joke. Had he watched it? What did he think? No, nothing, came the reply again and again. He insisted he hadn't even cracked it open, heaping scorn on the very notion that it might actually do him good. As far as I know, he still has the video.

THE EXERTIONS OF PUNK PERFORMANCE

As one vocalist in a Mexico City band explained, "Screaming in a band is very hard work. You have to dedicate to it a lot of time, years, a lot of energy, a lot of brain power, and really it's a great effort physically and mentally. Like any work, it's very exhausting but equally very satisfying."[17] The comment demonstrates not only his own linkage of punk performance with hard work but also his valorization of hard work as a source of fulfillment. His engagement with punk performance is work that is external to his daily hustle, the task of getting by in the neoliberal Mexican economy. But in addition to its personal satisfactions, the extra work of punk performance is like a labor of love, an affective labor that accomplishes relational work, transforming rage into love-and-rage, an affective intensity that ideally fuels the efforts of autogestión.

At a performance in 2011, at the top of a crumbling squat not far from the Paseo de la Reforma, one of the large, palm-lined avenues that runs through the center of Mexico City where several government and corporate offices are located, I

FIGURE 4.1. Punk show featuring the band Decomposed Society at the
Vieja Escuela in Tlalnepantla. Photo by Yaz "Punk" Núñez.

observed one band's exertions from an especially close vantage point. The band
was playing at a benefit party, and in the tightly packed, enthusiastic crowd, the
musicians simply cleared a space for themselves as the audience clustered around.
A small man, the band's vocalist appeared even more compact in performance,
despite the power of his sound. He often stooped forward slightly, back and
abdominal muscles taut with exertion as he took a broad stance, legs planted
firmly apart. His shiny, sweaty face contracted around his wide-open mouth,
and he was almost motionless as he delivered his lines, his focus exclusively on
his airflow. Being close to him, I could see him taking quick, deep breaths, his
head merely bobbing a bit between lines. When a real pause came in the lyrics,
he burst briefly into motion, springing upright and glancing down at his guitar
as he bounced on the balls of his temporarily liberated feet. As he moved around
the tight circle of space that barely provided a barrier between the audience and
the performers, he stirred the humid air, seeming to infuse it with a new source
of heat. Swiping quickly at his face with his soaked T-shirt and flashing a wet
midriff, he suddenly tensed up again, clenching his fist around the microphone
as he crouched into his next verse.[18] Meanwhile, holding down a tight battery of
noise to anchor the band, the group's drummer played with characteristic focus,
her mouth compressed into a frown-like expression. Head tilted back and eyes

often closed in performance, she let fly a stream of beats, the occasional angular rhythm, and multiple noisy timbres, all at an impressive level of volume and resonance, a bandana on her forehead catching copious sweat.

Performing in a punk band is an intense effort for all involved. Even with the purposeful simplicity of some hardcore punk, punk performance requires speed and stamina, as well as the physical exertion necessary to stimulate an almost incandescent energy that whips audiences up until they perform an appropriate expression of keen feeling. The powerful energy of punk is one of the music's hallmarks, and punk performance is highly energetic most everywhere it occurs.[19] This loud, vibrant, frenetic quality characterizes punk performance with the "density and intensity" akin to what Steven Feld (2012, 142) describes as key to the aesthetics of certain modern jazz performances, with the sweat of figures like Ghanaian percussionist Nii Otoo Annan and his hero Elvin Jones indexing their incredible musical imagination and dexterity as well as their physical exertion. Sweat is just one among other strong indexes of hard work for punk performers, with those signs of effort shared among all of a band's performers, and not just the drummer—nor just the vocalist, as I may have suggested unintentionally in previous writing.[20]

For punk performers, other aspects of performance that provide indexes of the intensity of their musical work include muscle tension, contorted bodily postures and facial expressions, and for vocalists, harsh, distorted vocal timbres that index not only the strain of their production but also the expression of important affects like rage. In fact, to stoke rage at a punk show, perhaps preparing the way for the love of friendship and solidarity to flow through embodied, participatory practices like the slam dance, punk performers enact a kind of affective labor that is inextricably tied to their strenuous physical effort. While much literature on affective labor in music has focused on the so-called creative labor of making music, some scholars have turned attention to the link between the clearly laboring bodies of musicians and the affective outcomes that such labor is intended to produce (Hofman 2015; Tochka 2017; Graber and Sumera 2020; Gray 2021).

In addition to that small body of work in ethnomusicology, anthropologists working with athletes, like boxers, have also demonstrated the links between hard physical work and its affective significance within and beyond the ring (Downey 2005; Trimbur 2013; Wacquant 2004). Writing about young men of color who have difficulty securing formal work and who struggle against the persistent possibility of incarceration, Lucia Trimbur sees the physical exertions of a committed boxing training regime as a kind of replacement for waged work.

"By engaging in amateur athletics, young men are able to see themselves as a different kind of laborer, and produce a new kind of work—bodywork—and attendant forms of value" (2013, 18).

The concept of "bodywork" is also useful for theorizing the place of hard physical effort in punk-scene participants' debates about labor, which happen through musical as well as extra-musical performances. Through the physical exertions of extreme musical practices, Mexico City's punk musicians also perform a kind of bodywork, though not as an overt, disciplined training regimen. Instead, the affective impact of their labor arises in the context of local punk performance. Linking hard physical work to the relational work of promoting autogestión among their audiences, punk performers mediate their lingering investments in a Fordist-era understanding of labor, transforming their hard physical work into a tool that they also use to reach toward an anarchism-inspired belief in autogestión. Through the dual physical and affective exertions of extreme musical performance, participants in Mexico City's punk scene explore alternative relationships to work and notions of value, using the hard work of their bodies to ground their imaginings of alternative ways to make meaningful social contributions, beyond earning a wage.

Being at the edge of their physical stamina, as well as at the borders of what's possible in terms of amplification, punk musicians perform bodywork as straining, struggling bodies, bodies fighting against their corporeal limitations and the great volume of sound surging around them. In doing this, they create the powerful, transformative sound-as-presence that physically impacts the bodies around them, causing drum beats to land thumping in participants' bellies while various forms and pitches of noise press in on their chests, limbs, and heads. To create this intense, tactile exchange of energy, particularly in cases where the acoustics of the space are not ideal and sound equipment is not functioning at peak capacity—frequent conditions that shape live performance of punk in Mexico City—musicians must work extremely hard. And so they present that effort, the sweat and straining muscles, breathlessness or hoarseness, in the sight, sound, and physical impact of their performance.

Through the bodywork of extreme vocalizations, punk musicians attempt to model an appropriate rage to their friends and listeners, encouraging them to work to better themselves through autogestión and to practice solidarity with one another, projecting their ire outward, toward powerful, exploitative figures and institutions. This is a twinned physical and affective exertion, a transfiguration of physical work through affective labor. Rather than celebrating a hardworking body as an icon of working-class masculinity, punk performance produces bodywork that links hard physical work to the relational work that performers attempt to create at punk shows, stimulating the rage and love that motivate others' social engagement.

While performers prompting rage ultimately can't direct it, friends voice the idea that punk performances can spark the motivation to continue the arduous work of autogestión. Ideally, this means participating in projects that reach beyond the punk show, from the creation of fanzines and song lyrics as outreach and training activities, to the practice of skill swapping as mutual aid, to the more contested notions of direct democracy and direct action that inform both the organization of punk-scene collectives and their choice of political method and action.

SEED: A PUNK SING-ALONG

The guitar had a name: Ixchel, for the Mayan moon goddess. It was a small, pink acoustic guitar, probably for marketing to little girls. Its owner, a grown-up male guitarist, had a fascinating way of strumming high over the bridge in an incredibly fast, consistently downward motion. It was astonishing how much noise he could compel from the fragile-looking instrument, which seemed to amplify the buzz of the strings more than the chords he formed with his leisurely left hand.

It was late on a Saturday afternoon, in the street across from the main corridor of the Chopo market, where those who didn't pack the cantinas packed the sidewalk outside, stealthily passing the caguama. The guitarist strummed at his strings, and a small group began to cohere around him— first, one person yelling a lyric, then another making a contribution, until everyone was yelling in unison. One woman's voice was especially hoarse and broken, strained after the previous afternoon at a rally. But together the crowd made a good, healthy noise, occasionally pumping their fists and making eye contact as they reached key lyrics, as if to confirm the truth of what they shouted.

OUTREACH AND TRAINING:
SONG LYRICS AND FANZINES

Sing-alongs were not infrequent occurrences during my early days of hanging out in the street with punk-scene participants. Street sociability is often slow, mundane, routine. "We're bored with our lives. Tell us about you," a woman commanded me in one of my first post-Chopo street hangs. A friend with a guitar provides a welcome distraction from the chatter, the mutual surveillance of the police, the stares of passersby. Singing together in a tight semicircle around the guitarist, participants ward off not only the boredom of a long evening in the street but also the potential for the disagreements that can suddenly flip the slow, friendly, but often edgy sociability into outright conflict and physical fighting.

Predictably, older songs are the focus at these impromptu singing events. Everyone already knows the words, and typically those lyrics present topics that everyone can agree with. Voicing old punk songs not only helps to stabilize a sense of commonality and goodwill among a brusque and argumentative social network, but also to refresh appropriately punk subjectivities through the embodiment of valued affects. Shouting well-known lyrics aids the preservation of memory and history among contemporary participants of the scene as they move the lyrics from the realm of sound recordings or written texts further along the spectrum from the "archive" to the "repertoire" of living performance, with all the potential for new meanings and change that the transformation represents (Taylor 2003; Gray 2013). Singing together, punk-scene participants reinvigorate old songs, performing not simply nostalgia but also a reevaluation and reinterpretation of materials that typically prove to retain their significance in the present moment as in the past (Boym 2001). Moments like these remake meaning, reinforcing a sense of friendship and belonging through active participation, warding off social fragmentation for a little while at least.

The street sing-along is also among the handful of punk performances that emphasize the equality between various members of the scene, refuting the kinds of hierarchies that may unintentionally develop at regular punk shows, such as those between musicians and non-musicians. There, audience members frequently shout along to song lyrics, and they may even be encouraged to take over the microphone to scream awhile. But while this is a time-honored and fairly regular practice, some vocalists quietly dread it. One confided to me that whenever he passes the mike, it comes back nasty and wet, covered in other peoples' saliva and sweat, increasing the chances of its malfunction. But not only is it important to trade roles, encouraging listeners to become vocalists and vocalists to listen awhile; tolerating others' bodily fluids and functions is also key to being banda, another way to assert egalitarianism. Sitting or standing on sidewalks and curbs in streets, parks, and plazas, various people commented approvingly that I was not squeamish about passing the caguama, a liter-sized bottle of beer—with or without a courtesy swipe at its mouth before sipping—or remarked about my nonchalance toward other intimate behaviors they antici-pated would offend my gringa sensibilities. Participating in street sing-alongs is another way to assert this basic equality between people, who share a repertoire of song lyrics preserved in their minds.

Additionally, street sing-alongs, like punk shows, help underscore the impor-tance of song lyrics and how they're recognized as key texts within the scene. Paying attention to song texts is one basic way to engage with a process of auto-gestión, particularly through the training and outreach opportunities that they may provide. Though some in Mexico City's punk scene dispute the best prac-tices of autogestión—particularly with regard to how to enact direct democracy and direct action—outreach, training, and mutual aid activities are especially emphasized in local punk-scene practice, educational materials like song lyrics and fanzines being virtually ubiquitous at events that scene participants create and frequent. Many autogestive punk projects that may be said to perform out-reach and training prioritize rhetoric, ideally in an attempt to spread anarchist ideas or the will to rebel against the status quo. The triple linguistic play that animates punk speech, song, and written words enables the construction of certain sanctioned, if not unanimous, voices, through these varied media (Feld and Fox 1994; Feld et al. 2004; Fox 2004; Weidman 2006). Rather than provid-ing a clear site of unified resistance, song lyrics and fanzines reveal mediations of prominent discourse within the scene, perhaps emphasizing commonly held ideas or perhaps encouraging others to question those.

A song by the now-defunct Mexico City band Rhuckuss, titled "Presos," dem-onstrates one way that song lyrics can illustrate prompts to rethink or perhaps discuss older ideas within the scene rather than the simple reiteration of shared beliefs. The issue of imprisonment is one that claims a lot of mental space in the local punk scene, but often the reference is more specifically to political pris-oners, people who have been unjustly imprisoned by the state because of their political activities or beliefs.[21] In the punk scene, this is made personal through the consequences of some participants' own activism. Among the demonstra-tions I attended, I occasionally joined protests outside of prisons, demanding the release of scene participants who were being held after detentions at marches, at tocadas that got unruly, or simply for being at the wrong place at the wrong time.

However, in the case of the song lyrics for "Presos," the text does not specifically take on the issue of political prisoners, but reframes the concept of imprisonment as a metaphor, directing it via a second-person address to suggest the imprisonment of all listeners. While the song does refer obliquely to political prisoners ("trapped behind bars, prisoners for thinking"), the song isn't simply about the need for the release of presos everywhere. Instead, it urges listeners to organize, to practice mutual aid and solidarity to escape their own prisons, like dependence on wages, entrapment in a corrupt political system, or unthinking adherence to dogma. It's a surprising take on a familiar topic, shifting the location of needed action from the public realm of policy and social justice initiatives to the realm of individuals, who are advised to reevaluate their participation in autogestive projects. While "Presos" briefly validates an opinion that many share about a disturbing political problem, the song subtly suggests that it's not enough to reiterate opposition to the state's practice of incarcerating dissidents. Song lyrics can function, then, not only as repositories of shared points of view, shared experiences, and shared sentiments, but as interventions into those as well, suggesting new ways to think about old problems.

In addition to song lyrics, fanzines are another important vehicle for autogestive interventions through linguistic as well as visual play. While fanzines are arguably descended from various self-published "little magazines" created around the world in the early twentieth century, dedicated to anything from poetry to science fiction writing, anthropologist Aída Analco Martínez also links them explicitly to the Mexican tradition of oppositional political writing that burgeoned at the beginning of the twentieth century before the Mexican Revolution. Here, she cites the important self-published periodical *Regeneración*, the work of Ricardo Flores Magón and his brothers, Enrique and Jesús, as particularly important to the Mexican tradition of fanzines, writing that "the life of Ricardo is a very big source of inspiration for those who make fanzines, because for many of them, he is a concrete example of a fighter and idealist who sustained his convictions and dreams up through the ultimate consequences" (Analco Martínez 2011, 56). Though others who have written about fanzines deny the link between them and alternative press publications, Analco Martínez sees the link concretely in the content of local fanzines themselves. She claims that references to Ricardo Flores Magón abound in punk fanzines, for example, far outpacing other key revolutionary-era figures like Emiliano Zapata or Pancho

Villa, who are perceived to have been co-opted by the PRI during its consolidation of power in the mid-twentieth century.[22]

Certainly, just as Flores Magón intended with his writing, fanzines are meant to sow ideas even as they entertain and provide outlets of self-expression (Lara Pacheco 2000; Wrekk 2014). The degree to which a fanzine is informational versus entertaining varies considerably. But as elsewhere in the global punk scene, the urge to create a fanzine means embracing a simple, do-it-yourself ethic and aesthetic (Triggs 2010; Dunn 2016, Bestley et al. 2019). On one visit to the Chopo market, a European woman who had been living in Mexico City and participating in its punk scene for some time urged me and other women to take a copy of a flier she had created by herself, informing readers of the various kinds of contraception available to us locally, along with their pros and cons. This document, a single sheet of white paper folded into thirds, was unusual in having been designed with little apparent thought to its appearance, but nevertheless shared some common ground with many other local punk zines by being handwritten and photocopied rather than created on computer software and home-printing technology.

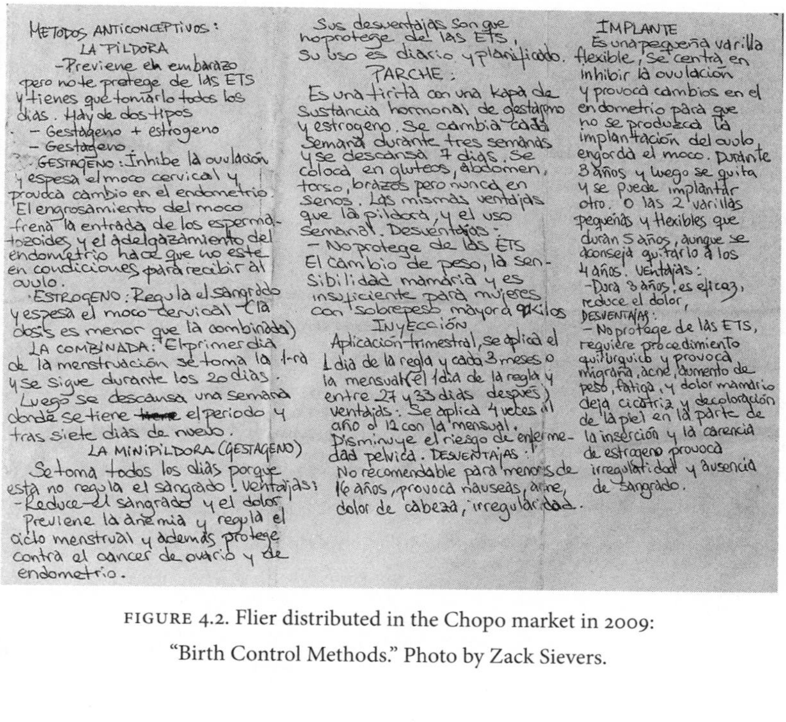

METODOS ANTICONCEPTIVOS:
LA PILDORA
-Previene en embarazo pero no te pretege de las ETS y tienes que tomarlo todos los dias. Hay de dos tipos
- Gestageno + estrogeno
- Gestageno.
· GESTAGENO: Inhibe la ovulación y espesa el moco cervical y provoca cambio en el endometrio. El engrosamiento del moco frena la entrada de los espermatozoides y el adelgazamiento del endometrio hace que no este en condiciones para recibir al ovulo.
· ESTROGENO: Regula el sangrado y espesa el moco cervical (la dosis es menor que la combinada)
LA COMBINADA: El primer dia de la menstruación se toma la 1-ra y se sigue durante los 20 dias.
Luego se descansa una semana donde se tiene ~~tiene~~ el periodo y tras siete dias de nuevo.
LA MINIPILDORA (GESTAGENO)
Se toma todos los dias porque esta no regula el sangrado! Ventajas:
-Reduce el sangrado y el dolor
Previene la anemia y regula el ciclo menstrual y ademas protege contra el cancer de ovario y de endometrio.

Sus desventajas son que no protege de las ETS, su uso es diario y planificado.
PARCHE:
Es una tirita con una kapa de sustancia hormonal de gestageno y estrogeno. Se cambia cada semana durante tres semanas y se descansa 7 dias. Se coloca en gluteos, abdomen, torso, brazos pero nunca en senos. Las mismas ventajas que la pildora, y el uso semanal. Desventajas:
- No protege de las ETS
El cambio de peso, la sensibilidad mamaria y es insuficiente para mujeres con sobrepeso mayor a 90 kilos
INYECCIÓN
Aplicación trimestral, se aplica el 1 dia de la regla y cada 3 meses o la mensual (el 1 dia de la regla y entre 27 y 33 dias después) ventajas: Se aplica 4 veces al año o 12 con la mensual.
Disminuye el riesgo de enfermedad pelvica. DESVENTAJAS:
No recomendable para menores de 16 años, provoca nauseas, acne, dolor de cabeza, irregularidad.

IMPLANTE
Es una pequeña varilla flexible, se centra en inhibir la ovulación y provoca cambios en el endometrio para que no se produzca la implantación del ovulo, engorda el moco. Durante 3 años y luego se quita y se puede implantar otro. O las 2 varillas pequeñas y flexibles que duran 5 años, aunque se aconseja quitarlo a los 4 años. Ventajas:
-Dura 3 años, es eficaz, reduce el dolor,
DESVENTAJAS:
- No protege de las ETS, requiere procedimiento quirurgico y provoca migraña, acne, aumento de peso, fatiga, y dolor mamario deja cicatriz y decoloración de la piel en la parte de la inserción y la carencia de estrogeno provoca irregularidad y ausencia de sangrado.

FIGURE 4.2. Flier distributed in the Chopo market in 2009: "Birth Control Methods." Photo by Zack Sievers.

If this particular example seems a bit simple and issue-specific to be included in the category of "fanzine," it bears pointing out that fanzines are often compilations of exactly this kind of information, along with editorials, poetry, reprints of newspaper writing, interviews with musicians and other well-known figures in the scene, song lyrics, vegan recipes, how-to articles for creating DIY objects, comic strips, and more, often helping to orient readers' experiences according to shared tastes and priorities. Some fanzines are far more elaborate than others. Most are also created by collectives rather than individuals.

While the sole author of "Metodos [sic] anticonceptivos" clearly prized information above creative expression, many fanzines try to strike a balance between the two, providing texts that contribute to debates within the scene or attempt a new consciousness-raising, while also drawing on more overtly "punk" aesthetics: stark black-and-white imagery, busy, crowded visual and textual collages, hand-drawn figures and photocopied imagery, or handwritten texts interspersed with newspaper cuttings or computer-generated copy. Precious items, fanzines are like song lyrics in that they also circulate long after their original creation. Many of the ones in my small collection are from before my own arrival in the local punk scene, purchased for *cooperación voluntaria*—whatever voluntary donation I thought appropriate—at the Chopo market or various shows and events.

People also gifted me fanzines, particularly friends who felt that the scene was at a low point in my early years in Mexico City. They wanted me to see the richness of the tradition from a few years back, compared to what was available in that slower moment. In such cases, fanzines provided me with a valuable, if small and personal, window onto the history of the scene, demonstrating the continuity or novelty of visual styles and tropes, as well as various themes that continued or no longer continued to animate conversation. However, I was also gifted fanzines that were created by people who do not participate in the punk scene, or by a mixture of people who do and don't. In such cases, the material was prized for its content, taking on themes that resonated with punk-scene participants. For some, using fanzines in the processes of autogestión can mean curating a collection from a variety of sources, emphasizing again that the punk scene is not a closed circuit but a network in constant flux.

Nevertheless, just as Desobediencia Civil's recording was pointed out to me as one that I needed to know if I wanted to learn about punk in Mexico City (see the prologue), certain fanzines were also recommended as essential scene reading. In early 2009, I bought a short stack of back issues of a punk fanzine produced in Mexico City—"a publication of anarcopunk affinity," it bills itself—called

FIGURE 4.3. Fanzine, *Pensares y sentires* (October 2006). Photo by Zack Sievers.

Pensares y sentires (Thoughts and feelings). One of these, from October 2006, makes a striking case for fanzines as a form of autogestión directly on its cover, a mint-green half-sheet of paper printed in stark black text and imagery, sheathing a ream of full-sized black-and-white pages within. The long, haphazardly punctuated run-on statement reads, "Creating and constructing, autogestive projects, with the intention of propelling the organization of this effort of social transformation, spread out and agitate, health and revolution in your insides."[23] Next to this block of text, a crude, hand-drawn cartoon of a "punk" shown from behind, urinating, harkens back to punk rock images of social rebellion. Elsewhere on this visually noisy page, there are woodcut-like portraits of Flores Magón and the masked EZLN Subcomandante Marcos with his pipe, as well as a number of other tiny images. Interestingly, while relatively few people in the punk scene still dress in the style presented here via the stereotypically rude "punk," with mohawks and spiked leather jackets, images of punk figures are often represented with that old-school look in zines.

As with the Rhuckuss song's lyrics, the fanzine's text frames the consuming of fanzines as a prompt for an individual's self-education and training, while the author of the zine engages in the outreach of creating them, encouraging others to do the same. Some writers argue that zines are inherently participatory, suggesting to readers that they make a zine of their own or go one better and do something even more ambitious (Lara Pacheco 2000, 21). The creator and consumer of the fanzine together plant the seeds of autogestión for themselves and others, uncertain and underdetermined though that body of processes may be.

Another look at the issue of presos and its frequent representation in fanzines suggests how their creators perform the outreach of autogestión, attempting to awaken readers' consciousness about particular issues. In the stack of *Pensares y sentires* I bought, encompassing issue numbers 28 to 32, each of the five issues contains some reference to this problem, one that is clearly close to the heart of this particular fanzine's authors, from a long article about the origins of prisons to updates about known activists who had been detained unjustly. Issue 30 prioritizes the problem of political prisoners throughout the fanzine, as well as on its front cover, sometimes privileging slogan-like text such as "Abajo los muros de las prisiones!" (Down with prison walls). Readers of this fanzine are repeatedly asked to think about the problem of political imprisonment, from its international aspect to how it may impact their own lives. How they choose to engage with the issue, or not, is left to their own initiative, though various possibilities emerge from the fanzine's pages as readers are introduced to anti-prison organizations, activists, and further resources for learning about the problem.

Like crafting song lyrics, creating fanzines involves a certain tension, an attempt to provoke thought, though ideally without suggesting an inappropriate or obnoxious authority, a sense that the creator has all the right answers. These accusations do fly, particularly about musicians, popular fanzine creators, people who have long been associated with key collectives, and anyone who is especially vocal or influential within the scene. There is a fine line to walk between embodying the self-improvement of autogestión and becoming self-important. While punk-scene participants may strive to be sembradores through autogestive practices, they continue to denigrate anyone who attempts to protagonizarse (to play the hero).

Meanwhile, at least some fanzine creators are explicit about wanting to include a plurality of voices, one tactic that can alleviate the problem of overbearing authorship in fanzines. In the last few years, some friends have been producing a fanzine called *Levantadxs* (Insurgents) and they asked me for a contribution in the summer of 2017. When I expressed surprise that they would want to include the writing of someone who is not seen as truly punk, my friend joked that their aim was to avoid being "amargopunk," a play on the word "anarcopunk," substituting *amargo*—bitter—for "anarco." Through his wordplay, he assured me that including my text was a strategy to downplay questions of who belongs to the scene and who can speak within it, which are often divisive and bitter.

Despite the difficulties of striking a balance of educating, not dictating, and entertaining while informing, putting out a fanzine is one of the primary tasks of individuals and groups within the scene. For some collectives, it is their only significant public instantiation, the means through which they voice their belonging to the greater punk scene by participating in its written economy, demonstrating its mastery of shared speech forms, as well as a similarity, if not uniformity, of opinion and purpose. In some fanzines, you may find a humorous, playful style of writing, as well as the use of specific language and spelling choices that connote belonging among la banda and other forms of code that appeal to specific identities and perspectives among their intended readers (Analco Martínez 2011). Many lo-

cal punk fanzines reproduce colloquial speech forms, from everyday rhetorical prose to the slogans that activists use at mass demonstrations. The interpenetration of written and performed speech and song is therefore evident in the pages of a fanzine. Because of the important place of linguistic performance through song lyrics and fanzines in punk-scene sociability, everyday

FIGURE 4.4. Fanzine, *Levantadxs* (2017). Photo by Zack Sievers.

FIGURE 4.5. A protest in solidarity with anarchist prisoners outside the Tribunal Superior de Justicia in August 2017. Photo by Yaz "Punk" Núñez.

exchanges between scene participants often draw not only on concepts but also on specific language choices derived from these sources.

The way that Mexico City's punk-scene participants engage in language choices that reflect one another, from song lyrics to written fanzine text to everyday speech, is similar to the process that Aaron Fox (2004) has noted among working-class country musicians. Linking the sociability of musical performance with ordinary talk through the ways that the poetics and performance of country music permeate everyday speech, Fox reveals the key role that music plays in constructing a shared expressive language among country music fans and practitioners, a language found not only in music, and not only in talk about music, but in talk generally. Through a triangulated relationship between musical performance, speech, and the written word of fanzines, a similar construction happens in the local punk scene. While taking care not to overplay the sembrador, fanzine creators, like those who write song lyrics, reinscribe important conceptual, linguistic, and even spelling choices that signify belonging, while also attempting to question and provoke, ideally stimulating an active self-education to mirror or exceed their own. These actions underscore the care underlying scene practices, the love that should prevail even when provoking rage about disturbing social justice issues, such as the unjust incarceration of political actors.

SEED: COOPERATE!

Clearly, my fellow organizers for the Femstival—a three-day festival organized by local women with ties to the punk scene to celebrate International Women's Day on March 8—were not very comfortable with delegating tasks. But I hated to find myself at loose ends while others were still working. Finally, we agreed that I would gather cooperación voluntaria (donations) from the audience at a nighttime show of music. Standing with an old coffee can pierced by a coin slot at the top, I found myself at the entrance to the event, wheedling and cajoling the mostly male audience to give up even a peso in support.

One guy looked over my shoulder at the women setting up instruments on the makeshift stage and, in a whiny, disappointed tone, asked if it would be all "chicas" performing that night.

"Yes," I said, locking my eyes on his, daring him to contradict me. "Isn't that fantastic?" I ignored the fact that there were men scheduled to perform as well—sadly, there weren't nearly enough all-female bands to fill our roster. I shook the little bit of change I had accumulated in the can, which made a bright, resonant noise totally out of proportion to how few coins were actually inside.

A bit sheepishly, he agreed as he dropped a few centavos in my jar.

MUTUAL AID: TRUEQUE, *COOPERACIÓN*, AND SKILL SWAPPING

When life is a hustle and securing everyday necessities a regular challenge, it pays to be generous with what you have. Sharing of all kinds is key to sociability in Mexico City's punk scene for that pragmatic reason, as well as for more high-minded principles derived from anarchist ideals. Mutual aid is an autogestive principle that governs several exchanges, as many participants engage in the task of ensuring their own wants and needs, in part by seeing to the wants and needs of others. The roots of practicing mutual aid are, like many other key activities in the scene, multiple. In the earliest days of the Chopo market, for example, middle-class regulars privileged the practice of trueque, trading precious cultural items that were hard to find in Mexico at the time, such as recordings of free jazz, rock, and other cosmopolitan musical styles not significantly produced by the national music industry. In this way, people could pursue expensive, hard-to-find cultural experiences without having to repeatedly lay out large sums of money for the privilege. Abraham Ríos Manzano (1999, 24) has noted the importance of the practice in his history of the Chopo market, before its removal to the street outside the Chopo museum, which hastened the arrival of more economically marginalized patrons from the metropolitan zones, including punk fans.

In the late 1980s, as the market became better established and more regulated, its leaders increasingly failed to provide a space for this type of exchange to occur, but persistent criticism from marketgoers eventually brought back the practice. During my fieldwork periods, people who wanted to swap items knew to go to the very back of the market, to an open space right next to the Espacio Anarcopunk. There, a shifting number of people milled about with a box of records, a handful of cassettes, a DVD, or whatever it was that they were looking to upgrade for someone else's cast-off treasures. The practice was important to punk-scene participants as well. I witnessed people engaging in trueque within the Espacio Anarcopunk itself, despite its puestos with items for sale, people sometimes bartering goods for services instead of goods for goods—by parting with a book or a T-shirt, the owner might have his hair neatly done in *rastas* (dreadlocks).

In addition to trueque, a few other time-honored practices are meant to alleviate financial obstacles to punk-scene sociability. I witnessed many, many instances in which people banded together to hacer la vaca, pooling money for anything from a caguama from the corner store to admission to a punk show. For most of my friends, it didn't matter that I was a privileged North American when it came time to buy the beers. Few people—though not literally zero—ever hinted, much less demanded, that I should pay the party tab, but rather wanted to see my own contributions to a group total. A little handmade change purse I'd bought in a street market broke, the zipper worn out from so much use when giving a few pesos here, a few pesos there. I would save up change over the course of the week, my pockets, too, weighted with coins before starting a weekend's worth of activities.

The practice of pooling money for admission to tocadas has become controversial at punk shows, however, particularly when there has been some layout on the sound equipment or on venue rental. Though there are a few organizers with ties to professional venues, and thus pricey punk shows featuring internationally known performers at those locations, many shows are organized through DIY friendship networks, the burden of costs shared by a small group of people who'd ideally like to have them reimbursed. These bands typically perform for nothing, or for free refreshments, but there are often incidental expenses to get them to the shows, housed, and fed, especially if they are not locals. All show organizers complain that there is plenty of money for beer, so why can't people pay what they're asked at the door?

Meanwhile, people at shows protest even the most minimal prices of twenty or thirty pesos for admission, which can be the lower range for more informally organized events. Given that the minimum daily wage in Mexico City hovered around fifty-five pesos per day during my early fieldwork period—for the minority of people who had salaried work at all—the idea that people who want to attend a show might not be able to hand over a chunk of that figure never seemed far-fetched to me. And perhaps, even with the grumbling, most people feel the same. Despite controversy, the practice of pooling money continues in a number of small ways and is still unquestioningly accepted at some punk shows. Of course, refusing the practice can also spur a portazo.

Another tradition related to the concept of mutual aid is the practice of asking for cooperación voluntaria rather than setting strict prices for items like fanzines or for entrance to events. In this way, fanzine creators attempt to recoup the costs of printing their product while ostensibly keeping it affordable for everyone. People certainly abused the practice on occasion, refusing to give at all. The Femstival was one of those occasions. Set at the Auditorio Che Guevara on the campus of the Ciudad Universitaria (UNAM), the events attracted both people who did and didn't typically hang out in the punk scene. But for the most part, scene participants operate according to unwritten rules about what things are worth, and perhaps what they could get away with offering for any particular item. Habitually stingy people were ridiculed to their faces at times, and certainly behind their backs.

A related, more widespread and less open practice that flourishes in the punk scene, as well as in tianguis broadly, is the sliding scale approach to pricing, according to the presumed social positioning of a buyer. Prices at ordinary street markets for someone like me were often far higher than they would be for people not so clearly marked as economically privileged. If I gathered for some activity with punk-scene friends, preparing to cook a meal together perhaps, they tended not to send me out to buy things for that very reason. We wouldn't necessarily get our collective money's worth if I took charge. On the other hand, it was a great compliment when anyone would offer me *precio banda*, the price that they would offer to other members of la banda, not because they believed I couldn't

FIGURE 4.6. The reinauguration of the Biblioteca Social Reconstruir
in 2015. Photo by Iván Torres.

afford something, but because they wanted to make me feel like I was banda for one fleeting moment of camaraderie at least.

Finally, my favorite among the various mutual aid practices in the punk scene is an emphasis on skill swapping, sharing one's learning with others, often in the form of *talleres* (informal workshops). Here, I could participate easily. Skill swapping can happen as sharing favors, such as various occasions on which I was asked to do some Spanish to English translation or vice versa. Or it can be the exchange of informal teaching services, such as the time when I traded a violin lesson for a primer on how to operate a sewing machine.

Though shared tastes guide the selection of skills that scene participants might wish to offer or encounter as learners, the breadth of knowledge that may be shared is vast. From bike maintenance to computer hacks to vegan cookery, punk-scene participants develop expertise not only for their own use and enjoyment but also for the edification of their friends. While formal higher education draws controversy because of its inaccessibility for many, and the ways that it fails to create better job prospects for even more, informal autogestive education is a tradition within the punk scene in which most people participate freely and gladly.

Additionally, punk- scene participants use institutions like the Biblioteca Social Reconstruir to offer workshops to people in nearby communities, a practice that bleeds into outreach as well. During my visit in August 2017, library regulars were brainstorming activities for the local community as the new school year neared, planning how they could support families in the area and simultaneously attract them to the anarchist library's network.

In my experience, the Femstival 2010 was the event where skill swapping was on clearest display, providing numerous talleres over the course of its three-day existence. The event in itself was inspired by the examples of Ladyfest and CLITfest, two series of DIY women's festivals with strong punk participation, held in various global locations starting in the year 2000.[24] The local take on this practice was organized by a loose collective of women friends, many who were fixtures in the local punk scene, though also including a significant number of women who were not.

Workshops featured activities ranging from self-defense training to making one's own herbal remedies and washable sanitary napkins. At Femstival 2010, there were also discussions, performances, an art exhibition, crafts sales, and the raffle of a menstrual cup, an eco-friendly object not easy to find in Mexico in those days. The workshops primarily brought women together to teach and learn with one another. But as with fanzine production, the purpose was to en-tertain as the event educated, providing fun and informative events for men as well as women. Children and pets were also welcome, though parental discretion was to be advised. Many events incorporated frank discussions about sexuality, and imagery of the female body was prominently displayed. At the entrance to the auditorium proper, women bunched pink tissue paper to create a vaginal womb-door, prompting numerous delighted attendees to perform full-body jokes, snapping pictures.

There was an open call for women who wanted to set up a booth, stage a performance, or offer a workshop. They proposed their ideas and we did our best to provide them with space and materials for following through. This was a messy, ad hoc process, but it mostly worked. An impressive diversity of women participated, often recruited through collective members' friendship networks, and by no means all linked to the local punk scene. A few friends of friends even came in from other parts of the country to lend a hand, including a female tattoo artist who provided her services during the event. While the festival was a huge amount of work, particularly for the two women who became the project's de facto leaders (more on this later), the rewards were great enough that ultimately a second Femstival was planned for 2011, again providing numerous chances for mutual aid, as well as outreach and autogestión more broadly, since the festival drew participants from beyond the punk scene.

SEED: FRIENDSHIP AND FEMINISM

Saturday afternoon, the second day of the 2010 Femstival, an unfortunate bit of drama occurred. On the auditorium stage, a performance had barely begun before the crowd became uproarious. From outside of the auditorium, where I was stationed to sell raffle tickets, I heard a confusing blend of angry shouts and wolf whistles.

The performers referred to themselves as a body-positive cabaret group, but they were said by those present to have performed a striptease. Many men in the audience were loudly supportive. But from what I was told later, a handful of the festival organizers were enraged at this affront to their feminist beliefs and rushed the stage, yelling in their fury, attempting to physically remove the act. While other women tried to plead for calm and tolerance, the scene erupted in chaos.

The incident ignited tensions that had been sizzling beneath the surface between various women organizers. There had been whisperings that the feminism represented by the event was not radical enough. Some were annoyed by other events included in the festival, such as the performance of a pair of women who claimed to represent Hindu women's culture and who were described to me as gyrating in sparkly, gauzy, midriff-exposing saris.

The problem was that would-be performers weren't vetted before the event. The cabaret act, like most other groups, simply had a member who was friendly with one of our central organizers and she had vouched for them, having seen a very different performance that they had done some time before. Many of the groups and individuals that participated in the event were bound to Las Cirujanas—"The Surgeons," as the collective was known—by friendship ties, and it was taken as a given that we would all be more or less on the same page when it came to our feminism.

DIRECT DEMOCRACY AND DIRECT ACTION:
ORGANIZING IN THE *COLECTIVO*

For decades, collectives have been the conventional way that people have orga-nized themselves within the punk scene, a form favored by lots of community-based activists in the city.[25] Within the local punk scene, collectives are thought to have originated in the gang culture in the city's marginalized neighborhoods in the 1980s, with early punk-scene collectives like the Mierdas Punk initially deriving its membership from that infamous Neza gang. The collective Punks Not Dead, known as the PND, also flourished in the 1980s, eventually edging out the Mierdas, gaining status as the real trendsetting people in the city's nascent punk scene, when Tijuana was still the epicenter of punk in Mexico and the capital's scene seemed provincial in comparison. Some authors have written about the Chavas Activas PUNK in the 1980s, a rare women's collective in the early punk scene, which attempted to make a space for female punk- scene participants, as well as to create outreach into their local community on women's issues.[26] Some of the women from this collective are still active today.

Other collectives have gained a certain prestige over the years, such as the JAR (short for Juventud Antiautoritaria Revolucionaria) in the 1990s, its influence continuing to fuel a great deal of controversy during my own time in the city. JAR members and ex-members were still active in the punk scene, using their organizational skills to provide performance venues and other resources for the community at that time. A now-tiny collective of just two to three people, Acción Libertaria, linked to the Biblioteca Social Reconstruir, has existed since the 1990s as well.

While collectives like these achieve longevity, others may come together solely for the purpose of creating a specific project, such as a series of talleres or fan-zines. Some collectives experiment with lifestyle projects, such as collective living arrangements, either in squatted locations or in rented accommodations.[27] Many collectives are founded on preexisting friendship networks, and the more open among them can mushroom as each friend invites new participants to join in. Though I attended meetings for several anarchist and punk-scene collectives as an observer, this was how I got my invitation to become an active member of Las Cirujanas. Among my fellow collaborators, the benefits as well as the pitfalls of forming collective organizations through friendship ties became apparent, which in turn highlighted the challenges of directly democratic practices of decision-making.[28] The trouble with achieving directly democratic groups via friendship organizations also hinted to me why I didn't witness much open discussion or planning of direct actions, which of the five principles of autogestión laid out in Acción Libertaria's pamphlet seemed to be on many people's lips while also being the least well defined.

Among the benefits of friendships within Las Cirujanas was the good feeling that dominated at the beginning of the event's planning, and again after the dust had settled following the event. Many of the women involved had known one another for years, and it showed. Conversation and ideas flowed, laughter abounded. Attending the meetings was fun and uplifting, despite and even because of the edgy coexistence of many strong women's personalities. This was particularly true in the early days of brainstorming, when everyone was excited to contribute her prodigious energy and creativity, dreaming the possibilities together. It was clear even then that two of the organizers were really at the center of the event, but that responsibility had not yet become burdensome to them, nor irksome to anyone else. Eventually, however, the situation grew tense as the two women at the center took on so many tasks that it became difficult for the rest of us to get a clear picture of what assistance was needed—for those of us who continued with regular attendance at all. As other friends in various collectives have remarked, this is often one of the major challenges with collective organizations to begin with. Relying on friends' voluntary time and work often involves the disappointment of their irregular participation. Some participants in the punk scene report shying away from collectives for exactly this reason, including the lone woman who created the contraception zine highlighted previously.

But in addition to the pleasure they may bring to their members, friendship-based organizations have other benefits. For one, organizations based on friendship mediate the desconfianza that collectives may face, particularly those that attempt more controversial goals or forms of activism. Some collectives fear the infiltration of porros, strangers who are paid to act the part of friendship and commitment to a group's goals but clandestinely serve the state's political ends (Pensado 2013). Friendship ties allow participants to skirt this issue, with members vouching for one another based on long acquaintance. Of course, exclusivity can happen for the same reason, when someone who is not well known to the group wants to participate and so may be excluded or sidelined.

Maybe even more important than fostering trust or mistrust, the pleasure of friendship ties heightens a sense that solidarity is possible between individuals, as well as between disparate groups of them. As Francesca Polletta (2002) has argued, the kind of egalitarianism that happens in friendships is more organic, more complex than the egalitarianism of a trade union, for example, which is a strategic choice. Egalitarianism within friendships is not based on the principle of equality, but is actively formed through a series of affective interactions that reveal not only friends' identities and backgrounds but also their personal strengths and weaknesses, their talents and failures. Extending equity to friends means being aware and accepting of their qualitative differences, valuing those distinctions as part of the interpersonal navigations of the relationship. While a more calculated, principled egalitarianism may appear to work best for a number of social movement organizations, friendship feels right and appropriate to others, being a radical act of mutual recognition between disparate individuals who are aware of their differences and choose to love one another anyway.[29]

However, some people suggest that friendships may impede difficult discussions within solidarity groups, as friends shy away from engaging in direct conflict with one another. For example, scholars of the feminist consciousness-raising movement of the 1970s in the u.s. have written about the potentially stifling dynamic of such groups. This type of wariness about internal conflict seemed less of an issue among the women of Las Cirujanas, and, indeed, other collectives that I witnessed, as part of the aesthetic and ethic of punk involves tolerating or enjoying a certain degree of conflict and argument. More problematic in this context, however, friends may assume that they already understand one another's opinions, feelings, and needs. In fact, an underlying feeling of shared beliefs may be what anchors friendship networks in the punk scene, allowing friends to quarrel over the particulars while feeling unified by big ideas like anti-authoritarianism. Unfortunately, however, the pleasure of friendship-based groups engaged in organizational purposes can vanish as they become too strained to function, both in terms of meeting goals and in terms of producing the kinds of horizontal relationships that friendships appear to promise.

For this reason, the problems that I witnessed among collectives within the punk scene, as well as a couple of anarchist collectives, could obstruct not only the directly democratic principles of autogestión but also the degree to which these organizations were able to engage in direct actions. The very definition of direct action was one that produced controversy and heated debate across collectives and among individuals. I once had two people explain direct action to me in strikingly different ways in a two-day period.

The first day, I got a mini-lecture on the topic by a speaker who highlighted the definition in a very concrete way. A direct action is exactly that, he said: it is an action taken directly by people who see a need for some kind of intervention. These people do not appeal to authorities or political representatives of any kind, but rather seek to accomplish whatever needs to be done between them and whoever else is involved, directly. In this way, direct action can be a very quotidian experience, an everyday means of carrying out autogestión. Unfortunately, he continued, some people had come to associate direct action with more violent or spectacular actions, like breaking the windows of a research lab that experiments on animals to send a message about animal rights. But direct action was not property damage and it was not violence, he opined. His definition then meandered into stern judgment of various people who wrongly considered themselves to be anarchists. He had some grudging respect for people who he described as sympathizers, he said, those who let themselves be distracted by work or romantic attachments but lent their time and money to the cause as they felt they could. But worst of all, he concluded, were the *pinches intelectuales* (fucking intellectuals) who spouted off about their anarchist beliefs before turning around and voting for the PRD (the more leftist Partido de la Revolución Democrática in power in Mexico City at that time), revealing an insidious faith in representative democracy.

The next day, another friend attempted to correct this vision, which he believed was based on the first speaker's well-known and—to him—wrong-headed pacifism. Direct action could indeed be violent, he informed me, far more concisely and mysteriously than the disquisition I had received the day before. The challenge was to match the degree of violence visited upon marginalized communities by the state or corporate capitalism with an appropriately violent reaction, he said, framing direct action as the response to a particular aggression. While direct actions can be informal and everyday, as my first discussant suggested, they can also be spectacular interventions into social and political situations.[30] In that case, they depend even more fully on careful, collaborative planning.

While some people argue that their highly conscious, caring lifestyles include numerous direct actions, others continue to see direct action as a more attention-grabbing intervention into a large-scale problem. Some people change their minds. During my visit in August 2018, one friend informed me that he no longer believed in the efficacy of certain kinds of spectacular direct actions and wanted creative work he'd done to promote them to stay out of contemporary conversations about punk's history in Mexico City. The debate about what direct action is therefore continues. Meanwhile, those who want to make a greater impact on their world through social justice initiatives may well be drawn away from the punk scene, joining networks that are clearer in their aims, methods, or definitions of direct action, perhaps expressing solidarity without depending on the affection of long-term friendships to ground it.[31]

Nevertheless, through both the hard work of punk performance and the various practices of autogestión, scene participants attempt to create and maintain strong affective ties in order to work toward their larger political objectives. In so doing, they perform an affective labor that mediates between older ideas about wage exchange and the solidarity born of a working-class identity, and newer ways to build solidarity through relational work, slowly shifting the valuation of work itself.[32] In the final chapter, I turn to larger questions that occupy attention in the punk scene: questions about freedom. I ask, what do punk-scene participants imagine when they think about the key anarchist goal of freedom from authority? Investigating the various ways of applying the intensities of love and rage stimulated in Mexico City's punk scene, I evaluate their efficacy for pursuing two different, if interrelated, concepts of how to change the world from the ground up: via dissent or autonomy.

FIVE

Autonomy

SEED: APATÍA NO!

It's a wet night during the rainy season in the normally dusty streets of Ecatepec, and hundreds of people have crowded into a long, narrow, cinderblock space, so densely packed that moving through them is an intimate game of force and friction, of bodies literally rubbing past one another. We have all gathered to hear a visiting hardcore punk band from Venezuela, Apatía No. Several local bands have warmed up the crowd during the marathon gig, and with the moisture of so many heated, excited bodies moving, sweating, and breathing in the tightly enclosed space, condensation gathers on the ceiling, dripping back onto the crowd below.

At the front of the room, there is a raised stage next to a pair of toilets, a never-ending line of would-be occupants jostling outside. Taking the stage, the four members of the band contribute to the intense heat and energy of the space as the crowd cheers and moves with renewed vigor. The music is fast, pared down, and distorted, guitarists strumming with impressive velocity, the drummer pounding a quick duple time, and the lead vocalist screaming a high-pitched static, while the bass player sketches a spare harmony and provides dialogic counterpoint, vocalizing in deep, growl-like tones. Between each song, the bass-vocalist begs the audience for water, but the crowd pays no attention to her, too focused on an intense sociability: yelling above the noise in conversation, screaming along with song lyrics, or hurling their bodies at one another in two circles of slam dancers cycling through the crowd like twin hurricanes.

With so many people crammed into a narrow, uncomfortable space, moving to frenetic, deafening music, there are problems. Fistfights repeatedly threaten to break out. Someone loses consciousness and is carried out of the building. And finally, one guy climbs to the top of the structure enclosing the toilets and dives from its height into the crowd below, knocking people down with the weight of his body.

The band stops, and immediately the roar of the crowd escalates, with taunting whistles piercing the din. Screaming in a different register—a seemingly testy speech yelled into his microphone—the main vocalist asks that everyone take better care, adding that violence should not happen among audience members but should be reserved for the state. Within the pause, the band again appeals to the crowd for water, this time successfully. As water bottles audibly pelt the stage, a voice in the crowd begins shouting, "Muerte al estado! Qué viva la anarquía!" (Death to the state! Long live anarchy!)

In a second, the entire crowd is yelling and moving in unison, fists upraised. The band's drummer rat-tats in time with the chant. After a few renditions, the slogan fades away. Refreshed, the band launches into their performance once more, and the show finishes, still in incredibly high spirits but without further disturbing incident. Despite continued physical discomfort, the atmosphere in the building had shifted.

LOVE AND RAGE: AN AFFECTIVE CIRCUITRY

The sequence of events with Apatía No that I recount here was one of the most striking that I experienced in the context of performance in Mexico City's punk scene. It was not often that participants at a show were so obviously and directly asked to control their reactions to intense musical stimulation. Such discussion of appropriate responses happened outside the confines of a musical event, but musicians seldom reproach or instruct audiences during performances. In the heat of the performative moment, and without criticism, Apatía No's vocalist found a way to channel the audience's energy back into a more acceptable set of behaviors by appealing to participants' ideals about how they should responsibly express their vehemence in the context of a cohesive punk scene.

In that moment, the audience at the tocada was able to demonstrate an appropriate rage while also remembering the importance of love, enacted on this occasion by treating one another with greater care. Not only did they curb their aggression while reacting to stimulating music in an uncomfortably overcrowded space, but they also remembered their compassion and hospitality, belatedly providing water to their hardworking and thirsty musical guests. Instead of dampening the energy and expression of the crowd, the musicians seemed more interested in flipping the affective circuitry of the moment. The vocalist's commentary suggested that the tocada was not too intense, but rather that the intensity was being experienced improperly in that particular moment. Briefly stopping the music allowed for a redirection of the intense affect already aroused and then restimulated as the band resumed playing the well-liked song that they had paused. The transformation was not necessarily to the feeling or feelings prompted, but to the ways the crowd behaved while experiencing it.[1]

Punk shows are prime places to experience this affective circuitry, though other common scene activities like the sing-along may also suggest how participants mediate strong affects like love and rage. Though naming "rage," "solidarity," or "friendship" may begin to suggest how such mediation occurs—the intensities of scene experiences being affixed with terms that help participants understand and articulate the feelings they share—they remain complex affective experiences that outrun such labels.[2] Love and rage bleed into one another, substitute for one another, and replace one another, all of an appropriate intensity to be savored within the high-energy punk scene.[3]

The slam, for example, is at one moment an aggressive free-for-all, fists and knees flying as participants excise their rage and then, at the next moment or even simultaneously, feel the euphoria of friendship and solidarity, their love for the same people who have been sustaining their blows. The moment with Apatía No provided a chance to identify a circuit breaker, a purposeful intervention that had the power to flip the charge, encouraging a better outcome to all that affective expenditure, redirecting it toward a mixture that better favored love while keeping rage at a simmer. With a quick reminder to the audience of their anarchist ideals, the band invoked the distinction between the allegedly lazy, gratuitous violence of the "destroy punk" and the more politically committed scene participant.

It was a stroke of luck that an audience member picked up on this cue so readily, prompting the crowd's slogan ("Death to the state! Long live anarchy!"), which underscored another concept that anarchists everywhere hold dear: libertad (freedom). But there appear to be two distinct visions of freedom that operate within Mexico City's contemporary punk scene: a "freedom from" negative forces like repression or poverty and a "freedom to" start from the here and now, building on a vision of radical equality without petitioning the state for enhanced benefits. While demanding freedoms and rights from government may be well fueled by the rage that scene participants value, to achieve the cooperative, horizontal relationships of autonomous organizations requires patience, compassion, and tolerance. Enacting equitable discussion and consensus-based decision-making, for example, can be slow, tedious, painstaking processes. Extending solidarity beyond immediate friendship networks may also feel challenging, involving a compromise of ideals, valuing one key similarity in a person or group over their multiple differences.

To conclude, then, I point out that a punk poetics that foregrounds oppositionality may not truly mirror the range of activities and behaviors that participants undertake as they attempt to promote autogestión within and beyond the punk scene. I emphasize that not only do diverse contexts shape different experiences within a global punk scene, but also that punk's famed "resistance" can look very different, not just across different scenes but within them (O'Connor 2016). While recognizing the rage that punk aesthetics and practices can ignite, motivating protest and self-defense initiatives as well as more destructive behaviors, I was also struck by the impressive variety of caring relationships that animate Mexico City's punk scene and how they encourage participants to reimagine complex ideas like "freedom." Interest in autonomous ideals of freedom may prompt a more serious investment in the slower, patient practices of autogestión like direct democracy, a practice that is key to autonomous communities. Knowing how to mediate the affective circuitry of love and rage while experimenting with these ideas and practices is an elusive but important skill.

SEED: A PUNK POETICS

My initial period of fieldwork in Mexico City took place during a tumultuous time in politics, in Mexico and internationally. From 2008 through 2011, there was always a great deal to talk about with my politically aware friends, from the global financial crisis to the Arab Spring, anti-austerity protests in Europe to the continued Israeli occupation of Gaza and the West Bank, to the creation of Occupy encampments in the United States.

In Mexico, there was the "war on drugs," paramilitary violence against Indigenous peoples, hunger strikes in the Zócalo staged by members of the Sindicato Mexicano de Electricistas, increasing numbers of femicides, the murders of journalists who covered political corruption and drug trafficking, Mexico's Bicentennial celebrations in 2010, and the run-up to the 2012 presidential elections, when it appeared certain that the PRI would regain federal power—and so they did with the presidency of Enrique Peña Nieto.

While all of the controversies that evolved in Mexico garnered attention and discussion, I was initially terrible at predicting what would spark my friends' interests in world politics. Despite following Los Indignados in Spain and especially anti-austerity protests in Greece, my friends revealed little interest in anti-austerity demonstrations in most other European nations, less still in Occupy encampments in the United States. Most people suspected the military involvement in Egypt's ouster of Hosni Mubarak too much to celebrate that as an accomplishment during the Arab Spring, though many revealed a sustained interest in Palestinian resistance movements, with an especially intense contempt for the state of Israel.

The commonalities between friends' interests suddenly snapped into place for me at a party I attended to inaugurate a new cultural space housing a library and meeting rooms that punk-scene participants were welcome to use. A good number of my friends were in attendance, eager to celebrate the new space on a Saturday evening after the Chopo market closed. Standing behind another partygoer who wore a provocative T-shirt comparing Israelis to Nazis, I shifted my gaze to a far wall as the lights dimmed, where images of larger-than-life, Molotov cocktail-throwing protestors started looping against its bright blank space. Together, the images and sounds of the party suddenly appeared to me of one piece, constructing a poetics of dissent that continued to shape punk-scene participants' attitudes about social justice work and notions of freedom, even while they had diverse ideas about what it might look like and how to pursue it.

SEED: FREEDOM AS AN ENDLESS MEETING

Because for a time there was a good bit of overlap between punk-scene participation and participation in the anarchist group Colectivo Autónomo Magonista (CAMA), I sometimes went to organizational meetings there. On

FIGURE 5.1. An individual's standoff with riot police at the May Day march in the centro histórico in 2018. Photo by Yaz "Punk" Núñez.

one occasion, I noticed that regular attendees were trying to reshape their process since my last attendance at a long meeting, identifying a moderator and imposing some further rules for discussion.

As the meeting began, the buzz of socialization ceased. We seated ourselves in rows, looking to the front of the room, where the moderator and other key members of the group sat. The first order of business was to decide what the day's business was, and in what order to tackle it. The moderator kept track of who wanted to speak and in what order they had asked permission to do so. For the next few hours, one solitary voice after another dominated the room, the rest of the attendees silently listening.

While the meeting was semi-structured, speakers didn't seem to feel a need to impose limits on their own contributions. There were several digressions, certain people speaking repeatedly, often for long periods of time. A quiet, and to my mind, incredible placidity reigned despite there being no sanctioned process for interjecting comments or for checking to see whether there was any consensus in the room. Carrying themselves with care, people wound their way through the rows of seated participants to the bathroom or stood along the walls to bounce briefly in place, seeking relief from the ache of motionlessness or the chill in the room. I was grateful to the person at my right, a stranger who wordlessly handed me an orange slice that momentarily quenched my thirst. Very few people abandoned their uncomfortable seats to stride for the door, as I repeatedly fantasized of doing. The meeting ended with a subdued wave of quiet chatter and a good deal of stretching, our energy spent.

IN PURSUIT OF FREEDOM: DISSENT AND AUTONOMY

Over the past few decades, "autonomy" has become a more prominent way of conceiving of social justice goals for many different groups around the world, from Indigenous communities to arts collectives to social movement organizations.[4] Mexico in particular has been a key locus of innovation for this type of political action, with the Zapatista uprising of 1994 and its aftermath being among the emerging models that have inspired people in the hemisphere and globally to embrace horizontal, non-hierarchical forms of organizing and to rethink their relationships with the state, simultaneously creating what was long ago termed a "pre-figurative politics."[5] Anarchists might call this form of politics "building a new world in the shell of the old," using the here and now as a means to re-create social and political relations from the grassroots up.

FIGURE 5.2. Conversation about anarchism in the Foro Alicia with the participation of the Biblioteca Social Reconstruir. Photo by Yaz "Punk" Núñez.

Autonomous political models may downplay the importance of dissent, as movements or communities attempt to circumvent rather than directly challenge the state (Dellacioppa 2009; Shantz 2011; Stahler-Sholk et al. 2014). In many nations, political dissent has been increasingly criminalized over the last several decades, costing activists their freedom, well-being, and, in the worst case, their lives. Often working in opposition to neglectful or repressive states, movement groups that embrace autonomy refuse to recognize state governments as the sole entities with the power to grant rights and freedoms, making autonomous politics less directly confrontational but also rooted in the present. The concepts of resistance and revolution begin to look quite different from the perspective of autonomous organizations. Without waiting or scheming for some far-off revolution, often with limited resources and means, activists and organizations that embrace an autonomous model can focus on what they need now to become the kinds of communities they would like to see in the world.

In an effort to model more equitable social organization, autonomous groups often embrace a horizontalist ethic, rejecting representative politics and actively engaging with their community's multiple, intersecting identities rather than building solidarity through one exclusive rubric. Arguably, as part of this shift, autonomous groups have paid greater attention to affect and to the role of the individual in grassroots politics, investigating the diverse social relationships that may lead to solidarity while embracing the need to embody changes to the power structures they promote. This attention to affect and the individual is evident in autonomous networking, despite a widespread, continued anxiety among some activists about the utility of so-called "lifestyle politics," in which an investment in individual freedoms is feared to overshadow the necessity of more large-scale social justice initiatives.[6]

In the Latin American region, the Zapatistas have continued to be one important example of autonomous politics for many, including some—though by no means all—members of Mexico City's punk scene. The original militarism of the Ejército Zapatista de Liberación Nacional, which forcibly took control of portions of San Cristóbal de las Casas, the capital city of the Mexican state of Chiapas, on January 1, 1994, soon began to morph into something else as the rebels were quickly overpowered by the Mexican state and its military. Simultaneously, however, the Zapatistas recognized that the vast majority of the Mexican public supported their uprising against a loathed federal government. They employed sharp media savvy to build further support around the world. In 1996, after the Mexican government's betrayal of the San Andrés Accords—which its representatives had signed alongside representatives of the EZLN, promising to grant new measures of autonomy to the Indigenous peoples of the republic—the EZLN increasingly refused to negotiate or collaborate with the federal government. Instead, they strengthened their autonomy by fine-tuning and formalizing their means of self-government, ultimately creating five *caracoles* (snail's shells), each of which organized diverse Indigenous communities according to region, containing Juntas de Buen Gobierno (Good Government Councils).[7]

These councils practiced horizontal organization, leading to increased collaboration among their members and creating greater freedoms for the members of each community, while also encouraging their solidarity across differences. Organizational responsibility, too, was distributed more widely among them than in hierarchical groups. Over time, the Zapatistas explicitly sought to address lingering inequities within their organizational structures, promoting the participation of women, for example, and downplaying the leadership of any one spokesperson in the media.

FIGURE 5.3. Anarchist graffiti created in the centro histórico during the October 2 march in 2019. Photo by Yaz "Punk" Núñez.

People around the world continued to take note of the Zapatistas' model, converging on the Lacandon jungle to attend workshops and solidarity meetings there, while also using autonomous organizational strategies in their own struggles. In 2006, the EZLN began to travel around the country as part of La Otra Campaña (The Other Campaign), an effort to strengthen grassroots solidarity within Mexico, beyond Indigenous communities in the south. Friends recounted that during these years, in the late 1990s and into the early 2000s, punk-scene participants welcomed the Zapatista Caravan on its visit to Mexico City, and several people either had visited Chiapas or were trying to raise funds for the trip during my periods in the city.

Even among those who consciously look to the Zapatistas and other autonomous communities as models, however, that admiration may not extend to an emulation of real, nitty-gritty horizontal practices like consensus-based decision-making (rather than majoritarian voting). Achieving more horizontal relationships requires minute attention to process over product, to the day-to-day interactions among activists rather than an exclusive focus on the outcomes they accomplish. With the aim of encouraging full participation, horizontal organization also attempts to get everyone talking, even though the punk-scene charge of "too much talk" has long been used as a way to invalidate social movement organizations that are perceived to be ineffective. As some anarchist organizations in Mexico City attempted to adopt measures that would bring about a greater equitability in their discussion and decision-making procedures, such attempts made those groups less viable in the eyes of some punk-scene commentators I knew. One day, a bookish punk-scene friend and I pored over the literature selection at a back table during a CAMA meeting, and I asked him why he didn't hang out with the strictly anarchist (as opposed to anarchist punk) collectives more often. "Because they're trapped in their books," he alleged. "All talk and no action."

To feel active and engaged, punk-scene participants ideally hang on to the rabia stimulated during encounters with punk as music. As Kevin Dunn (2016) has argued, punk in scenes around the world often stimulates "oppositional identities," a key part of how global punk scenes encourage political awareness and perhaps action within individuals. An oppositional stance is also particularly useful in situations requiring self-defense or those more oriented toward a politics of dissent, something in which punk-scene participants have long enjoyed engaging (see chapter 3).

Autonomous communities, too, may require toughness and the capacity for self-defense, but also patience, calm, tolerance, and, often, an ability to withstand the tedium of drawn-out negotiations. While I don't wish to present dissent and autonomy as opposing poles on a spectrum of organizational tactics, my experience did suggest that they require the harnessing of different affective states to be achieved. In fact, I suspect that the Zapatistas continued to form a model for some punk-scene participants in Mexico City exactly because they model both sets of qualities. Having engaged in horizontal organizing and military resistance, the autonomous Zapatista communities have demonstrated something that looks a lot like the righteous rage and self-defense that scene participants respect while also being renowned for their communalist, equitable organizational methods and social justice innovation.[8]

Attempting to illuminate directly democratic practices in a different context—in u.s. social justice movements since the mid-twentieth century—Francesca Polletta investigates the "differences in 'tastes' for organizational styles," which can encourage or prevent activists from relating to social movement groups that feel affectively different to them even if they share common ideological backgrounds or political goals (2002, 216). She also emphasizes the role of friendship in social movements as part of a larger project to theorize a triangular model of direct democracy founded on interpersonal "relationships," along with "rules" and "rituals." This model recognizes both rational and affective elements that, ideally, allow social movements to cohere and work effectively toward their goals.

For Polletta, "tastes" or "styles" for certain kinds of organizing emerge especially in rituals large and small. She provides the example of facilitators in the Direct Action Network (DAN), a group that formed after the Seattle World Trade Organization protests in 1999, organizers who revealed a squeamishness about possibly crossing a line into a "Californian" or "new age" style of politics. Among other manifestations of this perceived style, agreement could be expressed via "twinkling" (wiggling the fingertips), along with a myriad of other small forms of gestural communication and "vibes monitoring" routinely used in DAN spokescouncil meetings. Union workers were uncomfortable with this "touchy-feely" quality, which they saw as the overly personal and expressive style of DAN meetings. This deterred them from participating in the group, despite the fact that DAN was actively seeking to partner with organizations like theirs (Polletta 2002, 216).

Such discrepancies between organizational tastes lead Polletta to conclude that "rules" and "relationships" are not enough to assure the health of participatory democracy among social movement networks. "Rituals" form the third point of her triangular model not only because through them specific organizational styles emerge, but also because their enactment can provide a Durkheimian effervescence, creating opportunities for social bonding within groups.[9] While I have argued that Mexico City's punk scene is not a social movement per se, it complicates the picture Polletta presents, in that rituals are key to scene sociability but they in no way guarantee social bonding or an increased possibility that individuals will join the more politically oriented projects or groups in the scene. Nor is there a clear separation between rational and affective realms, when a taste for rabia informs not just rituals but also interpersonal relationships and the unwritten rules for sociability within collectives as well.

In Mexico City's punk scene, not only does a taste for rage shape ritualistic practices like the slam, but it also helps to inform the brusque, edgy tension through which participants conduct their friendships. People value the edginess in others, savoring a friendship that can survive regular contestation. Someone who shies away from conflict entirely is unlikely to have many friends in the punk scene. My own friendships there deepened when I learned to express both my own anger and feelings of friendship with more clarity and insistence. The fraught love of friendship among punk-scene participants emerges not only from long-standing affective ties, however, but also via conceptual associations with the importance of solidarity in the context of Mexican history, politics, and aesthetics. Different individuals' preferences for the affective experiences of rage and love, how they balance in the affective circuitry of various punk-scene experiences, also help to determine what kinds of approaches they will take to enact their anarchist politics, itself informed by shifting ideas about what freedom might look like.

And to be fair, despite the circulation of anarchist ideals like autogestión in Mexico City's punk scene, some participants never make it beyond the camaraderie and the catharsis of their early involvement in punk practices. For these participants, punk remains a hedonistic pleasure, a much-needed escape from the grind of daily life among like-minded friends. Beyond a vague orientation to anti-authoritarianism, they may be little touched by more complex ideas that punk songs and fanzines present. Some people have long been more active in the punk scene, forming bands, writing songs, and creating fanzines, but perhaps remaining in the same configurations as always, trying to summon the love of friendship or solidarity to support the latest projects of their long-lived punk-scene collective. Meanwhile, others decide that punk is retrograde, juvenile, too focused on rage and self-destruction—that all punk is "destroy" oriented.

Maybe they retire in bitterness to more mainstream lifestyles (as some scene stalwarts allege), but occasionally attend a punk show. Maybe they focus on strictly anarchist collectives, moving on from the anarcopunk of their younger years. Some people sever or retain connections to the punk scene while joining more established social movements or social justice organizations in the city, in other parts of Mexico, or in other parts of the world.

This diversity and diffusion of ideas, practices, and influences among punk-scene participants is exactly what makes it such a vital, interesting presence in Mexican social and political life. While for some, the punk scene is simply an opportunity to encounter some much-needed pleasure, for others, it becomes a springboard, propelling them into activity with other activist networks that may or may not overlap with the punk scene, joining groups and participating in activities that align with their anarchist ideals, whether they work through protest, seek to build autonomous communities that hold state intervention at bay, or both.

The coexistence of the various sounds, affective practices, and political-organizational ideals linked to love and rage create productive frictions, prompting continued debate and inspiring individuals to seek connections within and beyond the punk scene as they determine how best to act on their ever-evolving personal and collective convictions.[10] The seeds that are sown in Mexico City's punk scene disperse widely, carried on currents that bring them to vastly different places with varied options for engagement.

SEED: COLLABORATIONS WITH A *BARRIO AUTÓNOMO*

During my days in Mexico City, I heard tell of one and then two local punk-scene participants who were so desirous to live and work with autonomous communities that they left, one reportedly moving to Oaxaca to engage in the ongoing aftermath of a massive uprising in the capital city in 2006. Their commitment to their politics was impressive, inspiring. Of course, not all scene participants can uproot themselves so easily.

But not everyone need do so. There are barrios autónomos, autonomous neighborhoods within Mexico City that experiment with autonomy, collectively creating and maintaining their own infrastructure. A punk-scene friend, who has long worked with local anarchist organizations, began collaborating with residents of one such neighborhood, which had called in her group for advice. Despite the fact that the neighborhood was more oriented toward an autonomous Marxism, my friend and her fellow anarchists held workshops and discussion groups with residents, attempting to help them set up their own system of security (rather than allowing the mistrusted police into their community). Just before the coronavirus pandemic struck, they were due to work further on the issue of intra-community resolutions for people found to have violated neighborhood rules. In the anarchist consultants' view, it would be key to abandon the punishment of criminal offenses, embracing instead a more restorative notion of justice in the community.

SEED: SOWING AN AUTONOMOUS LIVING SPACE

In the enormity of Mexico City, with its many twinkling electric lights—not to mention its obscuring smog—few stars appear to dazzle the night sky. Some of my punk-scene friends pine for the chance to escape the bright city permanently, to leave behind its bustle and chaos, its pollution and grime. A few years ago, a number of them banded together, recruiting a small group of friends to save money until they could collectively buy a little plot of land in a more rural area, from a family that had been farming it for generations. Together, the friends divided the portions into lots, imagining that over the years, they would slowly build up their own little community, living somewhat off the grid in a bucolic little settlement that they would design themselves. One friend sent me pictures of her little piece of land, excitedly pointing out every mature tree and maguey plant, every pretty vista that enhanced her own little portion.

Some people have barely visited since contributing their individual down payment. (There is grousing about those who don't pitch in.) Others visit regularly, though even with their commitment, preparing the land and building homes and infrastructure is painfully slow, especially without the ability to set aside a substantial amount of income and time for the project each year. The monster city continues to beckon with its promise of work, albeit low-waged and precarious labor. I hear that opportunities are even scarcer in the small city closer by.

While the dream remains of building a new home on the land, the plot functions as a garden and refuge for the city dwellers, who periodically meet up at the site, germinate new plants, clear brush, swim in a little man-made pond, socialize with the salt-of-the-earth farming family that evidently enjoys having them nearby, and brainstorm the various features they'd like to see on their patch of earth in years to come. They wonder how they can delicately suggest to their neighbors that they stop drinking Coca-Cola, a habit that supports a particularly nasty corporate profit machine. They learn, largely through the trial-and-error training of autogestión, as well as through their neighbors' advice, how to do necessary things: construct an earth toilet, rig up portable sources of electric power, and interpret the sounds and sights around them, signals that come from a distance that seems vast compared to the close quarters of the city.

SEED: THE VALUE OF "DESTROY PUNK"?

"Licenciado!" cried some of the youngest punk-scene participants whenever they spotted him. They were kids who liked to hang in the street post-Chopo, and they always honored him with the term for a college graduate, though technically he wasn't one. Like several people in the punk scene, he had some college education but had not been able to finish his degree. People respected him anyway, for being banda but attaining so much education. Undoubtedly, they also appreciated his generosity. Whenever he went to the Chopo or to punk shows, he was always up for the sociability, always ready with a joke and liberal with the coins he shared for beer.

Nevertheless, some people argued that he was only ever there for the party, apolitical, and that he could get nasty when he was really wasted. They told me not to give him any of my time, that he was not a "true punk," that I had nothing to learn from him. Increasingly, I saw that he could indeed be a divisive figure, even among those who enjoyed a debate. But apart from his kindness to me, what I found hardest to ignore was the admiration of young punk-scene participants, kids who were learning to deal with the precarity of life in el DeFectuoso, trying to find purpose and pleasure despite its difficulties, and encountering friendship and guidance through a variety of role models in the scene. While many people in Mexico City's punk scene valorize hard work, perhaps he is among those who show another way by also openly treasuring free time, refusing a blurring of work and leisure so endemic to life in neoliberalizing capitalist economies that many people hardly notice it.

SEED: MUTUAL AID, TRANSNATIONALLY

Even when I returned to the States, I was never far from connections to Mexico City's punk scene, especially when I moved to Chicago. In a building that once housed a metal-recycling business, out in the western part of the city, I attended a benefit show for the Biblioteca Social Reconstruir in 2017, an annual event organized for a few years running by people with ties to Mexico City's punk scene. Their aim was to raise funds for the venerated institution that had faced so much precarity in the decades since its founder's death in 1997.

When in early 2021 one of the library's most loyal caretakers—who had started out in the punk scene and had become a stalwart figure in Mexico City's anarchist circles—contracted COVID-19, the Chicago connections made use of their previous attention to the library, as well as their extensive, global punk-scene network, calling on friends near and far to raise money to support him in his illness. To everyone's demonstrable grief, he died before it could be delivered to him. The substantial funds they raised went to his family for his funeral services instead.

SEED: REGENERATION

One of the scene's most respected long-term participants has become one of its most respected historians. Having played in some of the key bands in Mexico City's punk-scene history, he is an expert on the music and has been part of many initiatives over the decades. He has long sold material in the Chopo market and has a vast collection of recordings and fanzines that he preserves and, increasingly, shares in person, on the radio, and streaming online.

As the coronavirus pandemic raged on in Mexico City, which was terribly hard-hit with high rates of illness and death, someone asked him in an interview what he hoped for after the crisis subsided. He noted the loss of venues that had occurred during the shutdowns, most of them hard-won spaces for punk performance that likely had vanished for good. Still, he struck a hopeful note. He remembered the beginning days of the city's punk scene, the days of especially intense repression and restriction.

He suggested that, if need be, everyone would draw on that history of strength and flexibility, meeting in whatever spaces they could claim. The seeds of a renewed punk scene were still there—pushed back underground, perhaps, but biding their time, waiting to regenerate in whatever climate might meet their scrappy will to flourish in a post-pandemic world.

NOTES

Prologue

1. Desobediencia Civil, *No hay libertad sin desobediencia* (Mexico City: Cryptas Records, Compact Disc, 2001). Lyrics may be found on http://www.musica.com/letras, accessed July 15, 2021. All translations in this text are my own, unless otherwise noted. Desobediencia Civil is one among several bands with impressive longevity in Mexico City's punk scene. Formed in the early 1990s, the group garnered a strong local fanbase and eventually an international one through DIY distribution of their material. In fact, the song begins with a fuzzy recording of a greeting at an international punk-solidarity gathering held in Uruguay in 1998.

2. The term *güera*, signifying a person (gendered feminine) with fair skin and often lighter hair color, is one among a range of terms to indicate differences in people's appearances, part of a legacy of colorism in Mexico as in Latin America broadly. See Dixon and Telles 2017; Dixon 2019; Reeskens and Velasco Aguilar 2020.

3. The term *autogestión* is a strange one, a word in use in other Spanish-speaking countries, but with a particular history in Mexican political life. For those familiar with punk scenes globally, autogestión may also appear to be like DIY, the do-it-yourself attitude that has been embraced by many "punks" around the world. While there is a similarity, the two terms are quite different in their contexts and intended scope. I'll explore this important term more fully in later chapters.

4. In the Mexican context, "libertarian" is a word more closely associated with anarchism than it is in the U.S. context, where it often has more free-market and socially conservative connotations.

5. As one example of the unwillingness among some anarchists to divide theory and practice, Jeff Shantz writes, "anarchism as a movement builds upon ways of living and relating that are already present in people's everyday lives rather than reflecting aspects of a future post-revolutionary society" (2011, 2).

6. Antifa is a global network of people who seek to combat fascism and do not shrink

from physical confrontation in doing so. In 2009, I attended an anti-fascist march in Mexico City, being made aware of it by punk-scene friends who identified themselves as Antifa. The black bloc is a tactic used among some activists, one that has been linked to anarchism in the mainstream media especially since its use in some anti-globalization protests in the 1990s and early 2000s. See Juris 2008. For more on Antifa, see Bray 2017.

7. A "squat" is a place that people occupy without owning or renting the property. This may occur among unhoused people seeking shelter and among people who want to make a statement against private property or the financial burden of rent. See, for example, Corr 1999.

8. For example, in the 1990s a transnational anarchist organization called Love and Rage/Amor y Rabia flourished in the U.S. and Mexico, with active members in Mexico City who also had ties to the local punk scene. See San Filippo 2003.

9. For an anthropological account of the impact of metaphors like these, see Delaney 1991.

ONE *Sowing*

1. In addition to some of my collaborators, several academics who write about punk also refer to it as a movement. See, for example, Bestley et al. 2019; Magaña 2020.

2. Other useful models include Juris (2008), an ethnographic exploration of the practice of networking in a transnational social movement organizational context. Gill (2017) uses the metaphor of the rhizome as both method and analytical tool to maintain fluidity when framing the "Turkish classical musicians" of her study.

3. These terms are not translated. Punk-scene participants use the English language terms "destroy" and "rocker" when denigrating those who enjoy early punk-rock sounds. The use of English in Mexican rock music has been controversial since the 1950s, something I'll explore further in the third and fourth chapters.

4. I adopt the terminology of "rockers" and "radicals" from a prominent member of the punk scene, an owner of the now-defunct club El Clandestino in Ecatepec, who used the terms in interviews for the documentary episode *Esquizofrenia: el microclima del punk*, directed by Gabriel Santander, which aired in Mexico City on Canal 22 in 2010.

5. Maurice Rafael Magaña (2020) has provided further confirmation of "punk" presence in social justice activity in his ethnography of autonomous organizing in Oaxaca since 2006.

6. I'm not alone in employing terms like "scene participants." See, for example, Kahn-Harris 2007; Jackson 2012.

7. Arias and Goldstein 2010. In contrast to previous scholarship, this interdisciplinary group of political scientists and anthropologists argue that violence is in fact constitutive of democracy in the Latin American region.

8. See Agren 2016, writing for the *Guardian*.

9. For seventy-one years, Mexico was dominated by the PRI, often referred to as a "soft dictatorship" that finally ended at the federal level in the year 2000, though the party remained powerful in various state and local governments. The PRI returned to federal power with the election of Enrique Peña Nieto to the presidency in 2012, though it was voted out again in the following *sexenio* (six-year presidential term). For more about politics in Mexico, see chapter 3.

10. Gallo 2004. Diane Davis explicitly links the city's problems with its populace's activism against the PRI. See 1994, 3.

11. Daniel M. Goldstein (2004) discusses this in the Bolivian context.

12. For an ethnographic account of a neighborhood that was settled by land invasion, see Matthew Gutmann, "The Invasion of Santo Domingo," in *The Meanings of Macho* (1996), 33–49.

13. For an account of how the growth of the metropolitan zone impacted the environment and quality of services in Mexico City, see Gamboa de Buen 1994.

14. Trash collection has long been a notoriously difficult problem in Mexico City, becoming the subject of various sociological and journalistic works. The classic account is Héctor Castillo Berthier's ethnographic research among *pepenadores* (garbage pickers), *La sociedad de la basura* (1990). See also Alma Guillermoprieto, *The Heart That Bleeds* (1995).

15. See "No Excuse," a report on the violence against journalists in Mexico, prepared by the Committee to Protect Journalists, published May 2, 2017, https://cpj.org, accessed March 4, 2020. The CPJ noted at the end of 2019 a drop in murdered journalists worldwide, though this needed development was not observed in Mexico.

16. Taibo 2010, 19. Despite this indictment, the essay concludes: "This is the best city on the planet, in spite of itself."

17. In more recent writing, Goldstein recounts his open availability to serve in this give-and-take role for local people as an important part of his research. For example, in his ethnography *Owners of the Sidewalk* (2016), an account of street vending in Cochabamba, he describes the ways that he solicited requests from his interlocutors to encourage their collaboration in his research, from writing publicly about the plight of street vendors in local media, to buying things for them, such as a Public Address system for their market.

18. Here, I refer to a passage in Aaron Fox's *Real Country*, in which he recounts that his relationships grew so comfortable that it was possible for him and his interlocutors to forget that he was doing research at all, symbolized by the seeming invisibility of his recording equipment (2004, xv).

19. My primary instruments at the time were viola and violin. Since I had hooked both of those instruments up to amps and effects pedals to play with rock and country bands previously, some friends and I did toss around the idea of my playing with a punk band in Mexico City. It never happened. A few scene participants were interested in more traditional violin sounds in styles like *huapango*, and so they came to me for violin lessons.

20. Like Goldstein, Carey writes persuasively about the propensity of his own inter-locutors in the Moroccan High Atlas to mistrust others, basing this not in the kind of calculated politics that Cochabambino street vendors demonstrate toward rain-making gringo outsiders, but rather in broader, more philosophical terms, in tune with deeply held local notions about the fundamental unknowability and inviolable independence of all people. He describes mistrust in the High Atlas context as a "rugged autonomy and moral equality that assumes other people to be both free and fundamentally uncontrol-lable" (2017, 10). For an examination of mistrust in another context, see Ashforth 2005.

21. The classic account is, of course, Dick Hebdige, privileging style as a subversive type of punk resistance in *Subculture: The Meaning of Style* (1979). The notion of punk-as-rebellion has currency in Mexico City's punk scene. See, for example, the (admittedly controversial) writings of local punk-scene veterans Detor Escobar and Hernández Sán-chez n.d. For a more recent and more scholarly approach, see Greene 2016.

22. For an in-depth analysis of the importance of friendship in the punk scene in Buenos Aires, see Rohrer 2014.

23. See, for example, Laitinen and Pessi 2015.

24. From Chaz Bufe and Mitchell Cowen Verter, eds. *Dreams of Freedom: A Ricardo Flores Magón Reader* (Oakland, CA: AK Press, 2005), 245.

25. In contrast, Magaña (2020) posits a "decolonial anarchism," inspired by Indigenous histories and practices as operative among the social movement groups he terms the 2006 Generation, whose initial resistance occurred in solidarity with APPO in Oaxaca's capital city. Though people did tell me about Indigenous precedents, I was more frequently re-ferred to texts by Flores Magón and classical European anarchists. As Magaña points out, however, Flores Magón was born in Oaxaca and was heavily influenced by Indigenous forms of anarchism there, in addition to his engagement with European and U.S. anarchists.

26. I wrote about another important source of information and sociability in the punk scene, the Biblioteca Social Reconstruir, which was closed for much of my initial, extended fieldwork period. See Tatro 2021.

27. Anarco-syndicalism is an anarchism linked to labor issues and trades unionism, while anarco-communism is based on collectivist community practices, such as hold-ing and working common lands (Hart 1978; Lida and Illades 2001; Ribera Carbó 2010).

28. Some of my friends located the word as descended from anarco-syndicalist tradi-tions, tracing its use back through the Biblioteca Social Reconstruir, the library amassed by Spanish Civil War exile Ricardo Mestre Ventura and then left in the care of punk-scene participants after his death in 1997 (Saño 1977; Arvon 1980; Tatro 2021). Anthropologist Livia Stone (2018) has attempted to trace the word's etymology and contemporary usage after learning it in the context of working with activists in solidarity with the people of Atenco, where, in 2002 and again in 2006, locals faced off with the government over land rights.

29. In his book on punk in Peru, Shane Greene comments on the usage of the term there, also contrasting it with DIY: "*autogestión* is the less literal way (compared to *hazlo-tu-mismo*) to translate the practical ideal of do-it-yourself (DIY). This is of course the term Anglo punks appropriated from the humdrum material but 'crafty' context of amateur house repair" (2016, 171).

30. Prompted by Francesca Polletta, whose book *Freedom Is an Endless Meeting* demonstrates the importance of direct democracy in the social movements of mid- to late twentieth-century North America, I trace the specific concept of rabia in local punk as it frames and reframes various "'tastes' for organizational styles that line up with differences in status" (2002, 216).

31. Interviewing does occasionally occur among punk-scene participants, however, especially in the production of fanzine content. Fanzine interviews (with band members, for example) are usually quite brief, emphasizing direct, firsthand knowledge that the interviewee alone can provide. As a genre that is part of the scene, they often read more like quick, chatty news bulletins than extended metacommunicative events that seek to unpack deeper cultural significance (Briggs 1986).

32. "Deep hanging" was the term that Louise Meintjes, my dissertation advisor, used to describe my methods.

33. Poma and Gravante (2016) also note this nadir.

34. Then, in the next *sexenio*, beginning in 2018, Andrés Manuel López Obrador (better known as "AMLO") was elected president. He has often been represented as a populist, and certainly the prospect of his administration provoked a great deal of hope for some people on the political left in Mexico. Sadly, a few years into his presidency, many who hoped his administration would bring sweeping changes to the country have lost that sense of optimism. For my friends in the punk scene—most of whom don't believe in representative democracy—AMLO never did raise their hopes, and so they have suffered less disillusionment since then.

35. After I left Mexico in 2011, the club changed ownership. It was renamed La Libélula and gradually began to present fewer shows of interest to my local friends.

36. The library was the work of Spanish Civil War refugee Ricardo Mestre Ventura, who left it in the care of young friends from the punk scene when he died in 1997. Clearly, the space helped breathe some new life and energy into the punk scene, which accounts for part of the revitalization that I mentioned. Currently housed in the local headquarters of the Frente Auténtico de Trabajo (FAT) labor union, the library provides not only books and other materials for learning but also a necessary space for socializing. Arguably, by providing tangible reminders of the punk scene's links to the Spanish exile community and now to the FAT, the space also legitimizes local punk-scene participants' history and politics. For more on the history of the FAT, an independent union created in midcentury Mexico, see Hathaway 1997.

37. The auditorium was occupied by students and affiliated groups during the university strike of 1999–2000. Since then, the continued "occupation" has caused controversy on campus, though the university tolerates the unauthorized use of the space as a community center and hangout for some students and campus employees, as well as people who have no official connection with the university. Student activism has been a contentious reality at UNAM since the 1960s. The university has also seen a fair share of *porrismo*, the practice of employing young "thugs for hire" or "agents provocateurs" to interfere in student activism (Pensado 2013).

38. Pulque is a pre-Hispanic drink made of the fermented sap of the maguey plant, a mildly alcoholic beverage experiencing a resurgence in popularity among young people during my early days in the city. In addition to the appeal of its native, precolonial roots, the drink is difficult to preserve and has not successfully been commercialized, another factor that makes it a favorite with politically conscious youth.

39. In fact, one friend informed me via WhatsApp message on September 10, 2018, that in the gentrified Plaza Garibaldi, even the mariachis have to make their living "*de volada*" (in flight), ducking the authorities as their informal means of earning a living becomes ever more precarious.

TWO *Rage*

1. While in many contexts, the term "moshing" has replaced the term "slam dancing," the latter remains viable in Mexico City's punk scene. People mostly refer to it simply as "the slam," however. In local Spanish pronunciation, this has two syllables: "*el eslam.*"

2. In contrast to stereotypes that describe a more individualistic and aggressive Mexican masculinity, I encountered a great deal of discussion in the punk scene about self-defense, often rooted in both self- and community protection. For more perspectives on masculinities in Mexico and Latin/x America (including the U.S.), see Lancaster 1992; Prieur 1998; Gutmann 1996, 2003; Adams and Savran 2002; McKee Irwin 2003; Macías-González and Rubenstein 2012; Hurtado and Sinha 2016; and Guidotti-Hernández 2021.

3. Also, as I noted in chapter 1, punk-scene participants are not necessarily very young people.

4. In 2018, the incoming mayor of Mexico City, Claudia Sheinbaum, announced the "dissolution" of the granaderos, who were to be incorporated into other security forces charged with "civil protection tasks." See González Alvarado and Cruz Flores 2018.

5. This is according to the Committee to Protect Journalists, which keeps track of journalists' deaths internationally, accessed at https://cpj.org on August 3, 2021. For more on the six students killed in Iguala and forty-three disappeared from Ayotzinapa, see Hernández 2016; Soloff 2019.

6. A newspaper story was published the day after the march, with "Anarco Furiosos"

as its headline. I interpret this phrase as a play on the term "anarcopunks," replacing the punks with the concept of "furious ones," creating a term that signifies "furious anarchists" but may still be understood to refer to punks in the context of other reporting on the events. See *El Gráfico*, October 3, 2009, 6.

7. This is the sub-headline of a two-page spread titled "Recuerdan '68 con desmán" (They remember '68 with excess) in *Metro*, October 3, 2009, 4–5. Both *El Gráfico* and *Metro* are sensationalist newspapers widely displayed on street newsstands. More rigorous news outlets mostly did not label protestors in the same manner.

8. *Diccionario de real academia Española*, "Rabia," accessed March 5, 2020, https://dle.rae.es/?w=rabia.

9. Rage and love are also linked in some U.S. feminist and anti-racist writing. Cornel West has characterized Malcolm X as "the prophet of black rage primarily because of his great love for black people," for example (1993, 95), while bell hooks has theorized rage (1995) as a healthy and necessary response to racism, and love (2000) as key to community and mutuality. See also Lorde 2007. Several books on rage authored by women and people of color were published after the 2016 U.S. presidential election, including Chemaly 2018; Cooper 2018; Traister 2018; and Owens 2020.

10. The hydraulic metaphor is consistent with the James-Lange theory of emotion, which imagines emotion as a force circulating within the body and potentially spilling over, particularly in the case of intense emotions such as anger. However, as Robert Solomon (1993) notes in his essay on the inadequacy of the James-Lange theory to account for "anger" cross-culturally, some cultures embrace a hydraulic understanding of emotion, and some do not.

11. Hahn 2006, 92. The susceptibility of the body to sound is also part of what can turn music into a weapon (Cusick 2006; Daughtry 2015).

12. Italics in the original.

13. This goes beyond timbre or the "grain" of the voice, as argued by Harkness 2014; Meintjes 2017. See also Tatro 2014.

14. Evan Rapport (2020, 194) provides a detailed stylistic analysis of hardcore punk, including its harmonic innovations, which resulted from practical performance considerations as well as the genre's fundamental orientation toward the guitar rather than the keyboard.

15. Visa costs and restrictions usually make touring in the U.S. impossible for these bands.

16. Blast beats are a running sixteenth-note beat played at extremely high speed, usually with most, if not all, of the elements of the drum kit emphasizing that rhythm, creating an intense, continuous blast of distortion and noise to anchor the grindcore band.

17. Nina Eidsheim explains the ways that musical vibrations are especially amplified within different regions of the body (2015, 172).

18. *Fresa* literally means "strawberry." I explicate this term alongside its opposite, *banda*, in the following chapter.

19. For a version of this history in the United States, see Paul Rachmann's (2006) film *American Hardcore*.

20. Roman (1988) is particularly clear on this point, based on her ethnographic focus on women who participated in midwestern punk scenes in the late 1980s.

21. Friends in the punk scene refer to music that has the right mixture of qualities with a variety of words: *dura* (hard), *gruesa* (fat), *maciza* (solid), and *pesada* (heavy). From these choices, I picked the term "hard" because it was one that could describe the sound according to my interlocutors' use, but it could also describe the ways that I saw participants reacting to the music and practices like the slam, by literally hardening their bodies.

22. Ironically, El Circo Volador is a special venue created to provide a space for the sociability of more economically marginalized young people. See Castillo Berthier 2004.

23. "Portazo en gatillazo en zapopan calle 2," YouTube video, www.youtube.com/watch?v=1MxOsU_IrR0, accessed July 17, 2021.

24. For a thoughtful meditation on the power and precarity of a white gringa positioning, see Nelson 1999.

25. *In Rage Becomes Her,* Soraya Chemaly discusses new research suggesting that women do not necessarily experience a "fight or flight" reaction to physical assault, an instinct often believed to be the normal and natural response to threats because much previous research was carried out on male subjects (2018, 146).

26. Following Elspeth Probyn in *Blush*, I understand the experience as what happens when the "feeling body outruns the cognitive capture of the habitus" (2005, 55).

27. Brittney Cooper (2018) discusses "white-girl tears," writing about how white women in the U.S. are conditioned to cry in the face of frustration and anger, a response that not only blunts their motivation to react but may also be weaponized in situations when they find themselves in conflict with people of color.

THREE *Dissent*

1. "Los derechos humanos; los violan en todas partes . . . en México es el destino."

2. "Debemos liberarnos; del dominio explotador; de puercos capitalistas; iniciemos una protesta."

3. The name of the PRI changed a few times over the course of this long period of consolidation, but this is the name that ultimately stuck.

4. However, Marroquín (1975) used the label "*jipiteca*," an amalgam of *jipi* and *azteca*, to recuperate Mexican hippies, who he believed were rediscovering their Indigenous roots through countercultural experience.

5. Public opposition to the PRI at the time was largely spearheaded by the Mexican

Communist Party. For a more detailed account of the negotiation of Marxist and anarchist traditions in the formation of the Partido Comunista Mexicano, see Carr 1983; Hodges 1995.

6. See, for example, Revueltas 1980.

7. For firsthand accounts of what transpired in the student movement leading up to the massacre of Tlatelolco, the events of the massacre itself, and its aftermath, see Poniatowska 1971.

8. For an account of what information has come to light over the years, see Katie Doyle, "Los muertos de Tlatelolco," trans. Lucía Luna, *Proceso*, October 1, 2006, 16–18, http://nsarchive.gwu.edu/NSAEBB/NSAEBB201/proceso.pdf.

9. The remembrance of October 2, 1968, has remained highly troubling for many Mexicans ever since, an open wound salted in 2014 after the disappearance of the forty-three normalistas from Ayotzinapa, Guerrero, an event that shares many disturbing parallels with the student massacre of 1968. Through an annual protest march from the Plaza de las Tres Culturas to the Zócalo, led by the survivors of the massacre and their families, many Mexicans continue to call for justice for the October 2, 1968, massacre. In 2016, the leaders of the student movement of 1968 ceded their place at the head of the annual march to the families of the forty-three normalistas, recognizing that link.

10. The massacre in June 1971 is also referred to as El Halconazo, after the name of the paramilitary unit that attacked protestors, *los halcones*. The massacre and the paramilitary training that preceded it were depicted in Alfonso Cuarón's award-winning film *Roma* (2018).

11. These stories emerge in the following documentary: *Rock 'n' Roll Made in Mexico: From Evolution to Revolution*, directed by Lance Miccio. Heatdrum Productions, 2008, DVD, 90 minutes. The story is also related in the Netflix documentary series *Rompan todo* (2020).

12. Agustín 2008, 99. He uses the English phrase "wishful thinking" directly in his text.

13. Urteaga Castro-Pozo, 155. The English-language names of these bands are the original ones, not translations, revealing a continued interest in English as a marker of musical authenticity among some fans.

14. For the emergence of DIY as an important value in the global punk scene, see O'Connor 2008. Urteaga Castro-Pozo (1998) recounts DIY practices of making and selling punk clothing in the early scene, for example.

15. People told me this personally, but you can also find accounts in Urteaga Castro-Pozo 1998; Detor Escobar and Hernández Sánchez n.d.

16. Her remembrances were originally published as a book in 1988. However, Poniatowska has repeatedly made this assertion in interviews and writings on the earthquake since that publication. In 2005, for example, Poniatowska recollected, "People like him helped in a more disinterested way. . . . They were young punks, *banda*, brothers and

friends who worked whole nights among the ruins, young guys marginalized by society, whom no one recognized and who nevertheless wanted to remain anonymous." See Poniatowska 2005.

17. In fact, many Spanish-language rock bands have employed a harder-edged style that recalls punk, such as Colombia's long-lived Aterciopelados (Morello 2012).

18. Bestley et al. 2019; Dunn 2016; Greene 2016; O'Hara 1999. Not all punk scenes embraced anarchist or even leftist positions, of course. And anarchism means something quite different in different contexts. See Marciniak 2015b, for example, on punk and anarchism in a post-Communist nation.

19. Spanish-language use remains a preference for Mexico City's punk-scene participants, as Alan O'Connor also noticed in his fieldwork in Mexico City (2002, 231).

20. Marshall 2010. Proudhon is credited with being the first to label himself an anarchist, meaning that previous authors like Godwin have been recognized for ideas that resembled what later came to be called anarchist theory. After the late nineteenth century, when anarchism became associated with violence, after a number of individuals who self-identified as anarchists carried out bombings and assassinations, some would refuse to label their ideas similarly. Tolstoy, a pacifist, was one of those people, while Mexican anarchist Ricardo Flores Magón did self-identify as anarchist but felt that it would be best to avoid publicly naming himself and his cohort as such because it might frighten away potential allies.

21. "Anarchy is usually defined as a society without government, and anarchism as the social philosophy which aims at its realization. . . . Today it has come to describe the condition of a people living without any constituted authority or government. From the beginning, anarchy has denoted both the negative sense of unruliness which leads to disorder and chaos, and the positive sense of a free society in which rule is no longer necessary" (Marshall 2010, 3).

22. Some "natural anarchists" work most directly from this kind of belief, offering animal behaviors and natural processes as models for "restoring" environmentally sound and equitable human interaction (Jones 2009). Prominent anarchist authors like James C. Scott and David Graeber have also been accused of writing from a similar bias, however, describing capitalism as the perverter of a fundamentally good human nature (Carey 2017).

23. Lida and Illades 2001. For anarchism in Latin America after 1900, see also Viñas 2004; Akemi et al. 2017.

24. For a history of the FAT, see Hathaway 1997.

25. For more on the event, see Ediciones Antorcha (website), www.antorcha.net, accessed November 30, 2020.

26. See "Presentación del Libro" on the Hormiga Libertaria website, http://hormig alibertaria.blogspot.com/, accessed November 30, 2020.

27. For information on the punk scene in the 1990s, including information on the

JAR and participants' opinions on the EZLN, see *La escena punk en* México, directed by Jesús Martín. 1994. Streaming video, 47 minutes, Sin Medios Producciones, https://www .youtube.com/watch?v=fDlhWWZ1GFU&t=492s, accessed December 1, 2020.

28. Though the autonomous university was tuition-free, that did not necessarily render it as accessible as it sounds. Many people I knew were not able to attend because they hadn't been educated through the preparatory high schools that serve to feed the university, partly by preparing students for its entrance exams. Among those I knew who had some university education, many recounted prohibitive costs such as library and transportation fees. Simply finding a way to balance study with the need to work formed another significant barrier to higher education for many.

29. Accessed online at https://www.wired.com/2008/03/anti-emo-riots/, August 31, 2021.

30. For a summary of this coverage, see Eduardo Aquevedo, "Tribus urbanas: qué son los emos?" *Ciencias sociales hoy*, blog post, March 26, 2008, http://jaquevedo.blogspot .com, accessed July 17, 2021.

31. In addition to accounts I heard from my own interlocutors, see also Daniel Hernandez, "Violence Against Emos Sweeps Across Mexico," *Intersections*, blog post, March, 22, 2008, http://danielhernandez.com, accessed March 5, 2020. This is one in a series of posts Hernandez did on punk-emo conflict in Mexico. See also Hernandez 2011.

32. One of the key provisions of the 1917 Constitution was land reform, whose aim was to ensure that peasant populations could not be forced from their traditional agricultural lifestyles through private ownership of land, a problem that had been pervasive since the colonial period.

33. Gamboa de Buen 1994; Harvey 2005; Joseph and Buchenau 2013. For more on the informal economy and the punk scene, see chapter 4.

34. See Blanco 2010.

35. "Esquizofrenia: el microclima del punk," YouTube video, www.youtube.com/ watch?v=jaRtaPzadxk, accessed March 5, 2020.

36. For more on the role of porros in Mexican politics and youth culture, see Pensado 2013.

37. While some recent scholarship has attempted to emphasize the diverse masculinities available to Mexican men over the course of the modern period, there is also a strong history of linking lower-class men of various racial and ethnic backgrounds with an excessive virility. See, for example, O'Malley 1986; McKee Irwin 2003; Macías-González and Rubenstein 2012.

FOUR *Love*

1. My choice to link love, friendship, and solidarity is primarily motivated by ethnographic information. However, in invoking friendship, I concur with Rohrer (2014), who

observes a relative lack of attention to friendship in anthropological literature and the influence of Western notions of friendship via globalization in a transnational punk scene.

2. In fact, there is also a third term I heard used to describe the slam with some regularity: *un baile de energía* (a dance of energy). See chapter 2 for more on the slam.

3. For a good summary of this classic view of solidarity, see Smith 2015.

4. For example, cultural anthropologist Diane Nelson coined the term "fluidarity" to counter a too-solid, rigid understanding of the term, mapping instead a complex network of shifting affective and strategic relationships in her study among local and international activists who drew global attention to the civil war in Guatemala in the 1980s (1999, 70). See also Laitinen and Pessi 2015.

5. Love, friendship, and solidarity are entangled in etymological, historical, and philosophical sources. Friendship and love share the same Latin root, which filters down into amistad and amor in contemporary Spanish. The ancient Greeks also loom large over the topic of love and friendship, with terms for different forms of strong interpersonal attachments ranging from *philia* (brotherly love) to *eros* (romantic love) and *agape* (a broad love for humanity). Meanwhile, some scholarship on solidarity links it to brotherhood (via the French revolutionary trio, *liberté, egalité, fraternité*), empathy, or moral recognition. Some authors discuss "universal," "global," or "human" solidarity, often described in terms that recall the concept of agape. See Solomon 1981; May 2011; Grayling 2013; Brunkhorst 2005; Scholz 2008; Rohrer 2014; and Laitinen and Pessi 2015.

6. Horvat 2016, 6 (italics in original). See also Derrida (2005) on friendship and politics, and Shirinian (2020) on love and revolution in Armenia.

7. There is no label affixed as consistently to more socially engaged punk-scene participants. Sometimes people refer to more committed punk-scene participants as "anarco-punks," though that term had fallen out of favor somewhat during my fieldwork period. Some people contrasted "rockers" with "radicals," though that was not a popular choice either. In fact, I would argue that the lack of a term to contrast with the widespread use of "destroy punk" underscores that label's facility in othering those who are perceived to fail scene ideals.

8. This debate is common among anarchists as well, dating back at least to the 1990s and the increasing prominence of so-called "lifestylism" in several social movement issues and organizations of the time. See, for example, Bey 1991; Bookchin 1995; L. Davis 2010; White 2011; and Portwood-Stacer 2013. Dunn (2016), meanwhile, posits lifestylism as key to a global punk politics.

9. One practice that could attract charges of a "destroy punk" orientation, for example, is that stereotypical punk habit of "sniffing glue." The abuse of solvents—a cheap and therefore accessible high—does occur among some punk-scene participants in Mexico City. While other forms of drug taking, such as marijuana use, are normalized in the punk scene, inhaling solvents is lamented and mocked for being highly dangerous to one's health

and safety, a stupid and literally self-destructive habit. Gilberto Rosas writes movingly about the practice among marginalized youth living precariously along the U.S.-Mexico border. They tell him about the pleasure they experience in huffing, its "freedoms," which include the knowledge that the habit makes them repulsive to others (2012, 116).

10. Weeks provides a history of work refusal in feminist and Marxist contexts as a narrative contrast with the broad historical prominence of the work ethic. She specifically names "punks" among a range of people from "youth subcultures" (2011, 80) who may have "failed to internalize the gospel of work" (79). It's important to note, however, that work refusal is not necessarily an attempt to refute the necessity of work or effort, but rather a refusal to prioritize waged labor as central to life, a common orientation to labor in capitalist societies.

11. Most interesting for my purpose in understanding the work ethic in relation to certain Mexican masculinities, Hurtado and Sinha's (2016) research with Latino men in the United States revealed an intense investment in providing for one's family, something that respondents themselves identified in open-ended questioning about defining masculinity. Though the researchers privileged college students and professionals in their study, many respondents were raised in working-class families, often by parents who had migrated from Latin America, with a high percentage being of Mexican descent.

12. In this chapter, I follow the practice of using "work" to refer broadly to productive action, while I use "labor" to denote the exchange of work for a wage. Affective labor may be waged or unwaged, as Muehlebach (2011) explores.

13. My observations accord with Alan O'Connor's findings in punk scenes in both Europe and North America. He argues that punks are not slackers, but hard workers who are "dropouts from the middle class" (2008, 58), people who were acculturated to value hard work, but want to direct it into alternate channels than those valorized by their largely middle-class families.

14. For more on the Bibiloteca Social Reconstruir and anarco-syndicalism, see chapter 3. I also wrote about the library and its links to a Chicago DIY cultural institution. See Tatro 2021. For more on the Frente Auténtico del Trabajo, see Hathaway 1997.

15. As I suggested earlier in the chapter, however, I think Mexico's economic reliance on remittances from migrants in the U.S. and elsewhere may help sustain an investment in working-class labor and its benefits. For a concise history of the Mexican economy, see Harvey 2005.

16. The video I refer to here is *The Art of Screaming*, directed by Susan Carr. Though the video offers good instruction on how to achieve breath support, I later found that *The Zen of Screaming*, created by Melissa Cross, contains more comprehensive information on how to produce various types of extreme vocalizations. For more on the mechanics of screaming, see Tatro 2014.

17. Email communication, October 14, 2013.

18. See Novak (2013, 36) for a description not only of the hard work of screaming but the skill involved in screaming effectively.

19. While most punk is fast, there are exceptions, and there have been since the increasing crossover between punk and metal in the 1990s. Some punk takes a slower, even "sludgy," pace, inspired by doom metal. See Kahn-Harris 2007.

20. One of the vocalists I spoke with for my article (Tatro 2014) was enthusiastic about writing, translating, and sharing portions of it. However, he insisted that my emphasis on vocalists was unfair because all of a band's performers work together to achieve the results that I'd noted. For another discussion of sweat in musical performance, see Steingo 2016, 50.

21. Interest in the punk scene regarding the problem of political prisoners also overlaps with a similar interest by other social justice groups in Mexico. Partly, this is a legacy of the 1968 movement, as its participants protested the detention of prominent labor leaders before many of them were also detained, as well as killed or "disappeared," by the authorities (Poniatowska 1971; Carey 2005; Draper 2018).

22. Analco Martínez, 205. Regarding her methodology, she clarifies that her study is based on an analysis of seventy fanzines created in the period from 1984 to 2002, including forty-six titles (117). While I agree that images and discussions of Ricardo Flores Magón are common in punk fanzines in Mexico City, my own observation was not undertaken as systematically as hers.

23. "Creando y construyendo, proyectos autogestivos, con la intención de impulsar la organización de este esfuerzo de transformación social, difunde y agita, salud y revolución en tu interior."

24. For more on the organization of Ladyfest, see Leonard 2007.

25. See, for example, Ríos Manzano 1999; Urteaga Castro-Pozo 1998. Also, O'Connor (2002) remarks on the tendency of Mexican punks to form collectives.

26. For example, Urteaga Castro-Pozo 1998.

27. The devastating earthquake of 1985 left a number of properties damaged and abandoned in the city center. Some of these properties became sites for squats in the ensuing decades, including a few in upscale neighborhoods. Despite the availability of abandoned buildings, squatting in Mexico City—particularly in the erstwhile Distrito Federal—has been exceptionally challenging, with the constant threat of forced eviction by the city, as well as abuse by police.

28. In their desire to be equitable, many collectives I witnessed tended to neglect to negotiate their organizational processes, leading to what Jo Freeman (1972) has termed a "tyranny of structurelessness" in the title of her article on the necessity to choose organizational structures consciously.

29. Very occasionally, the word *afinidad* (affinity) would crop up in discussions in the punk scene. Affinity groups represent another organizational model, often a more

temporary and diverse one, in which small groups come together, despite personal, identity-based differences, in the pursuit of a common goal. They may well disband after achieving that one narrow objective. The history of the term "affinity" did in fact link to friendship groups in nineteenth-century Spain, however, in which such groups—also called tertulias (chats)—were based on friendships and federated with other small friendship groups, instead of forming part of larger solidarity organizations. For more on affinity as an organizing principle, see Day 2001; Polletta 2002; and Dupuis-Déri 2010.

30. Even spectacular direct actions need not be violent, however. Peaceful direct action, such as "tree sitting"—camping in treetops in forests slated for razing by developers—has been a tactic deployed particularly by environmental justice groups, though they may face retaliation from the law or bodily harm from law enforcement. See Carter 2005; Graeber 2009.

31. Magaña (2020) describes the participation of "anarcopunks" on the barricades in Oaxaca City, following actions that began there in 2006, noting the difficulties some had in building trust with members of groups who didn't embrace their anti-authoritarianism and their desire for more "horizontal" organizational practices.

32. Drawing on her research on activist choirs in the former Yugoslavia, Ana Hofman (2020a; forthcoming) argues that scholars should privilege leisure rather than affective labor as a necessary counterbalance to neoliberal, totalizing notions of labor that continue to place work—whether waged or not—at the center of life. However, I believe that both masculine gendering and a working-class positioning specific to the Mexican economic context keep punk-scene participants' focus on work through a refashioning of the work ethic. Though post-Yugoslavian activist choir singers privilege leisure and Mexico City punk-scene participants privilege labor, I think both groups contribute meaningfully to a reevaluation of the place of work and labor in modern life.

FIVE *Autonomy*

1. For an exploration of how the "vibe" of an electronic dance music event may be experienced and manipulated, see Garcia 2020.

2. This reflects some affect-theory scholarship that understands affect as operating in a kind of dialectical tension between a social, but pre-subjective "intensity," and the qualifications that the acculturated subject imposes on those immanent states. See, for example, Massumi 1995; Mazzarella 2009.

3. See also Probyn (2005), who provides a thoughtful meditation on how shame is experienced in the body and in connection with other affective and cognitive states.

4. At the XXXVI Latin American Studies Association International Congress in Barcelona on May 23, 2018, I participated on a panel with an interdisciplinary group of scholars—Jeffrey S. Juris, José Martínez-Reyes, Michelle Tellez, Andrew Green, Livia

Stone, and Maurice Rafael Magaña—to explore "interstitial autonomies," autonomous politics emerging in urban areas and among groups like artists' and women's collectives.

5. This term was used to describe the practices of the New Left in the 1960s as they attempted to model the kinds of equitable organizational strategies they wanted to see. Polletta characterizes the choice as a refusal to bend to political expediency, which would force a sacrifice of broader ideals (2002, 6). For more on the Zapatista's influence, see Olesen 2005.

6. An important instantiation of this debate may be found starting with Murray Bookchin's inflammatory essay of 1995, in which he contrasts "social anarchism" with "lifestyle anarchism." See, for example, Bookchin 1995; Erlich 1996; Day 2001, Polletta 2002, Amster et al. 2009, Davis 2010; Shantz 2011; White 2011; Portwood-Stacer 2013; and, in the context of global punk scenes, Dunn 2016.

7. Zapatista communities have continued building their autonomous organizational capacity since then, creating new municipalities as well as expanding the number of caracoles and Juntas de Buen Gobierno.

8. In an interview, Subcomandante Marcos of the EZLN explained the relationship of the Zapatista movement to militarism: "We were formed in an army, the EZLN. . . . But our army is very different from others, because its proposal is to cease being an army. A soldier is an absurd person who has to resort to arms in order to convince others, and in that sense the movement has no future if its future is military" (Mertes 2004, 4).

9. Polletta 2002, 224. "As Emile Durkheim observed, rituals strengthen group solidarity by taking people out of the routine of daily life and reenacting their essential groupness. Rituals may be used to strengthen new forms of group solidarity as well as older ones, infusing new relationships with a power and appeal that transcend narrow calculations of interest. One can imagine rituals and symbols used to foster norms of solidarity and dissent, respect and self-confidence, trust and accountability, all of which are necessary to successful participatory democracies."

10. See Biehl and Locke (2017) on the anthropology of becoming. On "productive frictions," see Sakakeeny (2013, 140) citing Anna Tsing, *Friction: An Ethnography of Global Connection*. Princeton, NJ: Princeton University Press, 2005, 5.

REFERENCES

Adams, Rachel, and David Savran, eds. *The Masculinity Studies Reader*. Oxford: Blackwell Publishers, 2002.

Agren, David. "Mexico City Officially Changes Its Name—to Mexico City." *Guardian*, January, 29, 2016.

Agustín, José. *El rock de la cárcel*. 2nd ed. Mexico City: Debolsillo, 2007.

———. *La contracultura en México: La historia y el significado de los rebeldes sin causa, los jipitecas, los punks y las bandas*. Mexico City: Debolsillo, 2008.

Akemi, Romina, Ángel J. Cappelletti, and Javier Sethness-Castro. *Anarchism in Latin America*. Translated by Gabriel Palmer-Fernández. Oakland, CA: AK Press, 2017.

Alarcón, Sandra. *El tianguis global*. Mexico City: Universidad Iberoamericana, 2008.

Amster, Randall, Abraham DeLeon, Luis A. Fernandez, Anthony J. Nocella II, and Deric Shannon, eds. *Contemporary Anarchist Studies: An Introductory Anthology of Anarchy in the Academy*. London: Routledge, 2009.

Anabel, Hernández. *La verdadera noche de Iguala: la historia que el gobierno trató de ocultar*. Mexico City: Grijalbo, 2016.

Analco Martínez, Aída. *Desde abajo y a contracorriente: el fanzine y los imaginarios juveniles urbanos*. Mexico City: Instituto Nacional de Antropología e Historia, 2011.

Arce Cortés, Tania. "Subcultura, contracultura, tribus urbanas y culturas juveniles: ¿homogenización o diferenciación?" *Revista Argentina de Sociología* 6, no. 11 (2008): 257–71.

Arendt, Hannah. *On Violence*. New York: Houghton Mifflin Harcourt, 1970.

Arias, Enrique Desmond, and Daniel M. Goldstein, eds. *Violent Democracies in Latin America*. Durham, NC: Duke University Press, 2010.

Arvon, Henri. *La autogestion*. Translated by David F. Álvarez Aub. Mexico City: Fondo de Cultura Económica, 1980.

Ashforth, Adam. *Witchcraft, Violence, and Democracy in South Africa*. Chicago: University of Chicago Press, 2005.

Avant-Mier, Roberto. *Rock the Nation: Latin/o Identities and the Latin Rock Diaspora*. New York: Continuum, 2010.

Baulch, Emma. *Making Scenes: Reggae, Punk and Death Metal in 1990s Bali*. Durham, NC: Duke University Press, 2007.

Bennett, Andy. "Punk's Not Dead: The Continuing Significance of Punk Rock for an Older Generation of Fans." *Sociology* 40, no. 2 (2006): 219–35.

Bennett, Andy, and Keith Kahn-Harris, eds. *After Subculture: Critical Studies in Contemporary Youth Culture*. New York: Palgrave Macmillan, 2004.

Bennett, Andy, and Richard A. Peterson, eds. *Music Scenes: Local, Translocal, and Virtual*. Nashville, TN: Vanderbilt University Press, 2004.

Bennett, Andy, and Jodie Taylor. "Popular Music and the Aesthetics of Ageing." *Popular Music* 31, no. 2 (2012): 231–43.

Berríos-Miranda, Marisol, Shannon Dudley, and Michelle Habell-Pallán. *American Sabor: Latinos and Latinas in Us Popular Music*. Seattle: University of Washington Press, 2018.

Bestley, Russ, Mike Dines, Alistair Gordon, and Paula Guerra, eds. *The Punk Reader: Research Transmissions from the Local and Global*. Chicago: Intellect, 2019.

Bey, Hakim. *T.A.Z.: The Temporary Autonomous Zone, Ontological Anarchy, Poetic Terrorism*. New York: Autonomedia, 1991.

Biehl, João, and Peter Locke, eds. *Unfinished: The Anthropology of Becoming*. Durham, NC: Duke University Press, 2017.

Blanco, José. "Ninis." *La Jornada*, January 5, 2010.

Bookchin, Murray. *Social Anarchism Versus Lifestyle Anarchism: An Unbridgeable Chasm*. Oakland, CA: AK Press, 1995.

Bourgois, Philippe, and Nancy Scheper-Hughes, eds. *Violence in War and Peace: An Anthology*. Malden, MA: Blackwell Publishing, 2004.

Boym, Svetlana. *The Future of Nostalgia*. New York: Basic Books, 2001.

Bray, Mark. *Antifa: The Anti-Fascist Handbook*. New York: Melville House Publishing, 2017.

Brennan, Teresa. *The Transmission of Affect*. Ithaca, NY: Cornell University Press, 2004.

Briggs, Charles L. *Learning How to Ask: A Sociolinguistic Appraisal of the Role of the Interview in Social Science Research*. Cambridge: Cambridge University Press, 1986.

Brunkhorst, Hauke. *Solidarity: From Civic Friendship to a Global Legal Community*. Cambridge, MA: MIT Press, 2005.

Bufe, Chaz, and Mitchell Cowen Verter, eds. *Dreams of Freedom: A Ricardo Flores Magón Reader*. Oakland, CA: AK Press, 2005.

Bustamante Lemus, Carlos. "El comercio informal en la estructura econónimca de la Ciudad de México. ealidades y perspectivas." In *Informalidad urbana e incertidumbre: cómo estudiar la informalización en las metrópolis?* edited by Felipe de Alba and Frédéric Lesemann, 73–107. Mexico City: Universidad Autónoma de México, 2012.

Carbó Darnaculleta, Margarita. "Viva la tierra y libertad! La utopía magonista." *Boletín americanista* 47 (1997): 91–100.

Carey, Elaine. *Plaza of Sacrifices: Gender, Power, and Terror in 1968 Mexico*. Albuquerque: University of New Mexico Press, 2005.

Carey, Matthew. *Mistrust: An Ethnographic Theory*. Chicago: Hau Books, 2017.

Carr, Barry. "Marxism and Anarchism in the Formation of the Mexican Communist Party, 1910–19." *The Hispanic American Historical Review* 63, no. 2 (1983): 277–305.

Carspecken, Lucinda, ed. *Love in the Time of Ethnography: Essays on Connection as a Focus and Basis for Research*. Lanham, MD: Lexington Books, 2018.

Carter, April. *Direct Action and Democracy Today*. Cambridge: Polity Books, 2005.

Cassaniti, Julia L., and Jacob R. Hickman. "New Directions in the Anthropology of Morality." *Anthropological Theory* 14, no. 3 (2014): 251–62.

Castillo Bernal, Stephen. *Música del diablo: imaginario, dramas sociales y ritualidades de la escena metalera de la Ciudad de México*. Mexico City: Instituto Nacional de Antropología e Historia, 2015.

Castillo Berthier, Héctor. "My Generation: Rock and La Banda's Forced Survival Opposite the Mexican State." In *Rockin' Las Américas: The Global Politics of Rock in Latin/o America*, edited by Deborah Pacini Hernandez, Héctor Fernández L'Hoeste, and Eric Zolov, 241–60. Pittsburgh, PA: University of Pittsburgh Press, 2004.

———. "De *emos*, tribus, e intolerancia." In "Topodrilo," *Tribus Juveniles* 8 (2008): 49–52.

Castillo Berthier, Héctor F. *La sociedad de la basura: caciquismo urbano en la Ciudad de México*. Cuadernos De Investigación Social. 2nd ed. Mexico City: Universidad Nacional Autónoma de México, Instituto de Investigaciones Sociales, 1990.

Chemaly, Soraya. *Rage Becomes Her: The Power of Women's Anger*. New York: Simon & Schuster, 2018.

Coffey, Mary K. *How a Revolutionary Art Became Official Culture*. Durham, NC: Duke University Press, 2012.

Cooper, Brittney. *Eloquent Rage: A Black Feminist Discovers Her Superpower*. New York: St. Martin's Press, 2018.

Corr, Anders. *No Trespassing! Squatting, Rent Strikes, and Land Struggles Worldwide*. Cambridge, MA: South End Press, 1999.

Cross, John C. *Informal Politics: Street Vendors and the State in Mexico City*. Stanford, CA: Stanford University Press, 1998.

———. "Mexico." In *Media Piracy in Emerging Economies*, edited by Joe Karaganis. New York: Social Science Research Council, 2011. http://piracy.americanassembly.org/wp -content/uploads/2011/06/MPEE-PDF-Ch6-Mexico.pdf.

Cusick, Suzanne G. "Music as Torture/Music as Weapon." *Trans: Revista Transcultural de Música* 10(2006).

Das, Veena, Arthur Kleinman, Mamphela Ramphele, and Pamela Reynolds, eds. *Violence and Subjectivity*. Berkeley: University of California Press, 2000.

Daughtry, J. Martin. *Listening to War: Sound, Music, Trauma, and Survival in Wartime Iraq*. Oxford: Oxford University Press, 2015.

Davis, Diane E. *Urban Leviathan: Mexico City in the Twentieth Century*. Philadelphia: Temple University Press, 1994.

———. "From the *Reforma-Peralvillo* to the *Torre Bicentenario*: The Clash of 'History' and 'Progress' in the Urban Development of Mexico City." In *Mexico City through History and Culture*, edited by Linda A. Newson and John P. King, 55–84. Oxford: Oxford University Press, 2009.

———. "The Political and Economic Origins of Violence and Insecurity in Contemporary Latin America: Past Trajectories and Future Prospects." In *Violent Democracies in Latin America*, edited by Enrique Desmond Arias and Daniel M. Goldstein, 35–62. Durham, NC: Duke University Press, 2010.

Davis, Laurence. "Social Anarchism or Lifestyle Anarchism: An Unhelpful Dichotomy." *Anarchist Studies* 18, no. 1 (2010): 62–82.

Day, Richard. "Ethics, Affinity and the Coming Communities." *Philosophy and Social Criticism* 27, no. 1 (2001): 21–38.

Delaney, Carol. *The Seed and the Soil: Gender and Cosmology in Turkish Village Life*. Berkeley: University of California Press, 1991.

Dellacioppa, Kara Zugman. *This Bridge Called Zapatismo: Building Alternative Political Cultures in Mexico City, Los Angeles, and Beyond*. Lanham, MD: Rowman & Littlefield, 2009.

Derrida, Jacques. *The Politics of Friendship*. New York: Verso, 2005.

Detor Escobar, Álvaro. *Caos urbano México punk*. Mexico City: Museo Universitario del Chopo (UNAM), 2016.

Detor Escobar, Álvaro, and Pablo C. Hernández Sánchez. *México punk: 33 años de rebelión juvenil*. Mexico City: n.p., n.d.

Dixon, Angela R. "Colorism and Classism Confounded: Perceptions of Discrimination in Latin America." *Social Science Research* 79 (2019): 32–55.

Dixon, Angela R., and Edward E. Telles. "Skin Color and Colorism: Global Research, Concepts, and Measurement." *Annual Review of Sociology* 43 (2017): 405–24.

Downey, Greg. *Learning Capoeira: Lessons in Cunning from an Afro-Brazilian Art*. Oxford: Oxford University Press, 2005.

Draper, Susana. *1968 Mexico: Constellations of Freedom and Democracy*. Durham, NC: Duke University Press, 2018.

Dunn, Kevin C. *Global Punk: Resistance and Rebellion in Everyday Life*. New York: Bloomsbury, 2016.

Dupuis-Déri, Francis. "Anarchism and the Politics of Affinity Groups." *Anarchist Studies* 18, no. 1 (2010): 40–61.

Eidsheim, Nina Sun. *Sensing Sound: Singing and Listening as Vibrational Practice*. Durham, NC: Duke University Press, 2015.

Erlich, Howard, ed. *Reinventing Anarchy, Again*. San Francisco, CA: AK Press, 1996.

Estrada, Tere. *Sirenas al ataque: historia de las mujeres rockeras mexicanas*. Mexico City: Océano, 2008.

Estrada, Tere, and Julia Palacios. "A Contra Corriente: A History of Women Rockers in Mexico." In *Rockin' Las Américas: The Global Politics of Rock in Latin/o America*, edited by Deborah Pacini Hernandez, Eric Zolov, and Héctor Fernández L'Hoeste, 142–59. Pittsburgh, PA: University of Pittsburgh Press, 2004.

Fales, Cornelia. "The Paradox of Timbre." *Ethnomusicology* 46, no. 1 (2002): 56–95.

Fales, Cornelia, and Harris M. Berger. "'Heaviness' in the Perception of Heavy Metal Guitar Timbres: The Match of Perceptual and Acoustic Features over Time." In *Wired for Sound: Engineering and Technologies in Sonic Cultures*, edited by Thomas Porcello and Paul D. Greene, 181–97. Middletown, CT: Wesleyan University Press, 2005.

Fast, Susan, and Kip Pegley. *Music, Politics, and Violence*. Middletown, CT: Wesleyan University Press, 2012.

Feixa, Carles. "*Tribus Urbanas* and *Chavos Banda*: Being a Punk in Catalonia and Mexico." In *Global Youth? Hybrid Identities, Plural Worlds*, edited by Carles Feixa and Pam Nilan, 149–66. New York: Routledge, 2006.

Feld, Steven. *Jazz Cosmopolitanism in Accra: Five Musical Years in Ghana*. Durham, NC: Duke University Press, 2012.

Feld, Steven, and Aaron A. Fox. "Music and Language." *Annual Review of Anthropology* 23, no. 1 (1994): 25–53.

Feld, Steven, Aaron A. Fox, Thomas Porcello, and David Samuels. "Vocal Anthropology: From the Music of Language to the Language of Song." In *A Companion to Linguistic Anthropology*, edited by A. Duranti, 321–46. Malden, MA: Blackwell Publishing, 2004.

Fox, Aaron A. *Real Country: Music and Language in Working-Class Culture*. Durham, NC: Duke University Press, 2004.

Freeman, Jo. "The Tyranny of Structurelessness." *Second Wave* 2, no. 1 (1972): 20–33.

Frith, Simon. "Why Do Songs Have Words?" *Contemporary Music Review* 5, no. 1 (1989): 77–96.

Furness, Zack, ed. *Punkademics: The Basement Show in the Ivory Tower*. Brooklyn, NY: Minor Compositions, 2012.

Gallo, Rubén. "Introduction: Delirious Mexico City." In *The Mexico City Reader*, edited by Rubén Gallo and Lorna Scott Fox, 3–32. The Americas. Madison: University of Wisconsin Press, 2004.

Gamboa de Buen, Jorge. *Ciudad de México: una visión de la modernización de México*. Mexico City: Fondo de Cultura Económica, 1994.

Garcia, Luis-Manuel. "Feeling the Vibe: Sound, Vibration, and Affective Attunement in Electronic Dance Music Scenes." *Ethnomusicology Forum* 29, no. 1 (2020): 21–39.

García-Robles, Jorge. *¿Qué transa con las bandas?* 14th ed. Mexico City: Editorial Porrúa, 2013.

Gaytán Santiago, Pablo. *Desmadernos: crónica suburpunk de algunos movimientos culturales en la submetrópoli defeña.* Toluca: Universidad Autónoma del Estado de México, 2001.

Gibler, John. *To Die in Mexico: Dispatches from inside the Drug War.* San Francisco: City Lights Books, 2011.

Gill, Denise. *Melancholic Modalities: Affect, Islam, and Turkish Classical Musicians.* Oxford: Oxford University Press, 2017.

Goldstein, Daniel M. "*Desconfianza* and Problems of Representation in Urban Ethnography." *Anthropological Quarterly* 75, no. 3 (2002): 485–517.

———. *The Spectacular City: Violence and Performance in Urban Bolivia.* Durham, NC: Duke University Press, 2004.

———. *Owners of the Sidewalk: Security and Survival in the Informal City.* Durham, NC: Duke University Press, 2016.

Gomezjara, Francisco A., ed. *Las bandas en tiempo de crisis.* Mexico City: Nueva Sociología, 1987.

———, ed. *Pandillerismo en el estallido urbano.* Mexico City: Fontamara, 1988.

Gonzales, Michael J. *The Mexican Revolution, 1910–1940.* Albuquerque: University of New Mexico Press, 2002.

González Alvarado, Rocío, and Alejandro Cruz Flores. "Sheinbaum desaparece a granaderos y fustiga a los gobiernos que espían." *La Jornada*, December 6, 2018, 31.

González Amador, Roberto. "Seis de cada 10 mexicanos que trabajan están en la informalidad." *La Jornada*, December 12, 2012, 27.

González Rodríguez, Sergio. *The Femicide Machine.* Cambridge, MA: MIT Press, 2012.

Graber, Katie J., and Matthew Sumera. "Interpretation, Resonance, Embodiment: Affect Theory and Ethnomusicology." *Ethnomusicology Forum* 29, no. 1 (2020): 3–20.

Graeber, David. *Direct Action: An Ethnography.* Oakland, CA: AK Press, 2009.

Gray, Lila Ellen. *Fado Resounding: Affective Politics and Urban Life.* Durham, NC: Duke University Press, 2013.

———. "Listening for Affect: Musical Ethnography and the Challenge of/to Affect." *Culture, Theory and Critique* (2021). doi:10.1080/14735784.2020.1857287.

Grayling, A. C. *Friendship.* New Haven, CT: Yale University Press, 2013.

Green, Andrew. "Autonomy, Solidarity and Collaboration in the Work of *Producciones Radioinsurgente.*" In *Latin American Studies Association International Congress.* Barcelona, 2018.

Greene, Shane. "The Problem of Peru's Punk Underground: An Approach to under-Fuck the System." *Journal of Popular Music Studies* 24, no. 4 (2012): 578–89.

———. *Punk and Revolution: Seven More Interpretations of Peruvian Reality*. Durham, NC: Duke University Press, 2016.

Gregg, Melissa, and Gregory J. Seigworth, eds. *The Affect Theory Reader*. Durham, NC: Duke University Press, 2010.

Guidotti-Hernández, Nicole M. *Archiving Mexican Masculinities in Diaspora*. Durham, NC: Duke University Press, 2021.

Guillermoprieto, Alma. *The Heart That Bleeds: Latin America Now*. New York: Vintage Books, 1995.

Gutmann, Matthew C. *The Meanings of Macho: Being a Man in Mexico City*. Berkeley: University of California Press, 1996.

———, ed. *Changing Men and Masculinities in Latin America*. Durham, NC: Duke University Press, 2003.

Hahn, Tomie. "'It's the Rush': Sites of the Sensually Extreme." *TDR: The Drama Review* 50, no. 2 (2006): 87–96.

Hardt, Michael. "Affective Labor." *boundary 2* 26, no. 2 (1999): 89–100.

Harkness, Nicholas. *Songs of Seoul: An Ethnography of Voice and Voicing in Christian South Korea*. Berkeley: University of California Press, 2014.

Hart, John M. *Anarchism and the Mexican Working Class, 1860–1931*. Austin: University of Texas Press, 1978.

Harvey, David. *A Brief History of Neoliberalism*. New York: Oxford University Press, 2005.

Hathaway, Dale. "Mexico's Frente Auténtico Del Trabajo: Organizing Beyond the PRI and across Borders." In *Latin American Studies Association*. Guadalajara, Mexico, 1997.

Hebdige, Dick. *Subculture: The Meaning of Style*. London: Methuen, 1979.

Hernández, Anabel. *La verdadera noche de Iguala: la historia que el gobierno trató de ocultar*. Mexico City: Grijalbo, 2016.

Hernandez, Daniel. "Emo Bashing: Mexico's Latest Urban-Youth Craze." *L.A. Weekly*, April 9, 2008.

———. *Down and Delirious in Mexico City: The Aztec Metropolis in the Twenty-First Century*. New York: Scribner, 2011.

Hodges, Donald C. *Mexican Anarchism after the Revolution*. Austin: University of Texas Press, 1995.

Hofman, Ana. "Music (as) Labour: Professional Musicianship, Affective Labour and Gender in Socialist Yugoslavia." *Ethnomusicology Forum* 24, no. 1 (2015): 28–50.

———. "The Affective Turn in Ethnomusicology." *Muzikologija*, no. 18 (2015): 35–55.

———. "Disobedient: Activist Choirs, Radical Amateurism, and the Politics of the Past after Yugoslavia." *Ethnomusicology* 64, no. 1 (2020a): 89–109.

———. "The Romance with Affect: Sonic Politics in a Time of Political Exhaustion." *Culture, Theory and Critique* (2020b). doi:10.1080/14735784.2020.1848603.

———. *Socialism, Now! Singing Activism after Yugoslavia*. Oxford: Oxford University Press, forthcoming.

Holler, Bootsy, dir. *The Art of Screaming*. 90 minutes, 2008.

hooks, bell. *Killing Rage: Ending Racism*. New York: Henry Holt and Company, 1995.

———. *All About Love: New Visions*. New York: HarperCollins, 2000.

Horvat, Srećko. *The Radicality of Love*. Malden, MA: Polity, 2016.

Hurtado, Aída, and Mrinal Sinha. *Beyond Machismo: Intersectional Latino Masculinities*. Austin: University of Texas Press, 2016.

Jackson, Travis. *Blowin' the Blues Away: Performance and Meaning on the New York Jazz Scene*. Berkeley: University of California Press, 2012.

Jones, Patrice. "Free as a Bird: Natural Anarchism in Action." In *Contemporary Anarchist Studies: An Introductory Anthology of Anarchy in the Academy*, edited by Randall Amster, Abraham DeLeon, Luis A. Fernandez, Anthony J. Nocella II, and Deric Shannon, 236–46. London: Routledge, 2009.

Joseph, G. M., and Jürgen Buchenau. *Mexico's Once and Future Revolution: Social Upheaval and the Challenge of Rule since the Late Nineteenth Century*. Durham, NC: Duke University Press, 2013.

Jun, Nathan. *Anarchism and Political Modernity*. New York: Continuum, 2012.

Juris, Jeffrey S. *Networking Futures: The Movements against Corporate Globalization*. Durham, NC: Duke University Press, 2008.

Kahn-Harris, Keith. *Extreme Metal: Music and Culture on the Edge*. New York: Berg, 2007.

Khasnabish, Alex. *Zapatistas: Rebellion from the Grassroots to the Global*. Black Point, Nova Scotia: Fernwood Publishing, 2010.

Korycki, Denise. "The Zen of Screaming: Vocal Instruction for a New Breed." Van Nuys, CA: Alfred Publishing/Loudmouth, 2005.

Kuhn, Gabriel. "Anarchism, Postmodernity, and Poststructuralism." In *Contemporary Anarchist Studies: An Introductory Anthology of Anarchy in the Academy*, edited by Randall Amster, Abraham DeLeon, Luis A. Fernandez, Anthony J. Nocella II, and Deric Shannon, 18–25. London: Routledge, 2009.

Laitinen, Arto, and Anne Birgitta Pessi, eds. *Solidarity: Theory and Practice*. Lanham, MD: Lexington Books, 2015.

Lancaster, Roger. *Life Is Hard: Machismo, Danger, and the Intimacy of Power in Nicaragua*. Berkeley: University of California Press, 1992.

Lara Pacheco, Clemente Gonzalo. "Los zines como un recurso bibliográfico." Universidad Nacional Autónoma de México, undergraduate thesis 2000.

Latour, Bruno. *Reassembling the Social: An Introduction to Actor-Network Theory*. Oxford: Oxford University Press, 2007.

Lawrence, Bruce B., and Aisha Karim, eds. *On Violence: A Reader*. Durham, NC: Duke University Press, 2007.

Léger, Marc James, and David Tomas, eds. *Zapantera Negra: An Artistic Encounter between Black Panthers and Zapatistas*. New York: Common Notions, 2017.

Leonard, Marion. "Ladyfest: Online and Offline DIY Festival Promotion." In *Gender in the Music Industry: Rock, Discourse and Girl Power*, 163–80. Aldershot: Ashgate, 2007.

Lida, Clara E. *Caleidoscopio del exilio: actores, memoria, identitdades*. Mexico City: Colegio de México, 2009.

Lida, Clara E., and Carlos Illades. "El anarquismo europeo y sus primeras influencias en México después de la Comuna de Paris: 1871–1881." *Historia Mexicana* 51, no. 1 (2001): 103–49.

Lomnitz, Claudio. *The Return of Comrade Ricardo Flores Magón*. New York: Zone Books, 2014.

Lorde, Audre. *Sister Outsider: Essays and Speeches by Audre Lorde*. Berkeley, CA: Crossing Press, 2007.

MacGregor, Josefina, and Eduardo Blanquel, eds. *Ricardo Flores Magón y la revolución mexicana, y otros ensayos históricos*. Mexico City: Colegio de México, 2008.

Macías-González, Victor M., and Anne Rubenstein, eds. *Masculinity and Sexuality in Modern Mexico*. Albuquerque: University of New Mexico Press, 2012.

Madrigal, Alexis. "Anti-Emo Riots Break Out across Mexico." *Wired*, March 23, 2008.

Maffesoli, Michael. *The Time of the Tribes: The Decline of Individualism in Mass Society*. Translated by Don Smith. London: Sage Publications, 1996.

Magaña, Maurice Rafael. "Constellations of Resistance and Creation: Networking Autonomies, Rebel Aesthetics and Urban Youth Collectives." In *Latin American Studies Association International Conference*. Barcelona, 2018.

———. *Cartographies of Youth Resistance: Hip-Hop, Punk, and Urban Autonomy in Mexico*. Oakland: University of California Press, 2020.

Marciniak, Marta. "Intergenerational Relations and Ageing in the Punk Subculture." *Studia Socjologiczne* 216, no. 1 (2015a): 211–18.

———. *Transnational Punk Communities in Poland: From Nihilism to Nothing Outside Punk*. Lanham, MD: Lexington Books, 2015b.

Marroquín, Enrique. *La contracultura como protesta: análisis de un fenemeno juvenil*. Mexico City: Joaquín Mortiz, 1975.

Marshall, Peter. *Demanding the Impossible: A History of Anarchism*. Oakland, CA: PM Press, 2010.

Massumi, Brian. "The Autonomy of Affect." *Cultural Critique* 31, The Politics of Systems and Environments, Part II, no. Autumn (1995): 83–109.

May, Simon. *Love: A History*. New Haven, CT: Yale University Press, 2011.

Mazzarella, William. "Affect: What Is It Good For?" In *Enchantments of Modernity: Empire, Nation, Globalization*, edited by Saurabh Dube, 291–309. London: Routledge, 2009.

McDonald, David A. "Poetics and the Performance of Violence in Israel/Palestine." *Ethnomusicology* 53, no. 1 (2009): 58–85.

McKee Irwin, Robert. *Mexican Masculinities*. Minneapolis: University of Minnesota Press, 2003.

Meintjes, Louise. "Shoot the Sargeant, Shatter the Mountain: The Production of Masculinity in Zulu Ngoma Song and Dance in Post-Apartheid South Africa." *Ethnomusicology Forum* 13, no. 2 (2004): 173–201.

———. *Dust of the Zulu: Ngoma Aesthetics after Apartheid*. Durham, NC: Duke University Press, 2017.

Meneses Reyes, Marcela. "La institucionalization del Tianguis Cultural del Chopo: un espacio de identidad y control social." Universidad Nacional Autónoma de Mexico, master's thesis, 2003.

Mertes, Tom, ed. *Movement of Movements: Is Another World Really Possible?* London: Verso, 2004.

Meyers, John Paul. "The Beatles in Buenos Aires, Muse in Mexico City: Tribute Bands and the Global Consumption of Rock Music." *Ethnomusicology Forum* 24, no. 3 (2015): 329–48.

Miccio, Lance, dir. *Rock 'n' Roll Made in Mexico: From Evolution to Revolution*. 90 minutes, DVD, Heatdrum Productions, 2008.

Minter, Sarah, dir. "Nadie es inocente M.P. by Sarah Minter 1/6." Posted by sonido pappos on April 30, 2010. YouTube video, 9:48, from the 57-minute film by Sarah Minter, https://youtube.com/watch?v=_zlo19-59U8.

Mondini, Mateus. "'I Like Punk and I Like to Suck Dick': Martin Sorrondeguy on the Queer Rebellion of Latinx Punk." *Remezcla*, October 4, 2016.

Morello, Henry. "Aterciopelados' Musical Testimony: Bearing Witness to Colombia's Traumas." *Studies in Latin American Popular Culture* 30 (2012): 38–53.

Muehlebach, Andrea. "On Affective Labor in Post-Fordist Italy." *Cultural Anthropology* 26, no. 1 (2011): 59–82.

Muggleton, David, and Rupert Weinzierl, eds. *The Post-Subcultures Reader*. New York: Berg, 2003.

Muñoz Cota, José. *Ricardo Flores Magón: corridos*. Mexico: Editorial Castalia, 1963.

Nateras, Alfredo. "Las violencias sociales o todos somos *emos*." In "Topodrilo," *Tribus Juveniles* 8, (2008): 57–62.

Nelson, Diane M. *A Finger in the Wound: Body Politics in Quincentennial Guatemala*. Berkeley: University of California Press, 1999.

Novak, David. *Japanoise: Music at the Edge of Circulation*. Durham, NC: Duke University Press, 2013.

O'Connor, Alan. "Local Scenes and Dangerous Crossroads: Punk and Theories of Cultural Hybridity." *Popular Music* 21, no. 2 (2002): 225–36.

———. "Punk Subculture in Mexico and the Anti-Globalization Movement: A Report from the Front." *New Political Science* 25, no. 1 (2003): 43–53.

———. "Punk and Globalization: Spain and Mexico." *International Journal of Cultural Studies* 7, no. 2 (2004): 175–96.

———. *Punk Record Labels and the Struggle for Autonomy: The Emergence of D.I.Y.* Lanham, MD: Lexington Books, 2008.

———. "Towards a Field Theory of Punk." *Punk & Post-Punk* 5, no. 1 (2016): 67–81.

O'Hara, Craig. *The Philosophy of Punk: More Than Noise.* Oakland, CA: AK Press, 1999.

O'Malley, Ilene V. *The Myth of the Revolution: Hero Cultures and the Institutionalization of the Mexican State, 1920–1940.* New York: Greenwood Press, 1986.

Ochoa, Ana Maria. "A manera de introducción: la materialidad de lo musical y su relación con la violencia." *Trans: Revista Transcultural de Música* 10 (2006).

Olesen, Thomas. *International Zapatismo: The Construction of Solidarity in the Age of Globalization.* New York: Zed Books, 2005.

Owens, Lama Rod. *Love and Rage: The Path of Liberation through Anger.* Berkeley, CA: North Atlantic Books, 2020.

Pacini Hernandez, Deborah, Héctor Fernández L'Hoeste, and Eric Zolov, eds. *Rockin' Las Americas: The Global Politics of Rock in Latin/o America.* Pittsburgh, PA: University of Pittsburgh Press, 2004.

Palmer, Craig T. "Mummers and Moshers: Two Rituals of Trust in Changing Social Environments." *Ethnology* 44, no. 2 (2005): 147–66.

Pensado, Jaime M. *Rebel Mexico: Student Unrest and Authoritarian Political Culture During the Long Sixties.* Stanford, CA: Stanford University Press, 2013.

Pieslak, Jonathan. "Sound Targets: Music and the War in Iraq." *Journal of Musicological Research* 26 (2007): 123–49.

Pillsbury, Glenn T. *Damage Incorporated: Metallica and the Production of Musical Identity.* New York: Routledge, 2006.

Pla Brugat, Dolores. "Refugiados españoles en México." In *La comunidad española en la Ciudad de México.* Mexico City: Instituto de Cultura de la Ciudad de México, 1999.

Polletta, Francesca. *Freedom Is an Endless Meeting: Democracy in American Social Movements.* Chicago: University of Chicago Press, 2002.

Poma, Alice, and Tommaso Gravante. "Fallas del Sistema: análisis desde abajo del movimiento anarcopunk en México." *Revista Mexicana de Sociología* 78, no. 3 (2016): 437–67.

Poniatowska, Elena. *La noche de Tlatelolco: testimonios de historia oral.* Biblioteca Era. 1st ed. México: Ediciones Era, 1971.

———. *Nada, nadie. Las voces del temblor.* Biblioteca Era. 1st ed. Mexico City: Ediciones Era, 1988.

———. "Nada, nadie: las voces del temblor, 20 años después." *La Jornada*, September 14, 2005.

Portwood-Stacer, Laura. *Lifestyle Politics and Radical Activism*. New York: Bloomsbury, 2013.

Prieur, Annick. *Mema's House, Mexico City: On Transvestites, Queens, and Machos*. Chicago: University of Chicago Press, 1998.

Probyn, Elspeth. *Blush: Faces of Shame*. Minneapolis: University of Minnesota Press, 2005.

Rachman, Paul, dir. *American Hardcore: The History of American Punk Rock 1980–1986*. 100 minutes, Sony Pictures Home Entertainment, streaming video, 2006.

Rapport, Evan. *Damaged: Musicality and Race in Early American Punk*. Jackson: University of Mississippi Press, 2020.

Rasmussen, Anthony W. "Sales and Survival Within the Contested Acoustic Territories of Mexico City's Historic Centre." In *Ethnomusicology Forum* 26, no. 3 (2018): 307–30.

Reeskens, Tim, and Rodrigo Velasco Aguilar. "Being White Is a Full Time Job? Explaining Skin Tone Gradients in Income in Mexico." In *Journal of Ethnic and Migration Studies* (2020), doi:10.1080/1369183X.2020.1775071.

Revueltas, José. *Ensayo sobre un proletariado sin cabeza*. Mexico City: Ediciones Era, 1980.

Ribera Carbó, Anna. *La Casa del Obrero Mundial: anarcosindicalismo y revolución en México*. Mexico City: Instituto Nacional de Antropología e Historia, 2010.

Ríos Manzano, Abraham. *Tianguis Cultural del Chopo: una larga jornada*. Mexico City: n.p., 1999.

Rohrer, Ingo. *Cohesion and Dissolution: Friendship in the Globalized Punk and Hardcore Scene in Buenos Aires*. Freiburg, Germany: Springer VS, 2014.

Roman, Leslie G. "Intimacy, Labor, and Class: Ideologies of Feminine Sexuality in the Punk Slam Dance." In *Becoming Feminine: The Politics of Popular Culture*, edited by Leslie G. Roman and Linda K. Christian-Smith, 143–84. London: The Falmer Press, 1988.

Rosaldo, Michelle Z. *Knowledge and Passion: Ilongot Notions of Self and Social Life*. Cambridge: Cambridge University Press, 1980.

Rosaldo, Renato. "Grief and a Headhunter's Rage: On the Cultural Force of Emotions." In *The Emotions: A Cultural Reader*, edited by Helena Wulff, 219–28. Oxford: Berg, 2007.

Rosas, Gilberto. *Barrio Libre: Criminalizing States and Delinquent Refusals of the New Frontier*. Durham, NC: Duke University Press, 2012.

Ross, John. *El Monstruo: Dread and Redemption in Mexico City*. New York: Nation Books, 2009.

Sakakeeny, Matt. *Roll with It: Brass Bands in the Streets of New Orleans*. Durham, NC: Duke University Press, 2013.

San Filippo, Roy, ed. *A New World in Our Hearts: Eight Years of Writings from the Love and Rage Revolutionary Anarchist Federation*. Oakland, CA: AK Press, 2003.

Saño, Heleno. *Sindicalismo y autogestión*. Madrid: G. del Toro, 1977.

Santander, Gabriel, producer. "Esquizofrenia-Ecatepec El Microclima Del Punk 1/2."

Posted by texkumbala on January 18, 2012. YouTube video, 12:32, from the Canal 22 television series *Esquizofrenia* episode originally aired in 2010, https://youtube.com /watch?v=qHefH4vUEoE.

Scholz, Sally J. *Political Solidarity*. University Park: Pennsylvania State University Press, 2008.

Shantz, Jeff. *Active Anarchy: Political Practice in Contemporary Movements*. Lanham, MD: Lexington Books, 2011.

Shirinian, Tamar. "Love and the Liminality of Revolution: Interpersonal Transformations in between the April-May Events in Armenia." *Anthropology and Humanism* 45, no. 2 (2020): 322–38.

Simon, Bradford Scott. "Entering the Pit: Slam-Dancing and Modernity." *Journal of Popular Culture* 31, no. 1 (1997): 149–76.

Smith, Nicholas H. "Solidarity and Work: A Reassessment." In *Solidarity: Theory and Practice*, edited by Arto Laitinen and Anne Birgitta Pessi, 155–77. Lanham, MD: Lexington Books, 2015.

Soloff, Andalusia K. *Vivos se los llevaron: buscando a los 43 de Ayotzinapa*. Mexico City: Plan B, 2019.

Solomon, Robert C. *Love: Emotion, Myth, and Metaphor*. New York: Anchor Press, 1981.

———. "Getting Angry: The Jamesian Theory of Emotion in Anthropology." In *Culture Theory: Essays on Mind, Self and Emotion*, edited by Robert A. LeVine and Richard A. Shweder, 238–54. Cambridge: Cambridge University Press, 1984.

Sotelo, Adrian, ed. *Yo soy huelgista y yo soy de la UNAM: analysis y reflexiones sobre el movimiento universitario de 1999–2000*. Mexico City: Editorial RedeZ, 2009.

Stahler-Sholk, Richard, Harry E. Vanden, and Marc Becker, eds. *Rethinking Latin American Social Movements: Radical Action from Below*. Lanham, MD: Rowman & Littlefield, 2014.

Steingo, Gavin. *Kwaito's Promise: Music and the Aesthetics of Freedom in South Africa*. Chicago Studies in Ethnomusicology. Chicago: University of Chicago Press, 2016.

Stone, Livia. "Autonomy and *Autogestión* in Mexico City." In *Latin American Studies Association International Congress*. Barcelona, 2018.

Taibo, Paco Ignacio, ed. Translated by Achy Obejas. *Mexico City Noir*. Akashic Noir Series. New York: Akashic Books, 2010.

Talarico, Picky, dir. *Rompan todo: la historia del rock en América Latina*. Netflix limited series, streaming video, 6 episodes, 5:04:00, released in 2020, https://netflix.com/watch /81034647?trackId=13752289.

Tatro, Kelley. "The Hard Work of Screaming: Physical Exertion and Affective Labor among Mexico City's Punk Vocalists." *Ethnomusicology* 58, no. 3 (2014): 431–53.

———. "Performing Hardness: Punk and Self-Defense in Mexico City." *International Journal of Cultural Studies* 21, no. 3 (2018): 242–56.

———. "DIY Versus Development: International Edition." *Chicago Reader,* June 24, 2021.

Taylor, Diana. *The Archive and the Repertoire: Performing Cultural Memory in the Americas.* Durham, NC: Duke University Press, 2003.

Taylor, Jodie. "Scenes and Sexualities: Queerly Reframing the Music Scenes Perspective." *Continuum: Journal of Media & Cultural Studies* 26, no. 1 (2012): 143–56.

Tellez, Michelle. "Autonomy in the Spaces of Neoliberal Neglect: The Women of Maclovio Rojas." In *Latin American Studies Association International Congress.* Barcelona, 2018.

Tochka, Nicholas. "Singing 'with Culture': Popular Musicians and Affective Labour in State-Socialist Albania." *Ethnomusicology Forum* (2017). Published electronically December 13, 2017. doi:10.1080/17411912.2017.1407950.

Traister, Rebecca. *Good and Mad: The Revolutionary Power of Women's Anger.* New York: Simon & Schuster, 2018.

Triggs, Teal. *Fanzines: The DIY Revolution.* San Francisco: Chronicle Books, 2010.

Trimbur, Lucia. *Come Out Swinging: The Changing World of Boxing in Gleason's Gym.* Princeton, NJ: Princeton University Press, 2013.

Tsitsos, William. "Rules of Rebellion: Slamdancing, Moshing, and the American Alternative Scene." *Popular Music* 18, no. 3 (1999): 397–414.

Turner, Victor. *The Anthropology of Performance.* New York: PAJ Publications, 1986.

Urteaga Castro-Pozo, Maritza. *Por los territorios del rock: identidades juveniles y rock mexicano.* Mexico City: Consejo Nacional para la Cultura y las Artes/Culturas Populares, 1998.

Valenzuela, José Manuel. *¡A la brava ése! cholos, punks, chavos banda.* Tijuana: El Colegio de la Frontera Norte, 1988.

Villoro, Juan. *Horizontal Vertigo: A City Called Mexico.* Translated by Alfred MacAdam. New York: Pantheon Books, 2021.

Viñas, David. *Anarquistas en América Latina.* Buenos Aires: Paradiso, 2004.

Vodovnik, Žiga, ed. *¡Ya Basta! Ten Years of the Zapatista Uprising: Writings of Subcomandante Insurgente Marcos.* Oakland, CA: AK Press, 2004.

Wacquant, Loïc. *Body and Soul: Notebooks of an Apprentice Boxer.* Oxford: Oxford University Press, 2004.

Waksman, Steve. *This Ain't the Summer of Love: Conflict and Crossover in Heavy Metal and Punk.* Berkeley: University of California Press, 2009.

Wallach, Jeremy. "Living the Punk Lifestyle in Jakarta." *Ethnomusicology* 52, no. 1 (winter 2008): 98–116.

Wallach, Jeremy, Harris M. Berger, and Paul D. Greene, eds. *Metal Rules the Globe: Heavy Metal Music around the World.* Durham, NC: Duke University Press, 2011.

Walser, Robert. *Running with the Devil: Power, Gender, and Madness in Heavy Metal Music.* Hanover, NH: Wesleyan University Press, 1993.

Weeks, Kathi. *The Problem with Work: Feminism, Marxism, Antiwork Politics, and Postwork Imaginaries*. Durham, NC: Duke University Press, 2011.

Weidman, Amanda. *Singing the Classical, Voicing the Modern: The Postcolonial Politics of Music in South India*. Durham, NC: Duke University Press, 2006.

West, Cornel. *Race Matters*. Boston: Beacon Press, 1993.

Wetherell, Margaret. *Affect and Emotion: A New Social Science Understanding*. London: Sage, 2012.

White, Daniel. "Affect: What Is It Good For?" *Cultural Anthropology* 32, no. 2 (2017): 175–80.

White, Stuart. "Social Anarchism, Lifestyle Anarchism, and the Anarchism of Colin Ward." *Anarchist Studies* 19, no. 2 (2011): 92–104.

Whitehead, Neil L. "Introduction: Cultures, Conflicts, and the Poetics of Violent Practice." In *Violence*, edited by Neil L. Whitehead, 3–24. Santa Fe: School of American Research Press, 2004.

Wrekk, Alex. *Stolen Sharpie Revolution: A DIY Resource for Zines and Zine Culture*. 5th ed. Portland, OR: Lunchroom Publishing, 2014.

Zolov, Eric. *Refried Elvis: The Rise of the Mexican Counterculture*. Berkeley: University of California Press, 1999.

INDEX

Page numbers in *italics* refer to the illustrations

Juris, Jeffrey, 170n2

Juventud Antiautoritaria Revolucionario (collective), 111, 147, 178n27

K (band), 58

Kagada de Perro (band), 62

La Jornada, 104, 115

La Libélula (club), *105*, 173n35

land invasion, 19, 27, 171n12

land reform, 33–34, 179n32

Latour, Bruno, 13

La Vieja Escuela (venue), *128*

Las Cirujanas (collective), 146–49

Le Corbusier (Charles-Édouard Jenneret), 19

Levantadxs, 138, *139*. See also fanzines

LGBTQ+ participation in punk scene, 14

libertarian, 6, 32, 169n4

lifestyle politics, 121, 159

love (amor), 29, 43, 119–21, 127, 131, 140, 153–55, 170n8, 175n9, 179n1, 180n5; and friendship and solidarity, 8, 30, 36, 56, 57, 65, 75, 129, 149, 163; See also Horvat, Srećko

Maffesoli, Michel, 12, 113, 117

Magaña, Maurice Rafael, 36, 170n5, 172n25, 183n31, 184n4

Marciniak, Marta, 178n18

Marroquín, Enrique, 176n4

Marshall, Peter, 106–7, 178n21

Marxism, 93, 106, 165, 176n5

Masacre (band), 58

Masacre 68 (band), 58, 63, 84

masculinity, 9, 44, 47, 51, 56, 117, 122, 126, 131, 174n2, 181n11, 183n32

massacres: Corpus Christi, 94, 95, 177n10; Tlatelolco, *15*, 52, 88, 93–94, *94*, 95, 102, 177nn7–9

Maximumrocknroll, 64

Metallica, 62

Mexico City: as CD.MX. 18–19; la Alameda Central, *53*; Azcapotzalco (municipality), *21*; centro histórico (historic city center)

15, 20, 39, 102, *157*, *160*; cinturones de miseria, 98; colonias populares ("popular" neighborhoods), 20, 100; Distrito Federal (Federal District), 18–20, 22, 27, 116, 124, 182n27; earthquake of 1985, 102, 177n16, 182n27; Ecatepec (municipality) 20, 22, 23, 39, 45, 49, 57, 71, 77, 104, 152; Estado de México, 71; Glorieta de Insurgentes, 11, 13, 115; Iztacalco (municipality), *21*; metropolitan zone, 3, 19–25, 28, 47, 58, 62, 78, 97, 101, 116, 142, 171n13; "monster city" (ciudad monstruo), 18,78, 122; Monumento a la Revolución, *57*, *87*; Nezahualcóyotl (municipality), 20, 100, 147; nicknamed el DeFectuoso 18, 82, 166; Palacio de Bellas Artes, 52, 105; Palacio de los Deportes, 88; Paseo de la Reforma, *17*, 127; Plaza Garibaldi, 42, 174n39; Tlalnepantla (municipality), 20, 39, *128*; Zócalo, 18, 52–53, 73, 156, 177. See also Tenochtitlán

Mexican "miracle," 90, 91, 116

Meintjes, Louise, 55–56, 173n32, 153n13

Mestre Ventura, Ricardo, 105, 109–110, 172n28, 173n36. See also Spanish Civil War

metal (music genre), 182n19, 14, 15, 60, 62–64, 70, 88, 99; metaleros (metalheads), 114–15

Metodos anti-conceptivos, 135–36. See also fanzines

Mexican Revolution, 32–34, 88, 90, 92, 109, 134

Mierdas Punk (gang), 101, 141

migration, 8, 9, 19, 20, 27, 34, 49, 91, 99, 114, 122, 181n15; and remittances, 181n15; and U.S.-Mexico border, 32, 67, 92, 99, 180n9

mordida (bribe), 26, 46

Muehlebach, Andrea, 126, 181n12

Museo del Chopo, 101, 110

Nadie es inocente, 100

Nelson, Diane, 176n24

neoliberalism, 9, 16, 111, 116, 120, 127, 167, 183n32

ninis, 116

Novak, David, 182n18

O'Connor, Alan, 35, 178n19, 181n13

Okupa Che, *41*. *See also* squats

oppositionality, 86–87, 117–18, 119, 155; and oppositional identities, 161

organizational tastes, 36, 162–63, 173n30

PAN (Partido de Acción Nacional), 26, 38

Peña Nieto, Enrique, 156, 171n9

Pensares y sentires, 137–38. *See also* fanzines

pogo, 66–67

police, 22, 26, 39, 40, 42, 50, 70–71, 72, 79, 93, 112, 117, 165; and corruption, 26–27, 45–46, 73–74, 95–96, 182n27; in punk songs, 46; and raids, 91; riot police (granaderos) *27*, 49, *53*, *53*, 93, *157*. *See also mordida*

Polletta, Francesca, 119, 148, 162–63, 173n30, 184n5, 184n9

Poniatowksa, Elena, 102, 177n7, 177n16

porros (agents provocateurs), 117, 148, 179n36, 174n37

portazo (storming the doors), 48, 65, 74, 76, 81, 82, 143; and "destroy punk," 122; history of, 73; and rage, 48, 52, 71, 72, 75; and violence, 76, 81

post-work imaginaries, 126

PRD (Partido de la Revolución Democrática), 73, 150

presos (incarcerated people), 94, 133, 182n21, *140*; in Pensares y Sentires fanzine, 138; in Rhuckuss song lyrics, 133–34

PRI (Partido Revolucionario Institutional): corruption, 26, 34; and Cuban Revolution, 92; and earthquake of 1985, 102; history of, 91–92, 109, 135, 176n3, 176n5; and Mexico City, 19, 73, 100, 171n10; and Mexico's presidency, 38, 94, 156, 171nn9; "soft dictatorship," 26, 91, 171nn9

Probyn, Elspeth, 176n26

protagonizarse (to make oneself a protagonist), 9, 138

Proudhon, Pierre Joseph, 107, 110, 178n20

pulque, 40, 174n38

punk: aesthetics, 9, 15, 29–30, 35, 48, 70, 104, 136, 155, 163; anarcopunk 1, 15–16, 36, 53, 59, 136, 139, 164, 174n6, 180n7, 183n31; crust punk, 58, 64; d-beat, 62, 64; "destroy punk," 15, 121–22, 154, 166, 180n7; field, punk as, 12–13; and grindcore, 58, 64, 175n16; "happy punk," 31, 51; hardcore punk, 15, 59–61, 62–64, 67, 84, 104, 106,129, 152, 175n14; "hipster punk," 31; international solidarity meeting, 169n1; as lifestyle, 2, 17, 18, 30, 121, 147; metal-punk, 15, 63; network, punk as, 9, 12–16, 29, 44, 48, 76, 101, 118, 120, 136, 164, 167; poetics, 87, 140, 155–56; punk rock, 14, 15, 45, 59, 64, 66, 67, 96, 97–100, 104, 106, 137, 170n3; punk studies, 12; radicals, 15, 74, 170n4, 180n7; "rockers," 15, 122, 180n7; as scene, 1, 2, 9, 12–13, 16; and sniffing glue, 180n9; in Spanish, 106, 178n19; and stereotypes, 28, 43, 47, 48, 50, 81, 117; and thrash metal, 62, 64

Punks Not Dead (collective), 147

rage (rabia), 8–9, 28–30, 77–78, 153–54, 170n8, 175n9; and catharsis, 56–57; and gender, 43, 51, 80–81, 146, 176n25; and grief, 56; and madness, 55; and moral anger, 55–56; and protests, 85–86; and punk shows, 47, 57, 60–61, 65–71, 75–76, 129–30; and self-defense, 47, 48, 78–82, 118, 162; and social bonding, 51; and social consciousness, 48, 51, 59, 85; and violence, 43, 47, 51, 54, 118

Rapport, Evan, 175n14

Regeneración, 31, 32, 134

representative democracy, 150, 173n34

Revuelta Anarko Punk (collective), 59

Revueltas, José, 93

Rhuckuss (band), 63–64, 133, 138

Ríos Manzano, Abraham, 73, 96, 104

rituals, 71, 87, 162–63, 184n9

rock music, 73, 87, 88; Avándaro festival, 94–95; and banda, 97, 99–103; and cafés cantantes, 91; and CREA program, 100; early history in Mexico, 88, 90–96, 170n3; and El Chopo, 3, 73, 104; en español, 103–4;

and hoyos fonquis, 96; and jipitecas, 91; lost
decade of, 73, 96, 98; and middle class, 66,
72, 103; and "new song," 92; and "La Onda,"
92–94; and portazos, 73; and rocanrol, 91.
See also *Rompan todo*
*Rock 'n' roll made in Mexico: from evolution to
revolution*, 177n11. *See also* rock music
Rohrer, Ingo, 119, 179n1
Roman, Leslie G., 176n20
Rompan todo (documentary), 89. *See also* rock
music
Rosaldo, Michelle, 55–56
Rosaldo, Renato, 55–56, 81
Rosas, Gilberto, 180n9

Salinas de Gortari, Carlos, 116
Scheinbaum Pardo, Claudia, 174n4
Scorpions (band), 88
seed: as metaphor, 8–10, 31, 34–35, 38, 138, 164,
168. *See also* sowing
self-defense, 36, 43, 47–48, 50, 75–76, 77, 78–82,
145, 155, 161–62, 174n2. *See also* violence
self-management, 5, 35. *See also* autogestión
Sex Pistols (band), 98, 106
Shantz, Jeff, 169n5
Sindicato Mexicano de Electricistas, 22, 112, 156
skill swapping, 126, 131, 141, 144–5
slam dance, 45, 59, 65–72, 77, 79, 81, 153; and
energy, 60, 180n2; and portazo, 72, 75–76,
82; and punk sound, 60, 63; and solidarity
and friendship, 52, 65, 119–20, 129, 154, 163;
as training, 48, 60, 82, 174n1
Slim Helú, Carlos, 116
sing-alongs, 2, 40, 131, 132–33, 154
social movements: and anarchism, 35, 172n25,
180n8; and networks, 9, 12, 30, 162, 164,
170n2; organizing of, 30, 36, 119, 149, 158,
162, 173n30; of the 1960s, 34, 94; punk and,
12, 16, 31, 36, 113, 126, 161, 163
solidarity (solidaridad): and affect, 28, 56, 65,
130, *140*, 154, 159; and anarco-syndicalism,
125, 151, 172n25; and la banda, 13, 97,
102–103, 120; with Cubans, 92; dance of,

65, 75, 120, 129; difficulties of, 36, 70, 82,
120; Durkheim and, 120, 163, 184n9; and
"fluidarity," 180n4; and friendship, 8, 29, 30,
57, 65, 117, 148–49, 154, 155, 163, 179n1, 180n5;
and global punk, 85, 111, 169n1; Hegel and,
120; history of, 120–21; and love, 8, 51, 57, 65,
117, 121, 129, 154, 163, 180n5; in movement of
1968, 93; in punk-scene discourse, 30, 38,
49, 75, 82, 120, 134, 163; and rituals, 184n9;
with university strike, 112; waged labor and,
120, 122; and the Zapatistas, 34,160–61
Solomon, Robert, 175n10
song lyrics, 45, 56, 61, 82, 131, 132–40, 153
Southern California, 67, 99
sowing: as metaphor, 1, 9, 31–33, 165. *See also*
seed
Spanish Civil War, 34, 39, 88, 105, 109–110,
172n28, 173n36. *See also* Mestre Ventura,
Ricardo.
squats (ocupas), 8, 39, *41*, 42, 126, 127, 147,
170n7, 182n27; Okupa Che, *41*, 143;
squatting as practice, 106, 182n27
Stone, Livia, 172n28, 183n4
Strangulation (band), 58
street vending, 3, 4, 124, 171n17; ambulatory
vendors, 125. *See also* tianguis
sweat, 69, 79, 128–9, 130, 132, 152

Taibo, Paco Ignacio, II (Francisco Ignacio
Taibo Mahojo), 25, 171n16
Tenochtitlán, 3, *61*. *See also* Mexico City
Tequila Crisis, 116
tianguis (street markets), 2, 2–5, 10, 14, 40, 43,
99, 101, 104, 110, 126, 143. *See also* El Chopo;
street vending
Tijuana, 99, 147
Tolstoy, Leo, 32, 106, 178n20
Trimbur, Lucia, 129–30
trueque (swapping), 4, 141–42

Universidad Nacional Autónoma de México
(UNAM), 40, *41*, 143; and 1999 strike, 40,
111, 112, 174n37. *See also* squats

urban tribe (tribu urbana), 12, 113, 115, 117, 152, 179n30

Urteaga Castro-Pozo, Maritza, 101, 102, 177nn13–15

violence: and democracy, 18, 49; and fight-or-flight reaction, 80, 176n25; and intimacy, 31, 80; everyday, 49, 82; music and, 54; and physical aggression, 80, 81; political, 49; sexual harassment, 49, 79, 96; spectrum of, 46, 49, 50; state, 49–50; structural, 49; and vehemence, 54–55, 82. *See also* self-defense

Wallach, Jeremy, et. al., 60

war against drugs, 9, 22, 27, 48–49, 116

Weeks, Kathi, 181n10

West, Cornel, 175n9

work ethic, 122, 125–6, 181nn10–11, 181n15, 183n32. *See also* affective labor

work refusal, 122, 125, 181n10

Whitehead, Neil, 54

Zapatistas, 34, 50, 111, 159–62. *See also* EZLN

MUSIC / CULTURE

A series from Wesleyan University Press
Edited by Deborah Wong, Sherrie Tucker, and Jeremy Wallach
Originating editors: George Lipsitz, Susan McClary, and Robert Walser

The Music/Culture series has consistently reshaped and redirected music scholarship. Founded in 1993 by George Lipsitz, Susan McClary, and Robert Walser, the series features outstanding critical work on music. Unconstrained by disciplinary divides, the series addresses music and power through a range of times, places, and approaches. Music/Culture strives to integrate a variety of approaches to the study of music, linking analysis of musical significance to larger issues of power—what is permitted and forbidden, who is included and excluded, who speaks and who gets silenced. From ethnographic classics to cutting-edge studies, Music/Culture zeroes in on how musicians articulate social needs, conflicts, coalitions, and hope. Books in the series investigate the cultural work of music in urgent and sometimes experimental ways, from the radical fringe to the quotidian. Music/Culture asks deep and broad questions about music through the framework of the most restless and rigorous critical theory.

Marié Abe
Resonances of Chindon-ya:
Sounding Space and Sociality
in Contemporary Japan

Frances Aparicio
Listening to Salsa: Gender, Latin Popular
Music, and Puerto Rican Cultures

Paul Austerlitz
Jazz Consciousness: Music, Race,
and Humanity

Shalini R. Ayyagri
Musical Resilience: Performing Patronage
in the Indian Thar Desert

Christina Baade and Kristin McGee
Beyoncé in the World: Making Meaning
with Queen Bey in Troubled Times

Emma Baulch
Genre Publics: Popular Music,
Technologies, and Class
in Indonesia

Praise for *Thinking with Data*

Thinking with Data

Max Shron

O'REILLY®   Beijing · Cambridge · Farnham · Köln · Sebastopol · Tokyo

THINKING WITH DATA
by Max Shron

Copyright © 2014 Max Shron. All rights reserved.

Printed in the United States of America.

Published by O'Reilly Media, Inc., 1005 Gravenstein Highway North, Sebastopol, CA 95472.

O'Reilly books may be purchased for educational, business, or sales promotional use. Online editions are also available for most titles (*http://my.safaribooksonline.com*). For more information, contact our corporate/institutional sales department: 800-998-9938 or *corporate@oreilly.com*.

Editors: Mike Loukides and Ann Spencer	**Cover Designer:** Karen Montgomery
Production Editor: Kristen Brown	**Interior Designer:** David Futato
Copyeditor: O'Reilly Production Services	**Illustrator:** Rebecca Demarest
Proofreader: Kim Cofer	

February 2014:   First Edition

Revision History for the First Edition:
    2014-01-16:   First release

See *http://oreilly.com/catalog/errata.csp?isbn=9781449362935* for release details.

ISBN: 978-1-449-36293-5
[LSI]

Contents

Preface

Working with data is about producing knowledge. Whether that knowledge is consumed by a person or acted on by a machine, our goal as professionals working with data is to use observations to learn about how the world works. We want to turn information into insights, and asking the right questions ensures that we're creating insights about the right things. The purpose of this book is to help us understand that these are our goals and that we are not alone in this pursuit.

I work as a data strategy consultant. I help people figure out what problems they are trying to solve, how to solve them, and what to do with them once the problems are "solved." This book grew out of the recognition that the problem of asking good questions and knowing how to put the answers together is not a new one. This problem—the problem of turning observations into knowledge—is one that has been worked on again and again and again by experts in a variety of disciplines. We have much to learn from them.

People use data to make knowledge to accomplish a wide variety of things. There is no one goal of all data work, just as there is no one job description that encapsulates it. Consider this incomplete list of things that can be made better with data:

- Answering a factual question
- Telling a story
- Exploring a relationship
- Discovering a pattern
- Making a case for a decision
- Automating a process
- Judging an experiment

Doing each of these well in a data-driven way draws on different strengths and skills. The most obvious are what you might call the "hard skills" of working with data: data cleaning, mathematical modeling, visualization, model or graph interpretation, and so on.[1]

What is missing from most conversations is how important the "soft skills" are for making data useful. Determining what problem one is actually trying to solve, organizing results into something useful, translating vague problems or questions into precisely answerable ones, trying to figure out what may have been left out of an analysis, combining multiple lines or arguments into one useful result...the list could go on. These are the skills that separate the data scientist who can take direction from the data scientist who can give it, as much as knowledge of the latest tools or newest algorithms.

Some of this is clearly experience—experience working within an organization, experience solving problems, experience presenting the results. But these are also skills that have been taught before, by many other disciplines. We are not alone in needing them. Just as data scientists did not invent statistics or computer science, we do not need to invent techniques for how to ask good questions or organize complex results. We can draw inspiration from other fields and adapt them to the problems we face. The fields of design, argument studies, critical thinking, national intelligence, problem-solving heuristics, education theory, program evaluation, various parts of the humanities—each of them have insights that data science can learn from.

Data science is already a field of bricolage. Swaths of engineering, statistics, machine learning, and graphic communication are already fundamental parts of the data science canon. They are necessary, but they are not sufficient. If we look further afield and incorporate ideas from the "softer" intellectual disciplines, we can make data science successful and help it be more than just this decade's fad.

A focus on *why* rather than *how* already pervades the work of the best data professionals. The broader principles outlined here may not be new to them, though the specifics likely will be.

---

[1]. See *Taxonomy of Data Science* by Hilary Mason and Chris Wiggins (*http://www.dataists.com/2010/09/a-taxonomy-of-data-science/*) and *From Data Mining to Knowledge Discovery in Databases* by Usama Fayyad et al. (AI Magazine, Fall 1996).

This book consists of six chapters. Chapter 1 covers a framework for scoping data projects. Chapter 2 discusses how to pin down the details of an idea, receive feedback, and begin prototyping. Chapter 3 covers the tools of arguments, making it easier to ask good questions, build projects in stages, and communicate results. Chapter 4 covers data-specific patterns of reasoning, to make it easier to figure out what to focus on and how to build out more useful arguments. Chapter 5 takes a big family of argument patterns (causal reasoning) and gives it a longer treatment. Chapter 6 provides some more long examples, tying together the material in the previous chapters. Finally, there is a list of further reading in Appendix A, to give you places to go from here.

Conventions Used in This Book

The following typographical convention is used in this book:

Italic
>   Indicates new terms, URLs, email addresses, filenames, and file extensions.

Safari® Books Online

Safari Books Online is an on-demand digital library that delivers expert content in both book and video form from the world's leading authors in technology and business.

Technology professionals, software developers, web designers, and business and creative professionals use Safari Books Online as their primary resource for research, problem solving, learning, and certification training.

Safari Books Online offers a range of product mixes and pricing programs for organizations, government agencies, and individuals. Subscribers have access to thousands of books, training videos, and prepublication manuscripts in one fully searchable database from publishers like O'Reilly Media, Prentice Hall Professional, Addison-Wesley Professional, Microsoft Press, Sams, Que, Peachpit Press, Focal Press, Cisco Press, John Wiley & Sons, Syngress, Morgan Kaufmann, IBM Redbooks, Packt, Adobe Press, FT Press, Apress, Manning, New Riders, McGraw-Hill, Jones & Bartlett, Course Technology, and dozens more. For more information about Safari Books Online, please visit us online.

How to Contact Us

Please address comments and questions concerning this book to the publisher:

O'Reilly Media, Inc.
1005 Gravenstein Highway North
Sebastopol, CA 95472
800-998-9938 (in the United States or Canada)
707-829-0515 (international or local)
707-829-0104 (fax)

We have a web page for this book, where we list errata, examples, and any additional information. You can access this page at *http://oreil.ly/thinking-with-data*.

To comment or ask technical questions about this book, send email to *book questions@oreilly.com*.

For more information about our books, courses, conferences, and news, see our website at *http://www.oreilly.com*.

Find us on Facebook: *http://facebook.com/oreilly*

Follow us on Twitter: *http://twitter.com/oreillymedia*

Watch us on YouTube: *http://www.youtube.com/oreillymedia*

Acknowledgments

I would be remiss to not mention some of the fantastic people who have helped make this book possible. Juan-Pablo Velez has been invaluable in refining my ideas. Jon Bruner, Matt Wallaert, Mike Dewar, Brian Eoff, Jake Porway, Sam Rayachoti, Willow Brugh, Chris Wiggins, Claudia Perlich, and John Matthews provided me with key insights that hopefully I have incorporated well.

Jay Garlapati, Shauna Gordon-McKeon, Michael Stone, Brian Eoff, Dave Goodsmith, and David Flatow provided me with very helpful feedback on drafts. Ann Spencer was a fantastic editor. It was wonderful to know that there was always someone in my corner. Thank you also to Solomon Roberts, Gabe Gaster, emily barger, Miklos Abert, Laci Babai, and Gordon Kindlmann, who were each crucial at setting me on the path that gave me math. Thank you also to Christian Rudder, who taught me so much—not least of which, the value of instinct. As always, all the errors and mistakes are mine alone. Thanks as well to all of you who were helpful whose names I neglected to put down.

At last I understand why every author in every book on my shelf thanks their family. My wonderful partner, Sarah, has been patient, kind, and helpful at every stage of this process, and my loving parents and sister have been a source of comfort

and strength as I made this book a reality. My father especially has been a great source of ideas to me. He set me off on this path as a kid when he patiently explained to me the idea of "metacognition," or thinking about thinking. It would be hard to be grateful enough.

Scoping: Why Before How

Most people start working with data from exactly the wrong end. They begin with a data set, then apply their favorite tools and techniques to it. The result is narrow questions and shallow arguments. Starting with data, without first doing a lot of thinking, without having any structure, is a short road to simple questions and unsurprising results. We don't want unsurprising—we want knowledge.

As professionals working with data, our domain of expertise has to be the *full problem*, not merely the columns to combine, transformations to apply, and models to fit. Picking the right techniques has to be secondary to asking the right questions. We have to be proficient in both to make a difference.

To walk the path of creating things of lasting value, we have to understand elements as diverse as the needs of the people we're working with, the shape that the work will take, the structure of the arguments we make, and the process of what happens after we "finish." To make that possible, we need to give ourselves space to think. When we have space to think, we can attend to the problem of *why* and *so what* before we get tripped up in *how*. Otherwise, we are likely to spend our time doing the wrong things.

This can be surprisingly challenging. The secret is to have structure that you can think through, rather than working in a vacuum. Structure keeps us from doing the first things to cross our minds. Structure gives us room to think through all the aspects of a problem.

People have been creating structures to make thinking about problems easier for thousands of years. We don't need to invent these things from scratch. We can adapt ideas from other disciplines as diverse as philosophy, design, English composition, and the social sciences to make professional data work as valuable as possible. Other parts of the tree of knowledge have much to teach us.

Let us start at the beginning. Our first place to find structure is in creating the scope for a data problem. A scope is the outline of a story about why we are working on a problem (and about how we expect that story to end).

In professional settings, the work we do is part of a larger goal, and so there are other people who will be affected by the project or are working on it directly as part of a team. A good scope both gives us a firm grasp on the outlines of the problem we are facing and a way to communicate with the other people involved.

A task worth scoping could be slated to take anywhere from a few hours with one person to months or years with a large team. Even the briefest of projects benefit from some time spent thinking up front.

There are four parts to a project scope. The four parts are the *context* of the project; the *needs* that the project is trying to meet; the *vision* of what success might look like; and finally what the *outcome* will be, in terms of how the organization will adopt the results and how its effects will be measured down the line. When a problem is well-scoped, we will be able to easily converse about or write out our thoughts on each. Those thoughts will mature as we progress in a project, but they have to start somewhere. Any scope will evolve over time; no battle plan survives contact with opposing forces.

A mnemonic for these four areas is CoNVO: *c*ontext, *n*eed, *v*ision, *o*utcome. We should be able to hold a conversation with an intelligent stranger about the project, and afterward he should understand (at a high level), why and how we accomplished what we accomplished. Hence, CoNVO.

All stories have a structure, and a project scope is no different. Like any story, our scope will have exposition (the context), some conflict (the need), a resolution (the vision), and hopefully a happily-ever-after (the outcome). Practicing telling stories is excellent practice for scoping data problems.

We will examine each part of the scoping process in detail before looking at a fully worked-out example. In subsequent chapters, we will explore other aspects of getting a good data project going, and then we will look carefully at the structures for thinking that make asking good questions much easier.

Writing down and refining our CoNVO is crucial to getting it straight. Clear writing is a sign of clear thinking. After we have done the thinking that we need to do, it is worthwhile to concisely write down each of these parts for a new problem. At least say them out loud to someone else. Having to clarify our thoughts down to a few sentences per part is extremely helpful. Once we have them clear (or at least know what is still unclear), we can go out and acquire data, clarify our understanding, start the technical work, clarify our understanding, gradually converge on

something smart and useful, and...clarify our understanding. Data science is an iterative process.

Context (Co)

Every project has a context, the defining frame that is apart from the particular problems we are interested in solving. Who are the people with an interest in the results of this project? What are they generally trying to achieve? What work, generally, is the project going to be furthering?

Here are some examples of contexts, very loosely based on real organizations, distilled down into a few sentences:

- This nonprofit organization reunites families that have been separated by conflict. It collects information from refugees in host countries. It visits refugee camps and works with informal networks in host countries further from conflicts. It has built a tool for helping refugees find each other. The decision makers on the project are the CEO and CTO.

- This department in a large company handles marketing for a shoe manufacturer with a large online presence. The department's goal is to convince new customers to try its shoes and to convince existing customers to return again. The final decision maker is the VP of Marketing.

- This news organization produces stories and editorials for a wide audience. It makes money through advertising and through premium subscriptions to its content. The main decision maker for this project is the head of online business.

- This advocacy organization specializes in ferreting out and publicizing corruption in politics. It is a small operation, with several staff members who serve multiple roles. They are working with a software development team to improve their technology for tracking evidence of corrupt politicians.

Contexts emerge from understanding who we are working with and why they are doing what they are doing. We learn the context from talking to people, and continuing to talk to them until we understand what their long-term goals are. The context sets the overall tone for the project, and guides the choices we make about what to pursue. It provides the background that makes the rest of the decisions make sense. The work we do should further the mission espoused in the context. At least if it does not, we should be aware of that.

New contexts emerge with new partners, employers, or supervisors, or as an organization's mission shifts over time. A freelancer often has to understand a new context with every project. It is important to be able to clearly articulate the long-term goals of the people we are looking to aid, even when embedded within an organization.

Sometimes the context for a project is simply our own curiosity and hunger for understanding. In moderation (or as art), there's no problem with that. Yet if we treat every situation only as a chance to satisfy our own interests, we will soon find that we have passed up opportunities to provide value to others.

The context provides a project with larger goals and helps to keep us on track. Contexts include larger relevant details, like deadlines, that will help us to prioritize our work.

Needs (N)

Everyone faces challenges. Things that, were they to be fixed or understood, would advance the goals they want to reach. What are the specific needs that could be fixed by intelligently using data? These needs should be presented in terms that are meaningful to the organization. If our method will be to build a model, the need is not to build a model. The need is to solve the problem that having the model will solve.

Correctly identifying needs is tough. The opening stages of a data project are a design process; we can draw on techniques developed by designers to make it easier. Like a graphic designer or architect, a data professional is often presented with a vague brief to generate a certain spreadsheet or build a tool to accomplish some task. Something has been discussed, perhaps a definite problem has even been articulated—but even if we are handed a definite problem, we are remiss to believe that our work in defining it ends there. Like all design processes, we need to keep an open mind. The needs we identify at the outset and the needs we ultimately try to meet are often not the same.

If working with data begins as a design process, what are we designing? We are designing the steps to create knowledge. A need that can be met with data is fundamentally about knowledge, fundamentally about understanding some part of how the world works. Data fills a hole that can only be filled with better intelligence. When we correctly explain a need, we are clearly laying out what it is that could be improved by better knowledge. What will this spreadsheet teach us? What will the tool let us know? What will we be able to do after making this graph that we could not do before?

When we correctly explain a need, we are clearly laying out what it is that could be improved by better knowledge.

Data science is the application of math and computers to solve problems that stem from a lack of knowledge, constrained by the small number of people with any interest in the answers. In the sciences writ large, questions of what matters within the field are set in conferences, by long social processes, and through slow maturation. In a professional setting, we have no such help. We have to determine for ourselves which questions are the important ones to answer.

It is instructive to compare data science needs to needs from other related disciplines. When success is judged not by knowledge but by uptime or performance, the task is software engineering. When the task is judged by minimizing classification error or regret, without regard to how the results inform a larger discussion, the task is applied machine learning. When results are judged by the risk of legal action or issues of compliance, the task is one of risk management. These are each valuable and worthwhile tasks, and they require similar steps of scoping to get right, but they are not problems of data science.

Consider some descriptions of some fairly common needs, all ones that I have seen in practice. Each of these is much condensed from how they began their life:

- The managers want to expand operations to a new location. Which one is likely to be most profitable?
- Our customers leave our website too quickly, often after only reading one article. We don't understand who they are, where they are from, or when they leave, and we have no framework for experimenting with new ideas to retain them.
- We want to decide between two competing vendors. Which is better for us?
- Is this email campaign effective at raising revenue?
- We want to place our ads in a smart way. What should we be optimizing? What is the best choice, given those criteria?

And here are some famous ones from within the data world:

- We want to sell more goods to pregnant women. How do we identify them from their shopping habits?

- We want to reduce the amount of illegal grease dumping in the sewers. Where might we look to find the perpetrators?

Needs will rarely start out as clear as these. It is incumbent upon us to ask questions, listen, and brainstorm until we can articulate them clearly and they can be articulated clearly back to us. Again, writing is a big help here. By writing down what we think the need is, we will usually see flaws in our own reasoning. We are generally better at criticizing than we are at making things, but when we criticize our own work, it helps us create things that make more sense.

Like designers, the process of discovering needs largely proceeds by listening to people, trying to condense what we understand, and bringing our ideas back to people again. Some partners and decision makers will be able to articulate what their needs are. More likely they will be able to tell us stories about what they care about, what they are working on, and where they are getting stuck. They will give us places to start. Sometimes those we talk with are too close to their task to see what is possible. We need to listen to what they are saying, and it is our job to go beyond listening and actively ask questions until we can clearly articulate what needs to be understood, why, and by whom.

Often the information we need to understand in order to refine a need is a detailed understanding of how some process happens. It could be anything from how a widget gets manufactured to how a student decides to drop out of school to how a CEO decides when to end a contract. Walking through that process one step at a time is a great tactic for figuring out how to refine a need. Drawing diagrams and making lists make this investigation clearer. When we can break things down into smaller parts, it becomes easier to figure out where the most pressing problems are. It can turn out that the thing we were originally worried about was actually a red herring or impossible to measure, or that three problems we were concerned about actually boiled down to one.

When possible, a well-framed need relates directly back to some particular action that depends on having good intelligence. A good need informs an action rather than simply informing. Rather than saying, "The manager wants to know where users drop out on the way to buying something," consider saying, "The manager wants more users to finish their purchases. How do we encourage that?" Answering the first question is a component of doing the second, but the action-oriented formulation opens up more possibilities, such as testing new designs and performing user experience interviews to gather more data.

If it is not helpful to phrase something in terms of an action, it should at least be related to some larger strategic question. For example, understanding how users of a product are migrating from desktop to mobile versions of a website is useful for informing the product strategy, even if there is no obvious action to take afterward. Needs should always be specified in words that are important to the organization, even if they're only questions.

Until we can clearly articulate the needs we are trying to meet, and until we understand how meeting those specific needs will help the organization achieve its larger goals, we don't know why we're doing what we're hoping to do. Without that part of a scope, our data work is mostly going to be fluff and only occasionally worthwhile.

Continuing from the longer examples, here are some needs that those organizations might have:

- The nonprofit that reunited families does not have a good way to measure its success. It is prohibitively expensive to follow up with every individual to see if they have contacted their families. By knowing when individuals are doing well or poorly, the nonprofit will be able to judge the effectiveness of changes to its strategy.

- The marketing department at the shoe company does not have a smart way of selecting cities to advertise to. Right now it is selecting its targets based on intuition, but it thinks there is a better way. With a better way of selecting cities, the department expects sales will go up.

- The media organization does not know the right way to define an engaged reader. The standard web metric of unique daily users doesn't really capture what it means to be a reader of an online newspaper. When it comes to optimizing revenue, growth, and promoting subscriptions, 30 different people visiting on 30 different days means something very different from 1 person visiting for 30 days in a row. What is the right way to measure engagement that respects these goals?

- The anti-corruption advocacy group does not have a good way to automatically collect and collate media mentions of politicians. With an automated system for collecting media attention, it will spend less time and money keeping up with the news and more time writing it.

Note that the need is *never* something like, "the decision makers are lacking in a dashboard," or predictive model, or ranking, or what have you. These are potential solutions, not needs. Nobody except a car driver needs a dashboard. The need is not for the dashboard or model, but for something that actually matters in words that decision makers can usefully think about.

This is a point that bears repeating. A data science need is a problem that can be solved with knowledge, not a lack of a particular tool. Tools are used to accomplish things; by themselves, they have no value except as academic exercises. So if someone comes to you and says that her company needs a dashboard, you need to dig deeper. Usually what the company needs is to understand how they are performing so they can make tactical adjustments. A dashboard may be one way of accomplishing that, but so is a weekly email or an alert system, both of which are more likely to be incorporated into someone's workflow.

Similarly, if someone comes to you and tells you that his business needs a predictive model, you need to dig deeper. What is this for? Is it to change something that he doesn't like? To make accurate predictions to get ahead of a trend? To automate a process? Or does the business need to generalize to a new case that's unlike any seen in order to inform a decision? These are all different needs, requiring different approaches. A predictive model is only a small part of that.

Vision (V)

Before we can start to acquire data, perform transformations, test ideas, and so on, we need some vision of where we are going and what it might look like to achieve our goal.

The vision is a glimpse of what it will look like to meet the need with data. It could consist of a mockup describing the intended results, or a sketch of the argument that we're going to make, or some particular questions that narrowly focus our aims.

Someone who is handed a data set and has not first thought about the context and needs of the organization will usually start and end with a narrow vision. It is rarely a good idea to start with data and go looking for things to do. That leads to stumbling on good ideas, mostly by accident.

Having a good vision is the part of scoping that is most dependent on experience. The ideas we will be able to come up with will mostly be variations on things that we have seen before. It is tremendously useful to acquire a good mental library of examples by reading widely and experimenting with new ideas. We can expand our library by talking to people about the problems they've solved, reading books

on data science or reading classics (like Edward Tufte and Richard Feynman), following blogs, attending conferences and meetups, and experimenting with new ideas all the time.

There is no shortcut to gaining experience, but there is a fast way to learn from your mistakes, and that is to try to make as many of them as you can. Especially if you are just getting started, creating things in quantity is more important than creating things of quality. There is a saying in the world of Go (the east Asian board game): lose your first fifty games of Go as quickly as possible.

The two main tactics we have available to us for refining our vision are mockups and argument sketches.

A mockup is a low-detail idealization of what the final result of all the work might look like. Mockups can take the form of a few sentences reporting the outcome of an analysis, a simplified graph that illustrates a relationship between variables, or a user interface sketch that captures how people might use a tool. A mockup primes our imagination and starts the wheels turning about what we need to assemble to meet the need. Mockups, in one form or another, are the single most useful tool for creating focused, useful data work (see Figure 1-1).

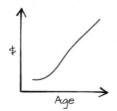

Figure 1-1. A visual mockup

Mockups can also come in the form of sentences:

Sentence Mockups

The probability that a female employee asks for a flexible schedule is roughly the same as the probability that a male employee asks for a flexible schedule.

There are 10,000 users who shopped with service X. Of those 10,000, 2,000 also shopped with service Y. The ones who shopped with service Y skew older, but they also buy more.

Keep in mind that a mockup is not the actual answer we expect to arrive at. Instead, a mockup is an example of the kind of result we would expect, an illustration of the form that results might take. Whether we are designing a tool or pulling data together, concrete knowledge of what we are aiming at is incredibly valuable.

Without a mockup, it's easy to get lost in abstraction, or to be unsure what we are actually aiming toward. We risk missing our goals completely while the ground slowly shifts beneath our feet. Mockups also make it much easier to focus in on what is important, because mockups are shareable. We can pass our few sentences, idealized graphs, or user interface sketches off to other people to solicit their opinion in a way that diving straight into source code and spreadsheets can never do.

A mockup shows what we should expect to take away from a project. In contrast, an argument sketch tells us roughly what we need to do to be convincing at all. It is a loose outline of the statements that will make our work relevant and correct. While they are both collections of sentences, mockups and argument sketches serve very different purposes. Mockups give a flavor of the finished product, while argument sketches give us a sense of the logic behind the solution.

For example, if we want to know whether women and men are equally interested in flexible time arrangements, there are a few parts to making a convincing case. First, we need to have a good definition of who the women and men are that we are talking about. Second, we need to decide if we are interested in subjective measurement (like a survey), if we are interested in objective measurement (like the number of applications for a given job), or if we want to run an experiment. We could post the same job description but only show postings with flexible time to half of the people who visit a job site. There are certain reasons to find each of these compelling, ranging from the theory of survey design to mathematical rules for the design of experiments.

Thinking concretely about the argument made by a project is a valuable tool for orienting ourselves. Chapter 3 goes into greater depth about what the parts of an argument are and how they relate to working with data. Arguments occur both in a project and around the project, informing both their content and their rationale.

Pairing written mockups and written argument sketches is a concise way to get our understanding across, though sometimes one is more appropriate than the other. Continuing again with the longer examples:

Example 1

- Vision: The nonprofit that is trying to measure its successes will get an email of key performance indicators on a regular basis. The email will consist of graphs and automatically generated text.

- Mockup: After making a change to our marketing, we hit an enrollment goal this week that we've never hit before, but it isn't being reflected in the success measures.

- Argument sketch: The nonprofit is doing well (or poorly) because it has high (or low) values for key performance indicators. After seeing the key performance indicators, the reader will have a good sense of the state of the nonprofit's activities and will be able to adjust accordingly.

Example 2

Here are several ideas for the marketing department looking to target new cities, depending on the details of the context:

Idea 1

- Vision: The marketing department that wants to improve its targeting will get a report that ranks cities by their predicted value to the company.

- Mockup: Austin, Texas, would provide a 20% return on investment per month. New York City would provide an 11% return on investment per month.

- Argument sketch: The department should focus on city X, because it is most likely to bring in high value. The definition of high value that we're planning to use is substantiated for the following reasons....

Idea 2

- Vision: The marketing department will get some software that implements a targeting model, which chooses a city to place advertisements in. Advertisements will be targeted automatically based on the model, through existing advertising interfaces.

- Mockup: 48,524 advertisements were placed today in 14 cities. 70% of them were in emerging markets.

- Argument sketch: Advertisements should be placed proportional to their future value. The department should feel confident that this automatic selector will be accurate without being watched.

Idea 3

- Vision: The marketing department will get a spreadsheet that can be dropped into the existing workflow. It will fill in some characteristics of a city and the spreadsheet will indicate what the estimated value would be.

- Mockup: By inputting gender and age skew and performance results for 20 cities, an estimated return on investment is placed next to each potential new market. Austin, Texas, is a good place to target based on age and gender skew, performance in similar cities, and its total market size.

- Argument sketch: The department should focus on city X, because it is most likely to bring in high value. The definition of high value that we're planning to use is substantiated for the following reasons....

Example 3

- Vision: The media organization trying to define user engagement will get a report outlining why a particular user engagement metric is the ideal one, with supporting examples; models that connect that metric to revenue, growth, and subscriptions; and a comparison against other metrics.

- Mockup: Users who score highly on engagement metric A are more likely to be readers at one, three, and six months than users who score highly on engagement metrics B or C. Engagement metric A is also more correlated with lifetime value than the other metrics.

- Argument sketch: The media organization should use this particular engagement metric going forward because it is predictive of other valuable outcomes.

Example 4

- Vision: The developers working on the corruption project will get a piece of software that takes in feeds of media sources and rates the chances that a particular politician is being talked about. The staff will set a list of names

and affiliations to watch for. The results will be fed into a database, which will feed a dashboard and email alert system.

- Mockup: A typical alert is that politician X, who was identified based on campaign contributions as a target to watch, has suddenly showed up on 10 news talk shows.

- Argument sketch: We have correctly kept tabs on politicians of interest, and so the people running the anti-corruption project can trust this service to do the work of following names for them.

In mocking up the outcome and laying out the argument, we are able to understand what success could look like. The final result may differ radically from what we set out to do. Regardless, having a rough understanding at the outset of a project is important. It is also okay to have several potential threads at this point and be open to trying each, such as with the marketing department example. They may end up complementing each other.

The most useful part of making mockups or fragments of arguments is that they let us work backward to fill in what we actually need to do. If we're looking to send an email of key performance indicators, we'd better come up with some to put into the email. If we're writing a report outlining why one engagement metric is the best and tying it to a user valuation model, we need to come up with an engagement metric and find or develop a user valuation model. The pieces start to fall into place.

At the end of everything, the finished work will often be fairly simple. Because of all of the work done in thinking about context and need, generating questions, and thinking about outcomes, our work will be the right kind of simple. Simple results are the most likely to get used.

Because of all of the work done in thinking about context and need, generating questions, and thinking about outcomes, our work will be the right kind of simple.

They will not always be simple, of course. Having room to flesh out complicated ideas is part of the point of thinking so much at the outset. When our work is complicated, we will benefit even more from having thought through some of the parts first.

When we're having trouble articulating a vision, it is helpful to start getting something down on paper or out loud to prime our brains. Drawing pretend graphs, talking through examples, making flow diagrams on whiteboards, and so on, are all good ways to get the juices flowing.

Outcome (O)

We need to understand how the work will actually make it back to the rest of the organization and what will happen once it is there. How will it be used? How will it be integrated into the organization? Who will own its integration? Who will use it? In the end, how will its success be measured?

If we don't understand the intended use of what we produce, it is easy to get lost in the weeds and end up making something that nobody will want or use. What's the purpose of all this work if it does nobody any good?

The outcome is distinct from the vision; the vision is focused on what form the work will take at the end, while the outcome is focused on what will happen when we are "done." Here are the outcomes for each of the examples we've been looking at so far:

- The metrics email for the nonprofit needs to be set up, verified, and tweaked. Sysadmins at the nonprofit need to be briefed on how to keep the email system running. The CTO and CEO need to be trained on how to read the metrics emails, which will consist of a document written to explain it.

- The marketing team needs to be trained in using the model (or software) in order to have it guide their decisions, and the success of the model needs to be gauged in its effect on sales. If the result ends up being a report instead, it will be delivered to the VP of Marketing, who will decide based on the recommendations of the report which cities will be targeted and relay the instructions to his staff. To make sure everything is clear, there will be a follow-up meeting two weeks and then two months after the delivery.

- The report going to the media organization about engagement metrics will go to the head of online business. If she signs off on its findings, the selected user engagement metric will be incorporated by the business analysts into the performance measures across the entire organization. Funding for existing and future initiatives will be based in part on how they affect the new engagement metric. A follow-up study will be conducted in six months to verify that the new metric is successfully predicting revenue.

- The media mention finder needs to be integrated with the existing mention database. The staff needs to be trained to use the dashboard. The IT person needs to be informed of the existence of the tool and taught how to maintain it. Periodic updates to the system will be needed in order to keep it correctly parsing new sources, as bugs are uncovered. The developers who are doing the integration will be in charge of that. Three months after the delivery, we will follow up to check on how well the system is working.

Figuring out what the right outcomes are boils down to three things. First, who will have to handle this next? Someone else is likely to have to interpret or implement or act on our work. Who are they, what are their requirements, and what do we need to do differently from our initial ideas to address their concerns?

Second, who or what will handle keeping this work relevant, if anyone? Do we need to turn our work into a piece of software that runs repeatedly? Will we have to return in a few months? More often than not, analyses get re-run, even if they are architected to be run once.

Third, what do we hope will change after we have finished the work? Note again that "having a model" is not a suitable change; what *in terms that matter to the partners* will have changed? How will we verify that this has happened?

Thinking through the outcome before embarking on a project, along with knowing the context, identifying the right needs, and honing our vision, improves the chance that we will do something that actually gets used.

Seeing the Big Picture

Tying everything together, we can see that each of these parts forms a coherent narrative about what we might accomplish by working with data to solve this problem.

First, let's see what it would look like to sketch out a problem without much structured thinking:

> We will create a logistic regression of web log data using SAS to find patterns in reader behavior. We will predict the probability that someone comes back after visiting the site once.

Compare this to a well-thought-out scope:

This media organization produces news for a wide audience. It makes money through advertising and premium subscriptions to its content. The person who asked for some advice is the head of online business.

This organization does not know the right way to define an engaged reader. The standard web metric of unique daily users doesn't really capture what it means to be a reader of an online newspaper. When it comes to optimizing revenue, growth, and promoting subscriptions, 30 different people visiting on 30 different days means something very different from 1 person visiting for 30 days in a row. What is the right way to measure engagement that respects these goals?

When this project is finished, the head of online business will get a report outlining why a particular user engagement metric is the ideal one, with supporting examples; models that connect that metric to revenue, growth, and subscriptions; and a comparison against other metrics.

If she signs off on its findings, the selected user engagement metric will be incorporated into the performance measures across the entire organization. Institutional support and funding for existing and future initiatives will be based in part on how they affect the new engagement metric. A follow-up study will be conducted in six months to verify that the new metric is successfully predicting revenue, growth, and subscription rates.

A good story about a project and a good scope of a project are hard to tell apart. It is clear that at the outset, we do not actually know what the right metric will be or even what tools we will use. Focusing on the math or the software at the expense of the context, need, vision, and outcome means wasted time and energy.

What Next?

With a basic understanding of the four areas of a project scope (context, needs, vision, and outcome), we turn our attention to filling in the details of the project. By thinking deeply before digging into the data, we maximize our chances of doing something useful as opposed to simply the first things that come to mind.

Working with data is a process that you lose yourself in. There is a natural tension between going into exploration as quickly as possible and spending more time thinking and planning up front. When balanced properly, they are mutually beneficial. However, diving in quickly and getting lost in the data exerts a natural siren song on those of us who work with data professionally. It takes effort and patience to put time into thinking up front, but it is effort that is duly rewarded.

Before we start down rabbit holes that may or may not take us somewhere useful, and after we have a rough project scope, we need to take some more steps to clarify the details of the problem we are working on. That process is the focus of this chapter. This includes important discussions with decision makers and implementers, figuring out how to define key terms, considering what arguments we might make, posing open questions to ourselves, and deciding in what order to pursue different ideas.

There is no particular order to these steps. A project might be so simple that every area is obvious and we don't need to engage with anybody else or do any more thinking before we dive into the data work. *This is rare.* More than likely, there will be things that need clarification in our own heads (and in the minds of others) to avoid wasted effort.

It's possible to know everything you need to know for a small, personal project before you even begin. Larger projects, which are more likely to cause something important to change, always have messier beginnings. Information is incomplete, expectations are miscalibrated, and definitions are too loose to be useful. In the same way that the nitty-gritty of data science presumes messier data than is given for problems in a statistics course, the problem definition for large, applied problems is always messier than the toy problems we think up ourselves.

As we move on to the rest of the project, it's critical to remember to take careful notes along the way. There are minor intellectual and technical decisions made throughout a project that will be crucial in writing the final documentation. Having a final, written version of the work we do means a much greater chance to reproduce our work again months or years down the line. It also means we are more likely to catch our own errors as we put our ideas down into words.

Refining the Vision

The vision we expressed in our first pass at a scope is often sufficient to get started, but not complete enough to guide our actions.

We refine our vision by improving our intuition about the problem. We improve our intuition by talking to people, trying out ideas, gathering questions, and running simple experiments. We want to spend time up front maximizing our understanding. It pays to make our early work investigative rather than definitive.

Pointed questions explore the limits of our current knowledge, and focusing on question generation is a good use of time. Good questions also offer up new ways to frame a problem. At the end of the day, it is usually how we frame the problem, not the tools and techniques that we use to answer it, that determine how valuable our work is.

Some of these questions will be preliminary and serve to illustrate the breadth of the problem, such as knowing whether there are ten thousand or ten million purchases per month to study. Others will form the core of the work we are looking to undertake, such as how exactly those purchases are related over time for the same customer.

One technique for coming up with questions is to take a description of a need or of a process that generated our data and to ask every question that we can think of—this is called *kitchen sink interrogation*. In a kitchen sink interrogation, we are generating questions, not looking for answers. We want to get a sense of the lay of the land. A few minutes up front can save days or weeks down the line.

If our customers leave our website too quickly, why do they leave? What does it mean to leave? At what points do they leave? What separates the ones who leave from the ones who stay? Are there things that we have done before that have changed customer behavior? Are there quick things we can try now? How do we know what their behavior is? How reliable is that source? What work has already been done on this problem?

If we're trying to understand user engagement, what metrics are already being used? Where do they break down? What are they good at predicting? What are some

alternative metrics that we haven't looked at yet? How will we validate what a good metric is? By collecting questions with a kitchen sink interrogation, we start to get a sense for what is known and what is unknown.

Another technique, *working backward*, starts from the mockups or argument sketches and imagines each step that has to be achieved between the vision and where we are right now. In the process of working backward, we kick up a number of questions that will help to orient us. When we're lucky, we will figure out that a certain task is not feasible long before we've committed resources to it.

The same techniques discussed in Chapter 1 do not go away once we have a basic sense of the vision. Mockups and argument sketches are continuously useful. Having a clear vision of what our goal looks like—whether it's in the form of a sentence describing what we would learn or a hand-drawn sketch of a graph—is incredibly instructive in its production and a wonderful guiding light when we are deep in the trenches. Having a clear idea of what numbers we expect to come out of a process before we start it also means that we will catch errors right away.

We can also borrow tactics that we used to refine needs. Walking through a scenario or roleplaying from the perspective of the final consumer is a good way to catch early problems in our understanding of what we are aiming at. If we are producing a map or a spreadsheet or an interactive tool, there is always going to be someone on the other side. Thinking about what their experience will be like helps keep us focused.

Once results start to come in, in whatever form makes sense for the work we are doing, it pays to continually refer back to this early process to see if we are still on track. Do these numbers make sense? Is the scenario we envisioned possible?

Techniques for refining the vision

Interviews
> Talk to experts in the subject matter, especially people who work on a task all the time and have built up strong intuition. Their intuition may or may not match the data, but having their perspective is invaluable at building your intuition.

Rapid investigation
> Get order of magnitude estimates, related quantities, easy graphs, and so on, to build intuition for the topic.

Kitchen sink interrogation
Ask every question that comes to mind relating to a need or a data collection process. Just the act of asking questions will open up new ideas. Before it was polluted as a concept, this was the original meaning of the term brainstorming.

Working backward
Start from the finished idea and figure out what is needed immediately prior in order to achieve the outcome. Then see what is prior to that, and prior to that, and so on, until you arrive at data or knowledge you already have.

More mockups
Drawing further and more well-defined idealizations of the outcome not only helps to figure out what the actual needs are, but also more about what the final result might look like.

Roleplaying
Pretend you are the final consumer or user of a project, and think out loud about the process of interacting with the finished work.

Deep Dive: Real Estate and Public Transit

An extended example will be instructive. Suppose that a firm in New York that controls many rental properties is interested in improving its profitability on apartment buildings it buys. It considers itself a data-driven company, and likes to understand the processes that drive rental prices. It has an idea that public transit access is a key factor in rental prices, but is not sure of the relationship or what to do with it.

We have a context (a data-driven New York residential real estate company) and a vague need (it wants to somehow use public transit data to improve its understanding of rental prices). After some deep conversation, and walking through scenarios of what it might do if it understood how transit access affects rental prices, it turns out the company actually has several specific needs.

First and simplest, it wants to confirm its hunch that rental prices are heavily dependent on public transit access in New York. Even just confirming that there is a relationship is enough to convince the company that more work in this area is warranted. Second, it wants to know if some apartments may be under- or overpriced relative to their worth. If the apartments are mispriced, it will help the

company set prices more effectively, and improve profitability. And third, the company would love to be able to predict where real estate prices are heading.

Note that the latter two needs did not mention public transit data explicitly. It may turn out in the process of working with this data that public transit data isn't useful, but all the other data we dig up actually is! Will the real estate company be disappointed? Certainly not. Public transit data will be the focus of our work, but the goal isn't so much to use public transit data as it is to improve the profitability of the company. If we stick too literally to the original mandate, we may miss opportunities. We may even come up with other goals or opportunities in the course of our analyses.

Before we go too far, what is our intuition telling us? Knowing the subject matter, or talking to subject matter experts, is key here. Reading apartment advertisements would be a good way to build up an understanding of what is plausible. Apartment prices probably are higher close to transit lines; certainly listings on real estate websites list access to trains as an amenity. Putting ourselves in the shoes of someone getting to work, we can realize that the effect likely drops off rapidly, because people don't like to walk more than 10 or 15 minutes if they can help it. The effects are probably different in different neighborhoods and along different transit lines, because different destinations are more interesting or valuable than others.

Moving on to the vision, we can try out a few ideas for what a result would look like. If our final product contained a graph, what would it be a graph of? Roughly speaking, it would be a graph of "price" against "nearness to transit," with price falling as we got farther away from transit. In reality it would be a scatterplot, but drawing a line graph is probably more informative at this stage. Actually sketching a mockup of a basic graph, with labels, is a useful exercise (Figure 2-1).

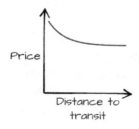

Figure 2-1. Mockup graph

We can recognize from this that we will need some way to define price and proximity. This presentation is probably too simple, because we know that the

relationship likely depends on other factors, like neighborhood. We would need a series of graphs, at least. This could be part of a solution to the first two needs, verifying that there is a strong relationship between public transit and the housing market, and trying to predict whether apartments are under- or overpriced.

Digging into our experience, we know that graphs are just one way to express a relationship. Two others are models and maps. How might we capture the relevant relationships with a statistical model?

A statistical model would be a way to relate some notion of transit access to some notion of apartment price, controlling for other factors. We can clarify our idea with a mockup. The mockup here would be a sentence interpreting the hypothetical output. Results from a model might have conclusions like, "In New York City, apartment prices fall by 5% for every block away from the A train, compared to similar apartments." Because we thought about graphs already, we know that one of the things we will need to control for in a model is neighborhood and train line. A good model might let us use much more data. For example, investigating the government data archives on this topic reveals that turnstile data is freely available in some cities.

A model has the potential to meet all three of our needs, albeit with more effort. Model verification would let us know if the relationship is plausible, outlier detection would allow us to find mispriced apartments, and running the model on fake data would allow us to predict the future (to some extent). Each of these may require different models or may not be plausible, given the data that is available. A model might also support other kinds of goals—for example, if we wanted to figure out which train line had the largest effect on prices.

If our vision is a transit map, it would be a heat map of apartment prices, along with clearly marked transit lines and probably neighborhood boundaries. There would need to be enough detail to make the city's layout recognizable. Depending on the resolution of the map, this could potentially meet the first two needs (making a case for a connection and finding outliers) as well, through visual inspection. A map is easier to inspect, but harder to calibrate or interpret.

Each has its strengths and weaknesses. A scatterplot is going to be easy to make once we have some data, but potentially misleading. The statistical model will collapse down a lot of variation in the data in order to arrive at a general, interpretable conclusion, potentially missing interesting patterns. The map is going to be limited in its ability to account for variables that aren't spatial, and we may have a harder time interpreting the results. Each would lend itself to a variety of arguments.

What we finally end up with will probably be more complicated than the basic things we outline here. There may actually be a combination of two or all three of these, or some output we haven't considered yet; maybe a website that the firm can use to access the model predictions with a few knobs to specify apartment details, or a spreadsheet that encodes a simple model for inclusion in other projects. Any graph, model, or map we make for this project will depend on additional bits of analysis to back up their conclusions.

Another way to explain this process is to say that we begin with strong assumptions and slowly relax them until we find something we can actually achieve. A graph of price against proximity, or a user interface with two buttons, is almost certainly too simple to be put into practice. To make such a project work requires much stronger assumptions that we can make in practice. That shouldn't stop us from trying to express our ideas in this kind of clean way. Sometimes the details, even when they take up most of our time, are only epicycles on top of a larger point that we will be worse off if we forget.

Don't forget the utility of a few concrete examples in spurring the imagination. Before building a map, we should try plugging a few intersections into real estate websites to get a feel for how the aspects of homes might vary with distance and price. The same goes for reading classifieds. There may be entire aspects of apartments that were not obvious at first glance, like proximity to highly regarded schools, that will be mentioned in the apartment description and could have a huge effect on price. Always seek to immerse yourself in some particular examples, even if it just means reading the first 10 or 20 lines of a table in depth before building a model.

Always seek to immerse yourself in some particular examples, even if it just means reading the first ten or twenty lines of a table in depth before building a model.

Deep Dive Continued: Working Forward

Having imagined the end of our work, it is helpful to think about what kind of data is appropriate for defining the variables. Having spread our wings, it is time to get a little realistic and start working forward from what we have.

What will we use for apartment prices? It is common in the real estate industry to use price per square foot, to normalize against differences in apartment size. Finding historical price-per-square-foot data across an entire city may be as simple

as purchasing a database, or it could be a much more involved process of connecting public and private data together.

And what is transit access? Note that, despite the easy way we were able to draw that initial graph, it is not clear at first blush how to even define the term transit access! A little kitchen sink interrogation is useful here.

First, what is transit? The initial conversation was sparked from subway lines. Do buses count? Bus access will be much harder to show on a map than train access, but buses are a necessity in areas that are less well connected to trains. Knowing where the company actually operates might be useful here. How long do people actually walk? Where do people in each neighborhood actually go? Is that information available? Are there people we could talk to about getting end-to-end transit data, maybe from existing surveys? Could employment records be useful?

"Transit access" itself could be about walking distance to train or bus lines, or it could be about average travel time from a point to important landmarks, like the Empire State Building or Wall Street in New York City. Which one we pick will make a big difference!

In refining the vision we can also recognize that this is a causal question of sorts (how much does being near a subway station increase prices *compared to an identical apartment that was farther away?*), and therefore calls for a causal argument pattern. Chapters 4 and 5 cover argument patterns in detail, but for our purposes we can recognize that we will, at a minimum, need to acquire additional information to help distinguish the effect of proximity to transit from, say, higher prices on more luxurious apartments. More luxurious apartments may have been built closer to the subway to take advantage of the better location, and so on.

Further refining the vision, we know that apartment prices will be a continuous variable, neighborhood will probably be an important confounder, and each transit line will probably contribute a different amount. We will need locations of apartments and transit stops, information on subways accessed by each stop, and, if we build a model, a reasonable distance or travel time function to tie things together. If we want to understand how these things change over time, we will need not only a snapshot, but also a historical record. The breadth of making a full model starts to become clear in a way it might not have been at the start.

At this stage we may become aware of the limitations we are likely to face. It will probably be hard to encode an "apartment quality" measure. A proxy metric, like some sense of how recently or frequently an apartment was refurbished, requires additional data like city records. Our results may be hard to interpret without a great deal of work, but it may be good enough for our needs. And if we want to

understand historical relationships between transit connectivity and apartment prices, we have to figure out how far back to go and how to handle the additional complexities inherent in working with time data.

Thinking hard about the outcome can clear this up. What will be different after we are done? Might the easiest need be sufficient for now? A more purely observational study would be fine. Or might there be enough buy-in to get this work widely used within the firm? And is the time component really that valuable? Each of these goals is different, the arguments that are needed are different, and they will call for different levels of investment of time and energy. If we don't think about how the work will be used after we finish, we may end up working on something pointless.

Who will maintain this work after we finish? Keeping a map up-to-date is probably easier than a model with a dozen separate data sources. Are all the sources we are interested in available programmatically, or would we have to take weeks of time to get them again next year?

How will we know if we have done a good job? How do we cross-check our results? For example, we could look at how quickly or slowly each apartment was rented, as a way of verifying that we predicted over- or underpricing correctly. Naturally, this is complicated by the speed with which the rental market moves in a big city, but it is worth a thought nevertheless.

Deep Dive Continued: Scaffolding

Having elaborated our vision and what the pieces are that we plan to work with, the next step is to consider our project's scaffolding. How can we go about our tasks so that at each step we can evaluate what is taking shape and see if we need to change direction? We want to avoid looking back in horror at having wasted our time on something useless.

Especially at the beginning, we want to find things to do that will be fast and informative. The simple truth is that we don't know in advance what will be the right things to pursue; and if we knew that already, we would have little need for our work. Before we do anything slow, or only informative at the margins, we want to focus on building intuition—and eventually that means poking around with data.

If we have already collected some data, simple tabulations, visualizations, and reorganized raw data are the best way to quickly build intuition. Just combining and slicing various relevant data sets can be very informative, as long as we do not get stuck on this as our main task.

Models that can be easily fit and interpreted (like a linear or logistic model), or models that have great predictive performance without much work (like random forests), serve as excellent places to start a predictive task. Using a scatterplot of latitude and longitude points as a first approximation map is a great way to start a geospatial project. And so on.

It is important, though, to not get too deep into these exploratory steps and forget about the larger picture. Setting time limits (in hours or, at most, days) for these exploratory projects is a helpful way to avoid wasting time. To avoid losing the big picture, it also helps to write down the intended steps at the beginning. An explicitly written-down *scaffolding plan* can be a huge help to avoid getting sucked deeply into work that is ultimately of little value. A scaffolding plan lays out what our next few goals are, and what we expect to shift once we achieve them.

It also helps when we understand the argument or arguments we are looking to make. Understanding the outline of our argument will lead us to discover which pieces of analysis are most central. Chapter 3 discusses the details of arguments, including transformation, evidence, justifications, and arranging claims. These let us solve potentially complicated needs with data. With a sketch of the argument in place, it is easier to figure out the most central thing we need to work on. The easiest way to perform this sketching is to write out our ideas as paragraphs and imagine how we will fill in the details.

In the case of the apartment prices and public transit, finding or plotting a map of apartment prices next to a base layer of transit connections is probably the easiest thing to do first. By looking at the map, we can see whether such a relationship seems plausible, and start to gain intuition for the problem of making scatterplots or building a model.

Building exploratory scatterplots should precede the building of a model, if for no reason other than to check that the intuition gained from making the map makes sense. The relationships may be so obvious, or the confounders so unimportant, that the model is unnecessary. A lack of obvious relationships in pairwise scatterplots does not mean that a model of greater complexity would not be able to find signal, but if that's what we're up against, it is important to know it ahead of time. Similarly, building simple models before tackling more complex ones will save us time and energy.

Scaffolding is the art of prioritizing our aims and not going too far down that rabbit hole. How can we proceed in a way that is as instructive as possible at every step?

Verifying Understanding

In any scaffolding plan, it is important to build in explicit checks with the partners or decision makers to ensure that we understand their needs properly. It keeps us focused, and it builds trust. It is better to overcommunicate, especially with new partners, than it is to assume that we are on the same page for a week only to find we have built something pointless.

Find a convenient medium and explain the partners' needs back to them, asking if you have understood things properly. Mention generally what your thoughts are around your vision, such as the form that the results would take, without going into too much detail. The goal is conceptual agreement, not a detailed critique of the project, unless they are data-savvy and particularly interested. The details will evolve throughout the project anyway.

Explicitly ask them if they agree that you have understood what they are looking for, and if they have any more questions. You should feel confident that you are doing something that they will use. This doesn't need to be a formal meeting; it can often be accomplished with a quick conversation.

If one or more people will be needed to implement the final work, talk to them and make sure that their requirements are being represented. If someone else will be installing a script we create into production software, who will be in charge of cleaning it up and keeping it running? Talk to them and make sure that you understand what they need.

We will go through basically the same process on a regular basis for large projects, and at least when all the work is done for a project of any size, so pay attention to how these discussions go.

Partners and decision makers often have intuitive understandings of the processes they are looking to understand better, or at least have some idea of what concrete examples of what they're interested in will look like. Intuition like that is invaluable, and should never be overlooked. Spending lots of time talking to people who deal with a process is a smart way to get the intuition needed to build a data-based argument that can create real knowledge.

We know that we have grasped the problem well when we can explain our strategy to these partners in terms that matter to them (even if they have no knowledge of data science), and we receive back enthusiastic understanding.

Getting Our Hands Dirty

Once we have data, we may find that our initial ideas were wrong or that the need can be met even more easily than we thought. Regardless, thinking explicitly before we dive into them will make what we do far more productive.

We need to spend time data gathering: actually acquiring the data we will need. This step might be easy, or it may take a long time. We might have one database or API call, or we may need to strategize about how to store all the data we will require. We may need to contact people in positions of authority in order to acquire data. We may need to make trade-offs of accuracy against price or time to acquire new data.

Once some data is gathered, we can begin the transformations. We usually put raw data into a common format, then transform the data into graphs, models, tables, and summaries that can serve as evidence for a larger argument. These steps can take the longest amount of time. As part of the scaffolding, we should plan to start with easy transformations (like exploratory graphs or summary statistics) and then easy models, before moving on to more sophisticated or complicated models. Often, easy transformations will serve well enough to make a valid argument and additional work is not necessary.

Once the data is transformed and ready to serve as evidence, we can evaluate the strength of our arguments. By updating the few paragraphs we wrote out at the beginning with new information, we will know if what we have done fits into the larger goal or not. Is there another thing we forgot to justify or that we need to explore? Do we need to continue on to make a more complicated model? Are there alternative interpretations of what we have found that require us to find something else to help us decide between them? Does this argument even make any sense, given the data we have collected?

Say, for example, that we're outlining our argument to ourselves after collecting public transit and apartment price, and we realize that we're not sure if we have an unbiased sample of apartments. We have choices; do we want to acknowledge that bias and claim the conclusions to be more limited? Or do we perhaps want to make an argument as to why the data we have is actually representative of the city as a whole? We might find that most apartments are actually listed on Craigslist, or that, for the demographic that will be interested in using this information, nearly all apartments are listed on Craigslist. Strong arguments will rarely consist only of a single piece of evidence, though other strands of the arguments around them may be implied or gestured at.

After we have arrived at a useful point, we can arrange the results into a pleasing form, keeping in mind the needs of our audience. Will we only show the most damning graph, or does it make more sense to present a chorus of models and summaries? Should we present a series of claims each chained to another, or present a number of claims in parallel? If we're building a tool, which things should be optional and which fixed? If we're writing a narrative, which examples should we use to reinforce our point?

Finally, we need to present what we've done. The actual written copy, the final form of the graphs, the neat table, the interactive tool with a carefully designed UI —these are all part of having a good presentation. Presentation matters tremendously. At the very least, there are genre conventions in every field that are worth following in order to be taken seriously; tone is important in presentation. Highly polished, beautiful graphics may be considered fussy in an academic setting, but are necessary for an earnings report for a design company. A very abstract problem presentation is inappropriate for a board meeting, but useful for demonstrating a technique to colleagues. And so on.

As in any creative field, working with data is not a linear process where we proceed from a grand statement of the problem at hand and gradually fill in the pieces until we are satisfied. Sometimes we are lucky and problems flow like that, but more often (and more interestingly), there is an interplay of clarification and action that slowly brings us to a better place than where we started.

Arguments

Data consists of observations about the world—records in a database, notes in a logbook, images on a hard drive. There is nothing magical about them. These observations may prove useful or useless, accurate or inaccurate, helpful or unhelpful. At the outset, they are only observations. Observations alone are not enough to act on. When we connect observations to how the world works, we have the opportunity to make knowledge. Arguments are what make knowledge out of observations.

There are many kinds of knowledge. Sometimes we have an accurate, unimpeachable mental model of how something works. Other times we have an understanding that is just good enough. And other times still, the knowledge is not in a person at all, but in an algorithm quietly puzzling out how the world fits together. What concerns us in working with data is how to get as good a connection as possible between the observations we collect and the processes that shape our world.

Knowing how arguments work gives us special powers. If we understand how to make convincing arguments, we can put tools and techniques into their proper place as parts of a whole. Without a good understanding of arguments, we make them anyway (we cannot help ourselves, working with data), but they are more likely to be small and disconnected.

By being aware of how arguments hang together, we can better:

- Get across complicated ideas
- Build a project in stages
- Get inspiration from well-known patterns of argument
- Substitute techniques for one another
- Make our results more coherent
- Present our findings
- Convince ourselves and others that our tools do what we expect

Thinking explicitly about arguments is a powerful technique, with a long history in philosophy, law, the humanities, and academic debate. It is a more fleshed-out example of using a structure to help us think with data. Thinking about the argument we are making can come into play at any point in working with a problem —from gathering ideas at the very beginning, to ensuring that we are making sense before releasing something into the wild.

Audience and Prior Beliefs

Only in mathematics is it possible to demonstrate something beyond all doubt. When held to that standard, we find ourselves quickly overwhelmed.

Our ideal in crafting an argument is a skeptical but friendly audience, suitable to the context. A skeptical audience is questioning of our observations, not swayed by emotional appeals, but not so skeptical as to be dismissive. The ideal audience is curious; humble, but not stupid. It is an idealized version of ourselves at our best, intelligent and knowledgeable but not intimately familiar with the problem at hand.

With the skeptical ideal in mind, it becomes easier to make a general argument, but it is also easier to make an argument to a specific audience. After making an argument for an ideal audience, it is easy to remove some parts and emphasize others to meet the needs of one or more particular audiences. Simplifying or expanding on certain things for an audience is fine, but lying is not. Something that good data work inherits from the scientific method is that it is bad form to cheat by preying on gullibility or ignorance. It is bad form, and in the long run it will cause the ruin of a business (or maybe a civilization).

An argument moves from statements that the audience already believes to statements they do not yet believe. At the beginning, they already agree with some statements about the world. After they hear the argument, there are new statements they will agree to that they would not have agreed to before. This is the key insight as to how an argument works—moving from prior belief to new belief to establish knowledge in a defensible way.

No audience, neither our ideal nor a real one, is 100% skeptical, a blank slate that doesn't already believe something. Many things are already background knowledge, taken for granted. Consider an argument that a rocket is safe to launch. There are certain statements that any reasonable audience will take for granted. The laws of physics aren't going to change mid-flight. Neither will multiplication tables. Whether those laws and our understanding of metallurgy and aerodynamics will result in a safe launch requires an argument. The background knowledge of the equations of motion and laws of chemistry do not.

Most of the prior beliefs and facts that go into an argument are never explicitly spelled out. To explicitly spell out every facet of an argument is silly. Russell and Whitehead famously took 379 pages to *set up the preliminaries* for the proof that 1+1=2[1]. If the audience lacks some knowledge, either because of ignorance or reasonable doubt, it is important to be able to provide that (while not going overboard).

Prior belief, knowledge, and facts extend to more than just scientific laws. Audiences have dense webs of understanding that pre-date any argument presented to them. This collection of understanding defines what is reasonable in any given situation.

For example, one not-so-obvious but common prior belief is that the data in an argument comes from the same source that the arguer says it does. This is typically taken for granted. On the other hand, there may have been corruptions in what was collected or stored, or an intruder may have tampered with the data. If these would be reasonable possibilities to our skeptical audience (say the analysis involves an experimental sensor, or the audience is full of spooks), then any argument will need to address the question of validity before continuing. There needs to be something that the audience is tentatively willing to agree to, or else there is no way forward.

The algebra or mathematical theory behind specific techniques constitute another kind of common prior knowledge. Most arguments can safely avoid discussing these. Some real audiences may need their hand held more than others, or will be at our throats for execution details. But for the most part, the details of techniques are safely thought of as background knowledge.

Another source of prior or background knowledge is commonly known facts. Chicago is a city in the United States of America, which is a nation-state in the Northern Hemisphere on Earth, a planet. When it is necessary to compare Chicago to the whole US, their explicit relationship is rarely brought up. Of course, what is commonly understood varies by the actual audience. If the audience is in India, the location of Chicago in America may be an open issue. At that point, the audience will believe the atlas, and we'll be back to something that is commonly accepted.

"Wisdom" is also taken for granted in many arguments. When I worked at an online dating site, it was commonly taken for granted in internal discussions that men are more likely to send messages to women than the other way around. It was something that we had verified before, and had no reason to think had changed drastically. In the course of making an argument, it was already commonly under-

---

1. Volume 1 of *Principia Mathematica* by Alfred North Whitehead and Bertrand Russell (Cambridge University Press, page 379). The proof was actually not completed until Volume 2.

stood by the audience and didn't need to be spelled out or verified, though it could have been.

Not all wisdom can be verified. In the online dating example, we assumed that most of the people who had filled out their profiles actually corresponded to genuine human beings. We assumed that, for the most part, their gender identity offline matched their identity online. It may be painful to take some ideas for granted, but it is a necessity. We should aspire to act reasonably given the data at hand, not require omnipotence to move forward. People rarely require omnipotence in practice, but it might surprise you how many people seem to think it is a prerequisite for an explanation of how arguments work.

Building an Argument

Visual schematics (lines, boxes, and other elements that correspond to parts of an argument) can be a useful way to set up an argument, but I have found that sentences and fragments of sentences are actually far more flexible and more likely to make their way into actual use.

Prior facts and wisdom will typically enter into an argument without being acknowledged, so there is not much to show here at this point. As we go through the parts of an argument, examples of how each idea is produced in written language will appear here, in these sidebars.

To make the ideas more transparent, I have also marked the concepts introduced in each section with tags like *(Claim)*. In a real argument, it's rare to explicitly call out claims and evidence and so on, but it is nevertheless instructive to try while developing an argument. One more thing to note: the following example is made up. It is plausible, but unresearched. Anybody found citing it as truth down the line will be publicly shamed in a future edition of this book.

Claims

Arguments are built around claims. Before hearing an argument, there are some statements the audience would not endorse. After all the analyzing, mapping, modeling, graphing, and final presentation of the results, we think they should agree to these statements. These are the claims. Put another way, a claim is a statement that could be reasonably doubted but that we believe we can make a case for. All arguments contain one or more claims. There is often, but not necessarily, one main claim, supported by one or more subordinate claims.

Suppose that we needed to improve the safety of a neighborhood that has been beset by muggings. We analyze the times and places where muggings happen, looking for patterns. Our main claim is that police officers should patrol more at these places and times. Our subordinate claims are that there is a problem with muggings; that the lack of police at certain places and times exacerbates the problem; and that the added cost of such deployments is reasonable given the danger. The first and last points may or may not require much of an argument, depending on the audience, whereas the second will require some kind of analysis for sure.

Note that the claim is in terms that the decision makers actually care about. In this case, they care about whether the lack of police in certain places and times exacerbates muggings, not what model we built and what techniques we used to assess that model's fit. Being able to say that our model has good generalization error will end up being an important part of making a tight argument, but it functions as support, not as a big idea.

In the details justifying our claim, we could swap out another technique for assessing the quality of our model to show that we had a reasonable grasp of the patterns of muggings. Different techniques[2] make different assumptions, but some might be chosen purely for practical reasons. The techniques are important, but putting them into an argument frame makes it obvious which parts are essential and which are accidental.

Let us turn our attention back to the task of predicting how public transit affects real estate prices over time. Here is where thinking about the full problem really shines. There is no single statistical tool that is sufficient to create confidence in either a causal relationship or the knowledge that a pattern observed should continue to hold in the future. There are collections of things we can do, held together by strong arguments (such as sensitivity analysis or a paired design) that can do the job and make a case for a causal relationship. None of them are purely statistical techniques; they all require a case be made for why they are appropriate beyond how well they fit the data.

---

2. In this case, for example, Bayes factors for cross-validation.

Claims

(Claim) A 5% reduction in average travel time to the rest of the city results in a 10% increase in apartment prices, with the reverse true as well, an effect which persists. *(Subclaim)* We know this is true because we have looked back at historical apartment prices and transit access and seen that the effect persists. *(Subclaim)* More importantly, when there have been big shocks in transit access, like the opening of a new train stop or the closing of a bus route, there have been effects of this magnitude on apartment prices visible within a year.

Evidence, Justification, and Rebuttals

A key part of any argument is evidence. Claims do not demonstrate themselves. Evidence is the introduction of facts into an argument.

Our evidence is rarely raw data. Raw data needs to be transformed into something else, something more compact, before it can be part of an argument: a graph, a model, a sentence, a map. It is rare that we can get an audience to understand something just from lists of facts. Transformations make data intelligible, allowing raw data to be incorporated into an argument.

A transformation puts an interpretation on data by highlighting things that we take to be essential. Counting all of the sales in a month is a transformation, as is plotting a graph or fitting a statistical model of page visits against age, or making a map of every taxi pickup in a city.

Returning to our transit example, if we just wanted to show that there is *some* relationship between transit access and apartment prices, a high-resolution map of apartment prices overlaid on a transit map would be reasonable evidence, as would a two-dimensional histogram or scatterplot of the right quantities. For the bolder claims (for example, that the relationship is predictable in some way and can be forecast into the future), we need more robust evidence, like sophisticated models. These, too, are ways of transforming data into evidence to serve as part of an argument.

Evidence and Transformations

A 5% reduction in average travel time to the rest of the city results in a 10% increase in apartment prices, with the reverse true as well, an effect which persists. We know this is true because we have looked back at historical apartment prices and transit access and seen that the effect persists. *(Transformation)* This graph, based on *(Evidence)* 20 years of raw price data from the City, demonstrates how strong the relationship is.

More importantly, when there have been big shocks in transit access, like the opening of a new train stop, or the closing of a bus route, there have been effects on apartment prices visible within a year. *(Transformation, Evidence)* Average prices of apartments for each of the following five blocks, with lines indicating the addition or closure of a new train route within two blocks of that street, demonstrate the rapid change. On average, closing a train stop results in a *(Transformation, Evidence)* 10% decline in apartment prices for apartments within two blocks away over the next year.

If I claim that the moon is made of cheese and submit pictures of the moon as evidence, I have supplied two of the necessary ingredients, a claim and evidence, but am missing a third. We need some justification of *why* this evidence should compel the audience to believe our claim. We need a reason, some logical connection, to tie the evidence to the claim. The reason that connects the evidence to the claim is called the *justification*, or sometimes the *warrant*.

The simplest justification of all would be that the claim is self-evident from the evidence. If we claim that Tuesdays have the highest average sales in the past year, and our evidence is that we have tabulated sales for each day over the past year and found that Tuesday is the highest, our claim is self-evident. The simplest factual arguments are self-evident; these are basically degenerate arguments, where the claim is exactly the evidence, and the justification is extraneous.

Consider a slightly more sophisticated example: that map of home prices laid over a transit map. For this map, more expensive homes read as brighter blocks. The claim is that transit access is associated with higher prices. The evidence is the map itself, ready to be looked at. The justification might be termed visual inspection. By looking at the areas where there are highly priced homes, and seeing that transit stops are nearby, we are making a somewhat convincing argument that the two are related. Not all arguments are solid ones.

Or consider a regression model, where, for example, average prices are modeled by some function of distance to each transit line. The evidence is the model. One possible subclaim is that the model is accurate enough to be used; then the justification is cross-validation, with accuracy measured in dollars.

Another subclaim is that distance from the Lexington Avenue line has the largest effect on prices; then the justification might a single-variable validation procedure[3]. This illustrates a crucial point: the same data can be used to support a variety of claims, depending on what justifications we draw out.

There are always reasons why a justification won't hold in a particular case, even if it is sound in general. Those reasons are called the *rebuttals*. A rebuttal is the yes-but-what-if question that naturally arises in any but the most self-evident arguments.

Consider an attempt to show that a medication is effective at treating warts. If our claim is that the medication cures warts; that our evidence is a randomized controlled trial; and our justification is that randomized controlled trials are evidence of causal relationships, then common rebuttals would be that the randomization may have been done improperly, that the sample size may have been too small, or that there may be other confounding factors attached to the treatment. It pays to be highly aware of what the rebuttals to our arguments are, because those are the things we will need to answer when we need to make a water-tight argument.

In the case that we are using visual inspection to justify our claim that there is a relationship between apartment prices and transit lines, the rebuttal is that visual inspection may not be particularly clear, given that the data will be noisy. There will be highly priced places that are not near public transit lines, and places that have low prices and are on public transit lines.

For a justification of cross-validation, a rebuttal might be that the data is outdated, that the error function we chose is not relevant, or that the sample size is too small. There are always some things that render even the best techniques incorrect.

Finally, all justifications provide some degree of certainty in their conclusions, ranging from possible, to probable, to very likely, to definite. This is known as the degree of *qualification* of an argument. Deductive logic (Tim O'Reilly is a man; All men are mortal; Therefore, Tim O'Reilly is mortal) provides definite certainty in its conclusions, but its use in practice is limited. Having some sense of how strong our result is keeps us from making fools of ourselves.

---

3. Such as bootstrapping or a t-test.

Adding Justifications, Qualifications, and Rebuttals

A 5% reduction in average travel time to the rest of the city results in a 10% increase in apartment prices, with the reverse true as well, an effect which persists. We know this is true because we have looked back at historical apartment prices and transit access and seen that the effect persists. The graph *(Justification)* shows the predictive power of a model trained on each year's data in predicting the following year (based on 20 years of raw price data from the City), and demonstrates that a relationship is *(Qualification)* very likely.

More importantly, when there have been big shocks in transit access, like the opening of a new train station or the closing of a bus route, there were effects on apartment prices visible within a year. *(Justification)* Because the changes are so tightly coupled and happen more frequently together by chance than other changes, we can conclude that the changes in transit access are causing the drop in apartment prices. *(Qualification)* This leads us to believe in a very strong probability of a relationship.

Average prices of apartments for each of the following five blocks, with lines indicating the addition or closure of a new train route within two blocks of that street, demonstrate the rapid change. On average, closing a train stop results in a 10% decline in apartment prices for apartments within two blocks away over the next year, a relationship which roughly holds in at least *(Qualification)* 70% of cases.

(Rebuttal) There are three possible confounding factors. First, there may be nicer apartments being built closer to train lines. *(Prior knowledge)* This is clearly not at issue, because new construction or widespread renovation of apartments (which would raise their value) or letting apartments decline (which would lower their value) all take place over longer time scales than the price changes take place in. Second, there may be large price swings, even in the absence of changing transit access. *(Prior knowledge)* This is also not an issue, because the average price change between successive years for all apartments is actually only 5%. Third, it might be the case that transit improvements or reductions and changes in apartment price are both caused by some external change, like a general decline in neighborhood quality. *(Prior knowledge)* This is impossible to rule out, but generally speaking, the city in question has added transit options spottily and rent often goes up regardless of these transit changes.

Deep Dive: Improving College Graduation Rates

Another extended example is in order, this one slightly more technical. Suppose that a university is interested in starting a pilot program to offer special assistance to incoming college students who are at risk of failing out of school (the context). What it needs is a way to identify who is at risk and find effective interventions (the need). We propose to create a predictive model of failure rates and to assist in the design of an experiment to test several interventions (the vision). If we can make a case for our ideas, the administration will pay for the experiments to test it; if they are successful, the program will be scaled up soon after (the outcome).

There are several parts to our work. The first major part is to build a model to predict the chance of failure. The second is to make a case for an experiment to test if the typical interventions (for example, guidance, free books on study habits, providing free tutoring) are effective for at-risk students. Just identifying students at risk of failing out isn't enough.

When we think about building the model and designing the experiment, we need to put our findings in terms that the decision makers will understand. In this case, that's probably a well-calibrated failure probability rather than a black-box failure predictor. It also entails presenting the experiments in terms of the range of cost per student retained, or the expected lift in graduation rates, not Type I and Type II errors.[4]

In order to make the experiment easy to run, we can restrict ourselves to students who fail out after the first year. If we're lucky, the majority of failouts will happen in the first year, making the experiment even more meaningful. Performing a quick analysis of dropout rates will be enlightening, as evidence to support the short time span of our experiment (or counter-evidence to support a longer experiment, if the dropouts tend to happen at the end of a degree program).

It would be prudent to interview the decision makers and ask them what they think a reasonable range of expense would be for raising the graduate rate by 1%. By setting goals, we can assess whether our models and experiments are plausibly useful. It is important to find the current and historical graduation rate for the university, the general cost of each intervention, and to play around with those numbers. Having a general sense of what success would look like for a model will help set the bar for the remaining work. It is also important to recognize that not

---

4. For more information on modeling and measurement in a business context, and other in-depth discussions of topics raised throughout this book, see *Data Science for Business* by Foster Provost and Tom Fawcett (O'Reilly Media, 2013).

all students who drop out should or could have been helped enough to stay enrolled. Some admitted students were actually false positives to begin with.

To make this project useful, we need to define "failout" and differentiate a failout from a dropout, which might not be caused by poor academic performance. If the university already has a good definition of failout, we should use that. If not, we have to justify a definition. Something like: a failout is a student who drops out either when he is forced to do so by failing grades, or when he drops out on his own accord but was in the bottom quartile of grades for freshmen across the university. To justify this definition, we can argue that students who drop out on their own and had poor grades are probably dropping out in part because they performed poorly.

Now we can turn our attention to the modeling, trying to predict the probability that someone will fail out in her first year. Based on some brainstorming, we identify some potentially predictive facts about each student, plan our next steps, and collect data. If we have access to student records and applications, we might start with 10,000 records, including each student's age, high school GPA, family history, initial courseload, declared major, and so on. This step, acquiring and cleaning the data, will probably account for half or three quarters of the time we spend, so it pays to make a series of mockups along the way to show what we expect to get out of our transformations.

Consider for a moment what we will find if we get a good classifier. Suppose that about 10% of first-year undergraduates fail out. A successful classifier will take that 10% and spread it among some people with a large risk and some with a small risk, retaining the average of 10% across all students. A good classifier will be as spread out as possible while simultaneously having a high correspondence with reality. So in the ideal scenario, for example, we can identify students with 50–60% risk of failing out according to the model, for whom 50–60% do actually fail out in reality.

Our argument will be the following: *(Claim)* We have the ability to forecast which students will fail out accurately enough to try to intervene. *(Subclaim)* Our definition of failout, students who drop out either because they are asked to leave due to poor grades or who are in the bottom quartile of their freshman year, is consistent with what the administration is interested in. *(Justification for the first claim)* We can group students we did not fit the model on and see that the predictions closely match the reality. The error in our predictions is only a few percent on average, accurate enough to be acceptable. *(Justification for the subclaim)* Students

who dropped out on their own but had poor grades have essentially failed out; this idea is consistent with how the term is used in other university contexts.

Let's return to our second need, which was to design an experiment. Depending on how much money we have, how many students we have to work with, and how expensive each intervention might be, there are different experimental designs we can pursue. At a high level, we can imagine splitting students into groups by their risk level, as well as by intervention or combinations of interventions. If money is tight, splitting students into just high- and low-risk groups and choosing students at random from there would be fine. Based on the expectations laid out in discussions with decision makers, we can set minimum thresholds for detection and choose our sample sizes appropriately. And using our risk model, we can set appropriate prior probabilities for each category.

With our model accuracy in hand, we can also estimate the range of effectiveness the various interventions might have, and the associated cost. If, for example, the best our risk model could do was separate out students who were above or below average risk, "at-risk" students could be anywhere from 11% to 100% likely to fail out. With the right distribution of students, it's plausible that almost all of the money will be spent on students who were going to pass anyway. With some thought, we can derive more reasonable categories of high and low risk. With those, we can derive the rough range of cost and benefit in the best- and worst-case post-intervention outcomes.

Our argument for the second need is as follows, assuming that the math works out: *(Claim)* The experiment is worth performing. *(Subclaim)* The high and low ranges of costs for our experiment are low compared to a reasonable range of benefits. *(Subclaim)* Furthermore, their cost is fairly low overall, because we are able to target our interventions with accuracy and we can design the experiment to fit within the budget. *(Claim)* The right way to perform the experiment is to break up students into high- and low-risk groups, and then choose students from the population at random to minimize confounding factors...and so on.

In a fully worked-out project, these arguments would have actual data and graphs to provide evidence. It is also not right to expect that we will arrive at these arguments out of the blue. Like everything else, arguments are best arrived at iteratively. Early versions of arguments will have logical errors, misrepresentations, unclear passages, and so on. An effective countermeasure is to try to inhabit the mind of our friendly but skeptical audience and see where we can find holes. An even better approach is to find a real-life friendly skeptic to try to explain our argument to.

Patterns of Reasoning

One of the great benefits of studying arguments is that we can draw inspiration from patterns that have been noticed and explored by others. Instead of bush-whacking our way through the forest, we have a map to lead us to well-worn trails that take us where we need to go.

We can't simply lift up the patterns that structure arguments in other disciplines and plop them down precisely into data science. There are big differences between a courtroom, a scientific dispute, a national policy debate, and the work that we do with data in a professional setting. Instead, it is possible to take insights from patterns in other fields and mold them to fit our needs.

There are three groups of patterns we will explore. The first group of patterns are called *categories of disputes*, and provide a framework for understanding how to make a coherent argument. The next group of patterns are called *general topics*, which give general strategies for making arguments. The last group is called *special topics*, which are the strategies for making arguments specific to working with data. Causal reasoning, which is a special topic, is so important that it is covered separately in Chapter 5.

Categories of Disputes

A very powerful way to organize our thoughts is by classifying each *point of dispute* in our argument. A point of dispute is the part of an argument where the audience pushes back, the point where we actually need to make a case to win over the skeptical audience. All but the most trivial arguments make at least one point that an audience will be rightfully skeptical of. Such disputes can be classified, and the classification tells us what to do next. Once we identify the kind of dispute we are dealing with, the issues we need to demonstrate follow naturally.

Ancient rhetoricians created a classification system for disputes. It has been adapted by successive generations of rhetoricians to fit modern needs. A point of dispute will fall into one of four categories: *fact, definition, value,* and *policy*.

Once we have identified what kind of dispute we are dealing with, automatic help arrives in the form of *stock issues*. Stock issues tell us what we need to demonstrate in order to overcome the point of contention. Once we have classified what kind of thing it is that is under dispute, there are specific subclaims we can demonstrate in order to make our case. If some of the stock issues are already believed by the audience, then we can safely ignore those. Stock issues greatly simplify the process of making a coherent argument.

We can also use any of these patterns of argument in the negative. Each list of stock issues also forms a natural list of rebuttals in the event that we want to argue against a policy or particular value judgment. It is a very flexible technique.

FACT

A dispute of fact turns on what is true, or on what has occurred. Such disagreements arise when there are concrete statements that the audience is not likely to believe without an argument. Disputes of fact are often smaller components of a larger argument. A particularly complicated dispute of fact may depend on many smaller disputes of fact to make its case.

Some examples of disputes of fact: Did we have more returning customers this month than the last? Do children who use antibiotics get sick more frequently? What is the favorite color of colorblind men? Is the F1 score of this model higher than that of the other model?

The typical questions of science are disputes of fact. Does this chemical combination in this order produce that reagent? Does the debt-to-GDP ratio predict GDP growth? Does a theorized subatomic particle exist?

What all of these questions have in common is that we can outline the criteria that would convince you to agree to an answer prior to any data being collected. The steps might be simple: count the people in group A, count the people in group B, report if A has more members than B. Or it might be highly complex, involving many parts: verify that a piece of monitoring machinery is working well, correctly perform some pipette work 100 times, correctly take the output of the monitoring machine, and finally, apply a Chi-square test to check the distribution of the results. We can make a case for why meeting such conditions would imply the claim.

There are thus two stock issues for disputes of fact. They are:

- What is a reasonable truth condition?
- Is that truth condition satisfied?

In other words, how would you know this fact was right, and did it turn out the way you expected?

We need to lay out the conditions for holding a fact to be true, and then show that those conditions are satisfied. If the conditions are already obvious and held by the audience, we can skip straight to demonstrating that they are satisfied. If they aren't, then our first task is to make a case that we identified a series of steps or conditions that imply the claim.

Take a famous example, the claim that a debt-to-GDP (gross domestic product) ratio of over 90% results in negative real GDP growth. That is, if a national government had debt equal to 90% or more of its GDP in one year, then on average its GDP in the following year would fall, even adjusting for inflation. For several years, this was taken as a fact in many policy circles, based on a paper by the Harvard economists Reinhart and Rogoff.[1]

Reinhart and Rogoff stipulated the following truth condition: collect debt-to-GDP ratios for a number of years, across dozens of countries. Group each country-year into four buckets by their debt-to-GDP ratio (30%, 30–60%, 60–90%, 90% and above). Calculate the growth between that year and the next year. Average across each country, and then average all countries together. Whatever the average growth was in each bucket is the expected growth rate.

Both their truth condition and claim to satisfy that condition turned out to be flawed. When the result was examined in depth by Herndon, Ash, and Pollin from the University of Massachusetts Amherst,[2] several issues were found.

First, the truth condition was misspecified. Data is not available equally for all countries in all years, so averaging first within each country and then across all averages could weigh one year in one country equally with several decades in another. Specifically, in Reinhart and Rogoff's data, Greece and the UK each had 19 years with a debt-to-GDP ratio over 90% and growth around 2.5%, whereas New Zealand had one year with −7.9% growth. The three numbers were simply averaged.

Second, their execution turned out to be flawed. Excel errors excluded the first five countries (Australia, Austria, Belgium, Canada, and Denmark) entirely from the analysis. Additional country-year pairs were also omitted from the whole data set, the absence of which substantially distorted the result.

1. Reinhart, Carmen M., and Kenneth S. Rogoff. *Growth in a Time of Debt.* NBER Working Paper No. 15639, 2010. *http://www.nber.org/papers/w15639.*

2. Herndon, Thomas, Michael Ash, and Robert Pollin. *Does High Public Debt Consistently Stifle Economic Growth? A Critique of Reinhart and Rogoff.* PERI Working Paper No. 322, 2013. *http://bit.ly/1gIDQfN.*

Herndon, Ash, and Pollin made a counter-claim. They declared that there is no sharp drop in GDP growth at a 90% debt-to-GDP ratio, and that in fact the growth slowly falls from an average of 3% per year to around 2%, in the 30% to 120% debt-to-GDP ratio range, beyond which the data volume falls out.

Their truth condition was simply a smoothed graph fit to the original data, without any bucketing. It is worth noting that Herndon, Ash, and Pollin carried out their examination in R, rather than Excel, which provided better statistical tools and far easier replication and debugging.

DEFINITION

Disputes of definition occur when there is a particular way we want to label something, and we expect that that label will be contested. Consider trying to figure out whether antibiotics reduce the incidence of sickness in kids. In the contemporary United States, children are humans under the age of 13 (or 18, in the case of the law). Antibiotics are a known class of drugs. But what does it mean to regard a child as having been sick? Viral load? Doctor's visits? Absence from school? Each of these picks up something essential, but brings its own problems. Quite a lot can be on the line for determining the right definition if you're a drug company. Definitions in a data context are about trying to make precise relationships in an imprecise world. If a definition is already precise and widely shared, there is nothing at issue and we will have nothing to defend.

Words also have prior meanings that are an important part of how we think about them. If humans thought with exact, axiomatic logic, naming things would make no difference. But, for the same reason, our ability to think would be rigidly stuck within narrowly defined categories. We would fall apart the moment we had to think through something outside our axioms.

There are two activities involving definitions that can happen in an argument. The first is making a case that a general, imprecise term fits a particular example. If we show some graphs and claim that they demonstrate that a business is "growing," we are saying that this particular business fits into the category of growing businesses. That is something we have to make a case for, but we are not necessarily claiming to have made a precise definition.

The second activity is a stronger claim to make in an argument: that we have made an existing term more precise. If we say that we have developed some rules to determine which programming language is the most popular, or which users should be considered the most influential on Twitter, we are clarifying an existing idea into something that we can count with.

"Popularity," "influence," "engagement," and the like are all loaded terms, which is a good thing. If we shy away from using meaningful language, it becomes difficult to make judgments in new scenarios. Meaningful definitions provide sensible default positions in new situations. There are certain things we expect of a "popular" language beyond it being highly used in open source code repositories, even if that is how we define popularity. And we have some mental model of how "engaged" users should behave, which can be very useful for debugging an argument.

A term that an audience has no prior understanding of, either in the form of examples (real or prototypical) or prior definitions, is not going to be contested. There will be no argument, because the word will be totally new.

There are three stock issues with disputes of definition:

- Does this definition make a meaningful distinction?
- How well does this definition fit with prior ideas?
- What, if any, are the reasonable alternatives, and why is this one better?

We can briefly summarize these as Useful, Consistent, and Best. A good definition should be all three.

First, consider the issue of whether a definition makes a difference *(Useful)*. What would you think of a definition that declared users to be influential on Twitter based on the result of a coin toss? It would add no predictive ability as to how a given tweet would be taken up by the larger network. Or a definition of a growing business that included every business that was not spiraling into bankruptcy? There have to be some useful distinctions made by the definition in order to be worthy of being cared about, and we often have to make a case for the utility of a definition.

Discussions about how well a definition fits with prior ideas can take many forms *(Consistent)*. One is: how well does this definition agree with previously accepted definitions? Another: how well does this definition capture good examples? To justify a definition of influence on Twitter, it helps to both cite existing definitions of influence (even if they aren't mathematically precise) and to pick out particular people that are known to be influential to show that they are accounted for. Our definition should capture those people. And if it does not, we should make a clear case for why their exclusion does not create a problem with fitting into precedent.

Finally, it makes sense to consider any alternatives *(Best)*, lest our audience do it for us. If there are obvious definitions or classifications that we are missing or not using, it behooves us to explain why our particular definition is superior (or why they are not in conflict).

Disputes of definition are closely related to the idea of construct validity used in the social sciences, especially in psychology and sociology. A construct is a fancy term for definition, and construct validity refers to the extent to which a definition is reliably useful for causal explanation. When psychologists define neuroticism, psychosis, or depression, they're trying to make a prior idea more precise and justify that definition to others.

Definitions are also where we typically introduce simplifying assumptions into our argument. For example, in our investigation into apartment prices and transit accessibility, we discussed sticking only to apartments that are advertised to the public. On one hand, that could be a failing of the final argument. On the other hand, it greatly simplifies the analysis, and as long as we are up front about our assumptions when a reasonable skeptic could disagree with them, it is better to have provisional knowledge than none at all.

VALUE

When we are concerned with judging something, the dispute is one of value.

For example, is a particular metric good for a business to use? We have to select our criteria of goodness, defend them, and check that they apply. A metric presents a balance of ease of interpretability, precision, predictive validity, elegance, completeness, and so on. Which of these values are the right ones to apply in this situation, and how well do they apply? At some point we may have to choose between this metric and another to guide a decision. Which is more important, customer satisfaction or customer lifetime value? We often have to justify a judgment call.

Consider the decision to pick a certain validation procedure for a statistical model. Different criteria[3] are useful for solving different problems. Which of these criteria are the right ones in a particular situation requires an argument. There are trade-offs involved between validity, interpretability, accuracy, and so on. By what criteria should our model be judged?

---

3. Such as cross-validation, external validation, analysis of variance, bootstrapping, t-tests, Bayesian evidence, and so on.

B

Kellogg

Pickup By:
6/25/2022

.

.

.

.

.

.

What else but by their fruits? For disputes of value, our two stock issues are:

- How do our goals determine which values are the most important for this argument?
- Has the value been properly applied in this situation?

For example, consider a scenario where we are deciding between two models (not validation procedures as before, but separate models), one of which is easy to interpret and another that is more accurate but hard to interpret. For some reason, we are restricted to using a single model.

Which values matter in this case will depend on what our goals are. If our goal is to develop understanding of a phenomenon as part of a longer project, the interpretable model is more important. Likewise, if our goal is to build something we can fit into our heads to reason off of in new situations, concision and elegance are important. Our next step would then be to make a case that the model in question is, in fact, interpretable, concise, elegant, and so on.

On the other hand, if our goal is to build something that is a component of a large, mostly or entirely automated process, concision and elegance are irrelevant. But are accuracy or robustness more important? That is, is it more important to be right often, or to be able to withstand change? When the US Post Office uses its handwriting recognition tools to automatically sort mail by zip code, accuracy is the most important value—handwriting is not likely to change substantially over the next few years. By contrast, when building an autonomous robot, it is more important that it can handle new scenarios than that it always walks in the most efficient way possible. Our values are dictated by our goals. Teasing out the implications of that relationship requires an argument.

POLICY

Disputes of policy occur whenever we want to answer the question, "Is this the right course of action?" or "Is this the right way of doing things?" Recognizing that a dispute is a dispute of policy can greatly simplify the process of using data to convince people of the necessity of making a change in an organization.

Should we be reaching out to paying members more often by email? Should the Parks Department do more tree trimming? Is relying on this predictive model the right way to raise revenue? Is this implementation of an encryption standard good enough to use? Does this nonprofit deserve more funding?

The four stock issues of disputes of policy are:

- Is there a problem?
- Where is credit or blame due?
- Will the proposal solve it?
- Will it be better on balance?

David Zarefsky distills these down into Ill, Blame, Cure, and Cost.[4]

Is there a problem? We need to show that there is something worth fixing. Is revenue growth not keeping up with expectation? Are there known issues with a particular algorithm? Are trees falling down during storms and killing people? In any of these cases, it is necessary to provide an argument as to why the audience should believe that there is a problem in the first place.

Where is credit or blame due? For example, is revenue not keeping up with what is expected because of weaker than normal growth in subscriptions? If the problem is that we have a seasonal product, as opposed to that our marketing emails are poorly targeted, proposing to implement a new targeting algorithm may be beside the point. We have to make the case that we have pinpointed a source of trouble.

Would our proposal solve the problem? Perhaps we have run some randomized tests, or we have compared before and after results for the same users, or we have many strong precedents for a particular action. We need to show that our proposed solution has a good chance of working.

Finally, is it worth it? There are many solutions that are too expensive, unreliable, or hard to implement that would solve a problem but aren't worth doing. If it takes three or four days to implement a new targeting model, and it will likely have clear gains, it is a no-brainer. If it might take weeks, and nobody's ever done something like this before, and the payoff is actually rather low compared to other things that a team could be doing...well, it is hard to say that it would be a good decision.

Many, many sticky problems actually turn out to be policy issues. Having a framework to think through is invaluable.

4. *Argumentation, The Study of Effective Reasoning,* 2nd ed. Audio course, *http://www.thegreatcour ses.com/tgc/courses/course_detail.aspx?cid=4294.*

General Topics

Discussions about patterns in reasoning often center around what Aristotle called general topics. General topics are patterns of argument that he saw repeatedly applied across every field. These are the "classic" varieties of arguments: *specific-to-general, comparison, comparing things by degree, comparing sizes, considering the possible as opposed to the impossible,* etc. Undergraduate literature courses often begin and end their discussion of patterns of argument with these.

Though these arguments might seem remote from data work, in fact they occur constantly. Some, like comparing sizes of things and discussing the possible as opposed to the impossible, are straightforward and require no explanation. Others, like specific-to-general reasoning, or reasoning by analogy, require more exposition.

SPECIFIC-TO-GENERAL

A specific-to-general argument is one concerned with reasoning from examples in order to make a point about a larger pattern. The justification for such an argument is that specific examples are good examples of the whole.

A particularly data-focused idea of a specific-to-general argument would be a statistical model. We are arguing from a small number of examples that a pattern will hold for a larger set of examples. This idea comes up repeatedly throughout this book.

Specific-to-general reasoning occurs even when reasoning from anecdotes. Whenever we make productive user experience testing, we are using specific-to-general reasoning. We have observed a relatively small amount of the user base of a given product in great detail, but by reasoning that these users are good examples of the larger user base (at least in some ways), we feel comfortable drawing conclusions based on such research.

Another example of this reasoning pattern is what might be termed an illustration. An illustration is one or more examples that have been selected to build intuition for a topic. Illustrations are extremely useful early in an argument to provide a grounding to the audience about what is relevant and possible for the subject matter.

There is an element of the imagination in every argument. If someone literally cannot imagine an example or the possibilities of the thing under discussion, it is less likely that they will be swayed by the more abstract bits of reasoning. Worse, it is less likely that the argument will actually stick with the person. Practically speaking, it is not enough to convince someone. They need to stay convinced when they

walk away from your argument and not forget it moments later. Concrete examples, sticky graphics, and explanations of the prototypical will help ground arguments in ways that improve the chance of a strong takeaway, even when they are incidental to the body of the argument.

GENERAL-TO-SPECIFIC

General-to-specific arguments occur when we use beliefs about general patterns to infer results for particular examples. While it may not be true that a pattern holds for every case, it is at least plausible enough for us to draw the tentative conclusion that the pattern should hold for a particular example. That is, because a pattern generally holds for a larger category, it is plausible that it should hold for an example.

For example, it is widely believed that companies experiencing rapid revenue growth have an easy time attracting investment. If we demonstrate that a company is experiencing rapid revenue growth, it seems plausible to infer that the company will find it easy to raise money. Of course, that might not be true; the revenue growth may be short-term, or funding may be scarce. That doesn't make it improper to tentatively draw such a conclusion.

This is the opposite of the specific-to-general pattern of reasoning. Using a statistical model to make inferences about new examples is a straightforward instance of general-to-specific results arising from reversing a specific-to-general argument. We use the justification of specific-to-general reasoning to claim that a sample of something can stand in for the whole; then we use general-to-specific reasoning when we go to apply that model to a new example.

The archetypal rebuttal of a general-to-specific argument is that this particular example may not have the properties of the general pattern, and may be an outlier.

Consider a retail clothing company with a number of departments. Menswear departments may overwhelmingly be in the business of supplying men, but a fair number of women shop in menswear departments for aesthetic reasons or on behalf of their partners or children. If we argued that sales of men's dress shirts are indicative of more male customers, we are probably right, but if we argue that because a *particular* customer purchased a men's shirt that the shopper is probably male, we may be wrong.

ARGUMENT BY ANALOGY

Arguments by analogy come in two flavors: literal and figurative. In a literal analogy, two things are actually of similar types. If we have two clients with a similar

purchasing history to date, it seems reasonable to infer that after one client makes a big purchase, the other client may come soon after. The justification for argument by analogy is that if the things are alike in some ways, they will be alike in a new way under discussion.

In a figurative analogy, we have two things that are not of the same type, but we argue that they should still be alike. Traditionally, these kinds of analogies are highly abstract, like comparing justice to fire. This may seem out of place in a book on data analysis, but actually, figurative analogies are constantly present in working with data—just under a different banner.

Every mathematical model is an analogy. Just as justice is not a flame, a physical object moving in space is not an equation. No model is the same as the thing it models. No map is the territory. But behavior in one domain (math) can be helpful in understanding behavior in another domain (like the physical world, or human decision-making).

Whenever we create mathematical models as an explanation, we are making a figurative analogy. It may be a well-supported one, but it is an analogy nonetheless.

The rebuttal for argument by analogy is the same as the rebuttal for general-to-specific arguments—that what may hold for one thing does not necessarily hold for the other. Physical objects experience second-order effects that are not accounted for in the simplified physical model taken from an engineering textbook. People may behave rationally according to microeconomic models, but they might also have grudges that the models didn't account for. Still, when the analogy holds, mathematical modeling is a very powerful way to reason.

Special Arguments

Every discipline has certain argument strategies that it shares with others. The special arguments of data science overlap with those of engineering, machine learning, business intelligence, and the rest of the mathematically inclined disciplines. There are patterns of argument that occur frequently in each of these disciplines that also pop up in settings where we are using data professionally. They can be mixed and matched in a variety of ways.

Optimization, bounding cases, and cost/benefit analysis are three special arguments that deserve particular focus, but careful attention to any case study from data science or related disciplines will reveal many more.

OPTIMIZATION

An argument about optimization is an argument that we have figured out the best way to do something, given certain constraints. When we create a process for recommending movies to someone, assigning people to advertising buckets, or packing boxes full of the right gifts for customers based on their taste, we are engaging in optimization.

Of course, optimization occurs whenever we fit a model through error minimization, but in practice we rarely talk about such activities as optimizations.

This is one of the least argument-laden activities in data science...assuming we already know what we are intending to optimize. If we don't, we first have a dispute of value to deal with. The question of making a value judgment about the right thing to be optimizing is often far more interesting and controversial than the process itself.

BOUNDING CASE

Sometimes an argument is not about making a case for a specific number or model, but about determining what the highest or lowest reasonable values of something might be.

There are two major ways to make an argument about bounding cases. The first is called *sensitivity analysis*. All arguments are predicated on certain assumptions. In sensitivity analysis, we vary the assumptions to best- or worst-case values and see what the resulting answers look like. So if we are making a case that the number of new accounts for a small business could be (based on historical data) as low as two per month and as high as five, and that each account could bring in as little as $2,000 and as much as $10,000 each, then the worst case under these assumptions is a new income of $4,000 a month and a best case is as high as $50,000 a month. That is a huge range, but if we're only concerned that we have enough growth in the next month to pay off a $2,000 loan, then we're already fine.

A more sophisticated approach to determining bounding cases is through *simulation* or *statistical sensitivity analysis*. If we make assumptions about the plausibility of each value in the preceding ranges (based on historical data), say that 2 and 5 clients are equally likely but that 3 or 4 are twice as likely as 2 or 5, and that $2,000 to $10,000 are uniformly likely, then we can start to say things about the lower and upper decile of likely results. The simplest way to do that would be to simulate a thousand months, simulating first a number of clients and then a value per client.

Based on a particular level of risk, we can calculate percentiles of revenue that suit the task at hand. Cost projections for investors might be based on median revenue, whereas cost projections for cash flow analysis may use the lower decile or quartile for safety reasons. Uptime calculations for mission-critical servers, meanwhile, are only considered well-functioning if they can provide service 9,999 seconds out of every 10,000 or better. Bounding cases need to be matched to the relevant risk profile of the audience.

Sensitivity analysis or simulation can provide rough bounds on where important numbers will go. Sometimes just providing orders of magnitude is enough to push a decision forward—for example, by demonstrating that the energy needs for a construction project are a hundred times higher than what is available.

COST/BENEFIT ANALYSIS

A variant on disputes of both value and policy is a cost/benefit analysis. In a cost/benefit analysis, each possible outcome from a decision or group of decisions is put in terms of a common unit, like time, money, or lives saved. The justification is that the right decision is the one that maximizes the benefit (or minimizes the cost). In some sense, such an argument also draws on the idea of optimization, but unlike optimization, there is not necessarily an assertion that the argument takes into account all possible decisions, or a mix of decisions and constraints. A cost/benefit analysis compares some number of decisions against each other, but doesn't necessarily say anything about the space of possible decisions.

For a cost/benefit analysis, there is some agreement on the right things to value, and those things are conveniently countable. It may be quite an achievement to acquire those numbers, but once they are acquired, we can compare the proposed policy against alternatives.

Cost/benefit analyses can also be combined with bounding case analyses. If the lowest plausible benefit from one action is greater than the highest plausible benefit from another, the force of the argument is extremely strong. Even if one is just higher than the other on average, already the evidence is in its favor, but questions of the spread start to matter.

The rebuttals to a cost/benefit analysis are that costs and benefits have been miscalculated, that this is generally not the right method to make such a decision, or that the calculations for cost and benefit do not take into account other costs or benefits that reorder the answers. Next-quarter cash earnings may conflict with long-term profitability, or with legal restrictions that would land a decision maker in jail.

Causality

Causal reasoning is an important and underappreciated part of data science, in part because causal methods are rarely taught in statistics or machine learning courses. Causal arguments are extremely important, because people will interpret claims we make as having a cause-and-effect nature whether we want them to or not. It behooves us to try our best to make our analyses causal. Making such arguments correctly gives far more insight into a problem than simple correlational observations.

Causal reasoning permeates data work, but there are no tools that, on their own, generate defensible causal knowledge. Causation is a perfect example of the necessity of arguments when working with data. Establishing causation stems from making a strong argument. No tool or technique alone is sufficient.

Cause and effect permeates how human think. Causation is powerful. Whenever we think about relationships of variables, we are tempted to think of them causally, even if we know better. All arguments about relationships, even about relationships that we know are only associative and not causal, are positioned in relation to the question of causation.

Noncausal relationships are still useful. Illustration sparks our imaginations, prediction allows us to plan, extrapolation can fill in gaps in our data, and so on. Sometimes the most important thing is just to understand how an event happened or what examples of something look like. In an ideal scenario, however, our knowledge eventually allows us to intervene and improve the world. Whenever possible, we want to know what we should change to make the world be more like how we want it.

We can think about causal arguments in terms of a spectrum, running from arguments that barely hint at causality to arguments that establish undeniable causality. On the near end of the causal spectrum are arguments that are completely observational and not really causal in nature. At most, they vaguely gesture in the direction of causality. They are very useful for building understanding of what a phenomenon is about. Taxonomies, clustering, and illustrative examples stand at

this end. Again, these are not causal methods, but they can hint at causal relationships that require further investigation.

The next step in the direction of a full causal explanation is an argument claiming to have found a relationship with predictive power. A predictive relationship allows for planning, but if those variables were different, the outcome might still change as well. Suppose that we understand how likely customers are to quit their subscription to a dating site based on how quickly they reply to messages from other users. We aren't claiming that getting people to reply more quickly would change the chance that they drop off, only that people who tend to behave like that tend to drop off sooner. Most statistical models are purely predictive.

Moving further along, we have a range of methods and designs that try to eliminate alternative explanations. A *design* is a method for grouping units of analysis according to certain criteria to try to reduce uncertainty in understanding cause and effect. This is where causal influence actually begins. Techniques like *within-subject designs* and *randomized controlled trials* fall here. These methods make an effort to create defensible causal knowledge of a greater or lesser degree, depending on the number of issues stymieing causal analysis that we can eliminate. Randomized controlled trials are at the far end of this part of the causal spectrum.

On the very far end of the causal spectrum are arguments for which a causal relationship is obvious, such as with closed systems (like components in a factory) or well-established physical laws. We feel no compunction in claiming that dropping a vase is the cause of it breaking. Physical examples provide us with our intuition for what cause and effect mean. They are the paragons of the phenomenon of causation, but unfortunately, outside of some particularly intensive engineering or scientific disciplines, they rarely arise in the practical business of data work.

No matter how many caveats we may put into a report about correlation not implying causation, people will interpret arguments causally. Human beings make stories that will help them decide how to act. It is a sensible instinct. People want analysis with causal power. We can ignore their needs and hide behind the difficulty of causal analysis—or we can come to terms with the fact that causal analysis is necessary, and then figure out how to do it properly and when it truly does not apply.

To be able to make causal statements, we need to investigate causal reasoning further. Causal analysis is a deep topic, and much like statistical theory, does not have a single school that can claim to have a monopoly on methodology. Instead, there are multiple canons of thought, each concerned with slightly different scenarios. Statistics as a whole is concerned with generalizing from old to new data;

causal analysis is concerned with generalizing from old to new scenarios where we have deliberately altered something.

Generally speaking, because data science as a field is primarily concerned with generalizing knowledge only in highly specific domains (such as for one company, one service, or one type of product), it is able to sidestep many of the issues that snarl causal analysis in more scientific domains. As of today, data scientists do little work building theories intended to capture causal relationships in entirely new scenarios. For those that do, especially if their subject matter concerns human behavior, a more thorough grounding in topics such as construct validity and quasi-experimental design is highly recommended.[1]

Defining Causality

Different schools of thought have defined causality differently, but a particularly simple interpretation, suitable to many of the problems that are solvable with data, is the *alternate universe perspective*. These causes are more properly referred to as "manipulable causes," because we are concerned with understanding how things might have been if the world been manipulated a bit.

Not all causal explanations are about examining what might have been different under other circumstances. Chemistry gives causal explanations of how a chemical reaction happens. We could alter the setup by changing the chemicals or the environment, but the actual reasoning as to why that reaction will play out is fixed by the laws of physics.

Suppose there is a tree on a busy street. That particular tree may have been trimmed at some point. In causal parlance, it has either been *exposed* or *not exposed* to a *treatment*. The next year it may have fallen down or not. This is known as the *outcome*. We can imagine two universes, where in one the tree was treated with a trimming and in the other it was not (Table 5-1). Are the outcomes different?

Table 5-1. Consider one tree

	Treatment (trimming)	Outcome (fall down)
Universe A	True	False
Universe B	False	True

1. For more information, see *Experimental and Quasi-Experimental Designs* by William Shadish, et al. (Cengage Learning, 2001).

We can see that the trimming caused the tree to not fall down, or alternatively, that the lack of trimming prevented the tree from falling down. The trimming was not sufficient by itself (likely some wind or storm was involved as well) and it was not necessary (a crane could also have brought the tree down), but it was nevertheless a cause of the tree falling down.

In practice, we are more likely to see a collection of examples than we are a single one. It is important to remember, though, that a causal relationship is not the same as a statistical one. Consider 20 trees, half of which were trimmed. These are now all in the same universe (see Table 5-2).

Table 5-2. Looking at many trees

	Fell down	Didn't fall down
Trimmed	0	10
Not trimmed	10	0

It looks at first like we have a clear causal relationship between trimming and falling down. But what if we were to add another variable that mostly explained the difference, as shown in Table 5-3?

Table 5-3. Confounders found

Exposed to wind

	Fell down	Didn't fall down
Trimmed	0	2
Not trimmed	8	0

Not exposed to wind

	Fell down	Didn't fall down
Trimmed	0	8
Not trimmed	2	0

More of the trees that are exposed to the wind were left untrimmed. We say that exposure to the wind *confounded* our potential measured relationship between trimming and falling down.

The goal of a causal analysis is to find and account for as many confounders as possible, observed *and* unobserved. In an ideal world, we would know everything we needed to in order to pin down which states always preceded others. That

knowledge is never available to us, and so we have to avail ourselves of certain ways of grouping and measuring to do the best we can.

Designs

The purpose of causal analysis, at least for problems that don't deal with determining scientific laws, is to deal with the problem of confounders. Without the ability to see into different universes, our best bet is to come up with *designs* to structure how we perform an analysis to try to avoid confounders. Again, a design is a method for grouping units of analysis (like people, trees, pages, and so on) according to certain criteria to try to reduce uncertainty in understanding cause and effect.

A design is a method for grouping units of analysis (like people, trees, pages, and so on) according to certain criteria to try to reduce uncertainty in understanding cause and effect.

Before we stray too far away from multiple universes, one more point is in order. If we had included wind into our investigation of one single tree under different universes, we might see something interesting. After all, there does have to be to be some external agent, like a wind storm, to combine with the trimming or lack thereof to produce a downed tree. This is an illustration of *multiple causation*, where more than one thing has to be true simultaneously for an outcome to come about.

For data about one tree, reference Table 5-4.

Table 5-4. Multiple causation

	Treatment (trimming)	Wind storm	Outcome (fall down)
Universe A1	True	True	False
Universe A2	True	False	False
Universe B1	False	True	True
Universe B2	False	False	False

Typically, our goal in investigating causation is not so much to understand how one particular instance of causation played out (though that is a common pattern in data-driven storytelling), but to understand how we would expect a treatment to change an outcome in a new scenario. That is, we are interested in how well a causal explanation generalizes to new situations.

Intervention Designs

A number of different design strategies exist for controlling for confounders. In a typical randomized controlled trial, we randomly assign the treatment to the subjects. The justification for the claim that we can infer generalizability is that, because the treatment was chosen randomly for each unit, it should be independent of potential confounders.

There are numerous rebuttals for randomized controlled trials, the details of which would take up many books. The randomization may have been done improperly. The proposed treatment might not be the only difference between groups (hence double-bind experiments). The sample size may not have been large enough to deal with natural levels of variation. Crucially, new subjects may be different in novel ways from those included in the experiment, precluding generalization. If the same people are included in multiple experiments over time, they are no longer necessarily similar to a brand-new person.

In the case of *nonrandom intervention*, consider observing the stress level of someone for an hour and applying an electrical shock at the 30-minute mark without warning them. It will show a clear evidence of a relationship, but randomization was nowhere to be found. This is an example of a *within-subject interrupted time series design*; see Figure 5-1.

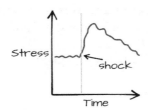

Figure 5-1. A shocking example of within-subject design

The causal relationship between shock and stress is justified on a number of levels. First, if we were carefully observing the subject and didn't see any other things that would have caused stress, such as a bear entering the laboratory, we have eliminated a large class of potential confounders. Second, we have prior intuition that shocks and stress should be related, so this result seems, prima facie, plausible. Third, the exact timing would be unreasonable to line up with another cause of stress, such as an unpleasant thought that lingered with the subject for the rest of the experiment. Finally, the magnitude of the jump was much larger than variation observed for the same subject prior to the shock.

Were we to perform this same experiment a dozen times, and each time see a similar jump in stress levels, then it would be reasonable to conclude that, for new subjects similar to the ones that we tested on, an unexpected shock would cause a jump in stress levels. That is, we could argue that the relationship is, to some extent, generalizable.

There may still be unmeasured confounders (if all of the experiment subjects were college students, they may have a lower pain threshold than, say, a construction worker) that would stymie generalization. But it is very important to note again that such unmeasured confounders can exist even in a randomized experiment. There may be important, unmeasured aspects of the subjects that can't be accounted for because all subjects are drawn from the same pool.

A truly randomized experiment would be randomized not only in the treatment, but also in the subjects, and in the pool of potential people or tools that would be carrying out an intervention. That is, we would be picking at random from the potential units (i.e., selecting people from the population at random) and executors of the treatment (i.e., if the treatment is applying a drug, choosing random doctors) in addition to applying the treatment at random. Random subjects and treaters are very rarely applied designs.

Observational Designs

In the case of purely *observational designs*, we are tasked with employing clever strategies for inferring generalizablity without the ability to intervene.

Observational designs are necessary when it is either impractical, costly, or unethical to perform interventional experiments. Most socially interesting causal estimation problems are of this kind. They frequently occur in business too; it may be advantageous for certainty's sake to take down a part of a business to see how it affects profit, but the downstream implications are almost always too great to consider doing so. Instead, we have to take advantage of natural differences in exposure or temporary outages to determine the causal effect of critical components.

Natural Experiments

Our best hope in setting up observational designs is to try to find natural experiments. Consider an effort to determine how being convicted of a crime in high school affects earnings from age 25 to 40. It isn't enough to just compare earning differences between those who were convicted and those who weren't, because clearly there will be strong confounding variables. A clever strategy would be to compare earnings between those who were arrested but not convicted of a crime,

and those who were convicted. Though there are obvious differences in the groups, they are likely to be similar on a number of other variables that serve as a natural control. This is what is known as a natural experiment: we try to argue that we have made a choice about what to compare that accounts for most alternative explanations.

When natural between-subject controls are not available, we can sometimes use methods such as *within-subject interrupted time series designs*, analogous to the electrical shock example. If sign-ups on a website are rising steadily, and when we introduce a new design for the sign-up page, sign-ups begin to drop immediately, it seems reasonable to assume that the redesign is at fault. But to claim so in good faith (and to make a strong argument), we have to eliminate other contenders. Did the site get slower? Is there a holiday somewhere? Did a competitor get a lot of coverage? By looking at bar charts and maps comparing the sign-ups for different groups of people in different regions, and confirming that the drop is fairly universal, we can strongly justify the redesign as the culprit. We are looking at the same subject and trying to account for alternatives.

The same methodology can also deal with fuzzier problems where we have no natural control group. If we are interested in whether changes in nutrition standards at schools improve test scores, we can go find test score data for many schools where we know that nutrition overhauls were put into place. If test scores (or test score ranking within a given region, to account for changes in the tests themselves) tend to be relatively flat before a nutrition change, then rise, and we have enough examples of this, it starts to be reasonable to implicate the nutrition changes. The justification for the claim of a causal relationship is that there are few reasonable alternative explanations, especially given the proximity in timing, so a causal relationship is the most logical explanation.

What we would have to do to make a good-faith effort is figure out all of the reasonable confounding factors and do our best to account for them. Our conclusion will necessarily be of a less definite kind than if we had somehow been able to randomly give individual kids more nutritious lunches—but such experiments would be not only unethical, but also self-defeating. How would you possibly enforce the restrictions of the experiment without unduly influencing the rest of the environment?

By comparison, just calculating the current test scores of schools that have booted nutrition standards against schools that have not would not be a particularly effective design, because there are likely to be a great number of confounding factors.

This, generally, paints the way for how we do causal reasoning in the absence of the ability to set interactions. We try to gather as much information as possible to find highly similar situations, some of which have experienced a treatment and some of which have not, in order to try to make a statement about the effect of the treatment on the outcome. Sometimes there are confounding factors that we can tease out with better data collection, such as demographic information, detailed behavioral studies, or pre- or post-intervention surveys. These methods can be harder to scale, but when they're appropriate, they provide us with much stronger tools to reason about the world than we are given otherwise.

Statistical Methods

If all else fails, we can turn to a number of statistical methods for establishing causal relationships. They can be roughly broken down into those based on causal graphs and those based on matching. If there have been enough natural experiments in a large data set, we can use statistical tools to tease out whether changes in some variables appear to be causally connected to others.

The topic of causal graphs is beyond the scope of this book, but the rough idea is that, by assuming a plausible series of relationships that would provide a causal explanation, we can identify what kinds of relationships we should *not* see. For example, you should never see a correlation between patient age and their treatment group in a randomized clinical trial. Because the assignment was random, group and age should be uncorrelated. In general, given a plausible causal explanation and a favorable pattern of correlations and absences of correlation, we have at least some measure of support for our argument of causality.[2]

The other variety of statistical causal estimation is matching. Of matching, there are two kinds: deterministic and probabilistic. In deterministic matching, we try to find similar units across some number of variables. Say we are interested in the effect drinking has on male fertility. We survey 1,000 men on their history and background, and measure their sperm count. Simply checking alcohol consumption history and comparing light and heavy drinkers in their sperm count is not sufficient. There will be other confounding factors like age, smoking history, and diet. If there are a small number of variables and a large number of subjects, we can reduce some confounding by finding *pairs* of men who match along many or all of the variables, but wherein only one of the two is a heavy drinker. Then we can

2. For more information on this topic, please see Judea Pearl's book *Causality* (Cambridge University Press, 2009).

compare the sperm count of the two men—and hopefully, if we have measured the right controls, it will be as if we had discovered a natural experiment.

If there are a large number of variables (say that diet is determined by a 100-question questionnaire, or we are introducing genetic data), it is more reasonable to use probabilistic matching. The most famous probabilistic matching methodology is *propensity score matching*. In propensity score matching, we build a model that tries to account for the probability that a subject will have for being treated, also called the propensity. In the alcohol example, we would model the probability of being a heavy drinker given age, smoking history, diet, genetics, and so on. Then, like in the deterministic matching example, we would again pair up similar subjects (this time, those who had roughly the same probability of becoming heavy drinkers) wherein one was a heavy drinker and one was not. We are seeking to create what might be termed an artificial natural experiment.

There are good theoretical reasons to prefer propensity score matching even in the case of a small number of variables, but it can sometimes be worthwhile to skip the added difficulty of fitting the intermediate model.

Putting It All Together

We should look at some extended examples to see the method of full problem thinking in action. By looking at the scoping process, the structure of the arguments, and some of the exploratory steps (as well as the wobbles inevitably encountered), we can bring together the ideas we have discussed into a coherent whole.

The goal of this chapter is not to try to use everything in every case, but instead to use these techniques to help structure our thoughts and give us room to think through each part of a problem. These examples are composites, lightly based on real projects.

Deep Dive: Predictive Model for Conversion Probability

Consider a consumer product company that provides a service that is free for the first 30 days. Its business model is to provide such a useful service that after 30 days, as many users will sign up for the continued service as possible.

To bring potential customers in to try its product, the company runs targeted advertisements online. These ads are focused on groups defined by age, gender, interests, and other factors. It runs a variety of ads, with different ad copy and images, and is already optimizing ads based on who tends to click them, with more money going toward ads with a higher click rate. Unfortunately, it takes 30 days or so to see whether a new ad has borne fruit. In the meantime, the company is spending very large amounts of money on those ads, many of which may have been pointlessly displayed. The company is interested in shrinking this feedback loop, and so asks a data scientist to find a way to shrink it. What can we suggest?

First, let us think a bit about what actions the company can take. It constantly has new users coming in, and after some amount of time, it can evaluate the quality of the users it has been given and choose whether to pull the plug on the advertisement. It needs to be able to judge quality sooner, and compare that quality to the cost of running the ad.

Another way of phrasing this is that the company needs to know the quality of a user based on information gathered in just the first few days after a user has started using the service. We can imagine some kind of black box that takes in user behavior and demographic information from the first few days and spits out a quality metric.

For the next step, we can start to ask what kind of behavior and what kind of quality metric would be appropriate. We explore and build experience to get intuition. Suppose that by either clicking around, talking to the decision makers, or already being familiar with the service, we find that there are a dozen or so actions that a user can take with this service. We can clearly count those, and break them down by time or platform. This is a reasonable first stab at behavior.

What about a quality metric? We are interested in how many of the users will convert to paid customers, so if possible, we should go directly for a probability of conversion. But recall that the action the company can take is to decide whether to pull the plug on an advertisement, so what we are actually interested in is the expected value of each new user, a combination of the probability of conversion and the lifetime value of a new conversion. Then we can make a cost/benefit decision about whether to keep the ad. In all, we are looking to build a predictive model of some kind, taking in data about behavior and demographics and putting out a dollar figure. Then, we need to compare that dollar figure against the cost of running the ad in the first place.

What will happen after we put the model out? The company will need to evaluate users either once or periodically between 1 and 30 days to judge the value of each user, and then will need some way to compare that value information to the cost of running the advertisement. It will need a pipeline for calculating the cost of each ad per person that the ad is shown to. Typical decisions would be to continue running an advertisement, to stop running one, or to ramp up spending on one that is performing exceptionally well.

It is also important to measure the causal efficacy of the model on improving revenue. We would like to ensure that the advertisements that are being targeted to be cut actually deserve it. By selecting some advertisements at random to be spared from cutting, we can check back in 30 days or so to see how accurately we have predicted the conversion to paid users. If the model is accurate, the conversion probabilities should be roughly similar to what was predicted, and the short-term or estimated lifetime value should be similar as well.

Context

A consumer product company with a free-to-try model. It wants people to pay to continue to use its product after the free trial.

Need

The company runs a number of tightly targeted ads, but it is not clear until around 30 days in whether the ads are successful. In the meantime, it's been spending tons of money to run ads that might have been pointless. How can it tighten up the feedback loop and decide which ads to cut?

Vision

We will make a predictive model based on behavior and demographics that uses information available in the first few days to predict the lifetime value of each incoming user. Its output would be something like, "This user is 50% less likely than baseline to convert to being a paid user. This user is 10% more likely to convert to being a paid user. This user....etc. In aggregate, all thousand users are 5% less likely than baseline to convert. Therefore, it would make sense to end this advertisement campaign early, because it is not attracting the right people."

Outcome

Deliver the model to the engineers, ensuring that they understand it. Put into place a pipeline for aggregating the cost of running each advertisement. After engineering has implemented the model, check back once after five days to see if the proportions of different predicted groups match those from the analysis. Select some advertisements to not be disrupted, and check back in one month to see if the predicted percentages or dollar values align with those of the model.

What is the argument here? It is a policy argument. The main claim is that the model should be used to predict the quality of advertisements after only a few days of running them. The "Ill" is that it takes 30 days to get an answer about the quality of an ad. The "Blame" is that installation probability (remember that we were already tracking this) is not a sufficient predictor of conversion probability. The "Cure" is a cost-predictive model and a way of calculating the cost of running a particular advertisement. And the "Cost" (or rather, the benefit) is that, by cutting out advertisements at five days, we will not spend 25 days worth of money on unhelpful advertisements.

To demonstrate that the Cure is likely to be as we say it is, we need to provisionally check the quality of the model against held-out data. In the longer term, we want to see the quality of the model for advertisements that are left to run. In

this particular case, the normal model quality checks (ROC curves, precision and recall) are poorly suited for models that have only 1–2% positive rates. Instead, we have to turn to an empirical/predicted probability plot (Figure 6-1).

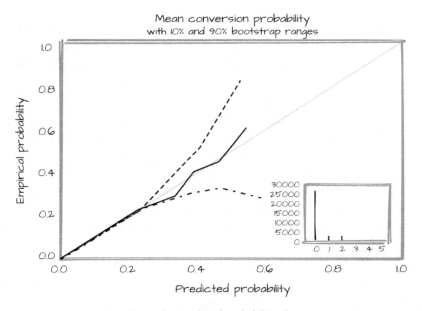

Figure 6-1. Predicted probability plot

To demonstrate the Cost, we need some sense of the reliability of the model compared to the cost range of running the ads. How does our predicted lifetime value compare to the genuine lifetime value, and how often will we overshoot or undershoot? Finally, is the volume of money saved still positive when we include the time cost of developing the model, implementing it, and running it? If the model is any good, the answer is almost certainly yes, especially if we can get a high-quality answer in the first few days. The more automated this process is, the more time it will take up front—but the more time it will save in the long run. With even reasonable investment, it should save far more than is spent.

In the end, what is the audience (in this case, the decision makers who will decide whether to proceed with this project and whether to approve the build-out) actually going to dispute? The Ill, Blame, and Cost may already be apparent, so the discussion may center on the Cure (how good is the model?). But if we were un-aware of the possibility that there could be other things to discuss (besides the quality of the model), it would be easy to be caught unaware and not be prepared

to coherently explain the project when pointed questions are asked by, for example, higher levels of management.

Deep Dive: Calculating Access to Microfinance

Microfinance is the provision of traditional bank services (loans, lines of credit, savings accounts, investments) to poor populations. These populations have much smaller quantities of money than typical bank customers. The most common form of microfinance is microloans, where small loans are provided as startup capital for a business. In poorer countries, the average microloan size is under $500. Most microloan recipients are women, and in countries with well-run microfinance sectors, the vast majority of loans are repaid (the most widely admired microfinance programs average over 97% repayment).

There is a nonprofit that focuses on tracking microfinance around the world. It has a relationship with the government of South Africa, which is interested in learning how access to microfinance varies throughout their country. At the same time, the nonprofit is interested in how contemporary tools could be brought to bear to answer questions like this.

From talking to the organization, it is clear that the final outcome will be some kind of report or visualization that will be delivered to the South African government, potentially on a regular basis. Having some summary information would also be ideal.

Context

There has been an explosion of access to credit in poor countries in the past generation. There is a nonprofit that tracks information about microfinance across the world and advises governments on how they can improve their microfinance offerings.

Needs

The South African government is interested in where there are gaps in microloan coverage. The nonprofit is interested in how new data sets can be brought to bear on answering questions like this.

Vision

We will create a map that demonstrates where access is lacking, which could be used to track success and drive policy. It will include one or more summary statistics that could more concisely demonstrate success. There would be bright spots around remote areas that were heavily populated. Readers of the map should be able to conclude where the highest priority places are, in order to

place microfinance offices (assuming they were familiar with or were given access to a map displaying areas of high poverty in South Africa).

Outcome

Deliver the maps to the nonprofit, which will take them to the South African government. Potentially work with the South African government to receive regularly updated maps and statistics.

Some immediate challenges present themselves. What does access mean? If a loan office is more than a half-day's journey away, it will be difficult for a lendee to take advantage of the service. Walking in rural areas for several hours probably progresses at around 3 kilometers per hour (about 1.86 miles per hour). If we figure that three or four hours is a reasonable maximum distance for a walk in each direction, we get about 10 kilometers as a good maximum distance for access to a microfinance office.

What do we mean when we say microfinance offices? In this particular case, the microfinance tracking organization has already collected information on all of the registered microfinance offices across South Africa. These include private groups, post office branches, and nonprofit microfinance offices. For each of these, we start with an address; it will be necessary to geocode them into latitude and longitude pairs.

What about population? A little digging online reveals that there are approximate population maps available for South Africa (using a 1 km scale). They are derived from small-scale census information. Without these maps, the overall project would be much more difficult—we would need to define access relative to entire populated areas (like a town or village) that we had population and location information from. This would add a tremendous amount of overhead to the project, so thankfully such maps can easily be acquired. But keep in mind that their degree of trustworthiness, especially at the lowest scale, is suspect, and any work we do should acknowledge that fact.

We are also faced with some choices about what to include on such a map. In practice, only a single quantity can be mapped with color on a given map. Is it more important to show gradations in access or the number of people without access? Would some hybrid of people-kilometers be a valid metric? After some consideration, demonstrating the number of people is the smarter decision. It makes prioritization simpler.

The overall argument is as follows. We claim that "has access to microfinance" can be reasonably calculated by seeing, for each square kilometer, whether that

square kilometer is within 10 kilometers of a microloan office as the crow flies. This is a claim of definition. To justify it, we need to relate it to the understanding about access and microfinance already shared by the audience. It is reasonable to restrict "access" to mean foot access at worst, given the level of economic development of the loan recipients. Using the list of microfinance institutions kept by the microfinance tracking nonprofit is also reasonable, given that they will be the ones initially using this map and that they have spent years perfecting the data set.

This definition is superior to the alternative of showing degrees of access, because there is not much difference between a day's round-trip travel and a half-day's round-trip travel. Only a much smaller travel time, such as an hour or so, would be a major improvement over a day's round-trip travel. However, such density is not achievable at present, nor is it going to provide a major discontinuity from mere half-day accessibility. As such, for our purposes, 10 kilometer distance to a microloan office is a sufficient cutoff.

We claim that a map of South Africa, colored by population, masked to only those areas outside of 10 kilometers distance to a microloan office, is a good visual metric of access. This is a claim of value. The possible competing criteria are legibility, actionability, concision, and accuracy. A colored map is actionable; by encouraging more locations to open where the map is currently bright (and thus more people are deprived of access to credit), the intensity of the map will go down. It is a bit less legible than it is actionable, because it requires some expertise to interpret. It is fairly accurate, because we are smoothing down issues like actual travel distance by using bird's-eye distance, but is otherwise reasonably reliable on a small scale. It is also a concise way to demonstrate accessibility, though not as concise as per-province summaries or, at a smaller level of organization (trade-off of accuracy for concision!), per-district and per-metropolitan area summaries.

To remedy the last issue, we can join our map with some summary statistics. Per-area summary statistics, like a per-district or per-metropolitan percentage of population that is within 10 kilometers of a microloan office, would be concise and actionable and a good complement to the maps. To achieve this, we need district-level administrative boundaries and some way to mash those boundaries up with the population and office location maps.

With this preliminary argument in mind, we can chat with the decision makers to ensure that what we are planning to do will be useful. A quick mockup drawing, perhaps shading in areas on a printout of a map of South Africa, could be a useful focal point. If this makes sense to everyone, more serious work can begin.

From a scaffolding perspective, it pays to start by geocoding the microloan offices, because without that information we will have to fall back on a completely different notion of access (such as one based on town-to-town distances). It pays to plot the geocoded microloan offices on a map alongside the population density map to get a sense of what a reasonable final map will look like. It is probably wise to work out the logic for assigning kilometer squares to the nearest microloan office, and foolish to use any technique other than brute force, given the small number of offices and the lack of time constraints on map generation.

After much transformation and alignment, we have something useful. At this point the map itself can be generated, and shared in a draft form with some of the decision makers. If everyone is still on the same page, then the next priority should be calculating the summary statistics and checking those again with the substantive experts. At this point, generating a more readable map (including appropriate boundaries and cities to make it interpretable) is wise, as is either plotting the summary statistics on a choropleth map or arranging them into tables separated by district.

Final copies in hand, we can talk again with the decision makers, this time with one or more documents that lay out the relevant points in detail. Even if our work is in the form of a presentation, if the work is genuinely important, there should be a written record of the important decisions that went into making the map and summary statistics. If the work is more exploratory and temporary, a verbal exchange or brief email exchange is fine—but if people will be making actual decisions based on the work we have done, it is vitally important to leave behind a comprehensive written record. Edward Tufte has written eloquently about how a lack of genuine technical reports, eclipsed instead by endless PowerPoints, was a strong contributing factor to the destruction of the space shuttle Columbia.

Wrapping Up

Data science, as a field, is overly concerned with the technical tools for executing problems and not nearly concerned enough with asking the right questions. It is very tempting, given how pleasurable it can be to lose oneself in data science work, to just grab the first or most interesting data set and go to town. Other disciplines have successfully built up techniques for asking good questions and ensuring that, once started, work continues on a productive path. We have much to gain from adapting their techniques to our field.

We covered a variety of techniques appropriate to working professionally with data. The two main groups were techniques for telling a good story about a project, and techniques for making sure that we are making good points with our data.

The first involved the scoping process. We looked at the context, need, vision, and outcome (or CoNVO) of a project. We discussed the usefulness of brief mock-ups and argument sketches. Next, we looked at additional steps for refining the questions we are asking, such as planning out the scaffolding for our project and engaging in rapid exploration in a variety of ways. What each of these ideas have in common is that they are techniques designed to keep us focused on two goals that are in constant tension and yet mutually support each other: diving deep into figuring out what our goals are and getting lost in the process of working with data.

Next, we looked at techniques for structuring arguments. Arguments are a powerful theme in working with data, because we make them all the time whether we are aware of them or not. Data science is the application of math and computers to solve problems of knowledge creation; and to create knowledge, we have to show how what is already known and what is already plausible can be marshaled to make new ideas believable.

We looked at the main components of arguments: the audience, prior beliefs, claims, justifications, and so on. Each of these helps us to clarify and improve the process of making arguments. We explored how explicitly writing down arguments can be a very powerful way to explore ideas. We looked at how techniques of transformation turn data into evidence that can serve to make a point.

We next explored varieties of arguments that are common across data science. We looked at classifying the nature of a dispute (fact, definition, value, and policy) and how each of those disputes can be addressed with the right claims. We also looked at specific argument strategies that are used across all of the data-focused disciplines, such as optimization, cost/benefit analysis, and casual reasoning. We looked at causal reasoning in depth, which is fitting given its prominent place in data science. We looked at how causal arguments are made and what some of the techniques are for doing so, such as randomization and within-subject studies. Finally, we explored some more in-depth examples.

Data science is an evolving discipline. But hopefully in several years, this material will seem obvious to every practitioner, and a clear place to start for every beginner.

Further Reading

Paul, Richard and Linda Elder. *The Miniature Guide to Critical Thinking*. Foundation for Critical Thinking, 2009.
A brief introduction to structures for thinking.

Wright, Larry. *Critical Thinking: An Introduction to Analytical Reading and Reasoning*. 2nd ed. Oxford University Press, 2012.
Readable, useful textbook on finding the essence of arguments.

Papert, Seymour. *Mindstorms: Children, Computers, and Powerful Ideas*. Basic Books, 1993.
A classic on how mental models open up the possibility of understanding new ideas.

Jones, Morgan D. *The Thinker's Toolkit: 14 Powerful Techniques for Problem Solving*. Crown Business, 1998.
A compendium of brainstorming and decision structuring techniques.

Moore, David T. *Critical Thinking and Intelligence Analysis*. CreateSpace, 2007.
Applications of argument and critical thinking with data in a wide-ranging and adversarial situation: national intelligence.

Toulmin, Stephen E. *The Uses of Argument*. Cambridge University Press, 2003.
Philosophical treatment of the foundations of argumentation.

Croll, Alistair and Benjamin Yoskovitz. *Lean Analytics*. O'Reilly, 2013.
In-depth guide to choosing the right metrics for a given organization at a given time.

Hubbard, Douglas W. *How to Measure Anything: Finding the Value of Intangibles in Business,*. Wiley, 2010.
Guide to measuring and acting on anything, including "intangibles" like security, knowledge, and employee satisfaction.

Provost, Foster and Tom Fawcett. *Data Science for Business*. O'Reilly Media, 2013.
   In-depth look at many of the same topics in this book, with a greater focus on
   the high-level technical ideas.

Tufte, Edward. *Envisioning Information*. Graphics Press, 1990.
   A classic in structuring visual thinking for both exploration and communication.

Shadish, William R., Thomas D. Cook, and Donald T. Campbell. *Experimental
and Quasi-Experimental Designs for Generalized Causal Inference*. Cengage Learning, 2001.
   Very readable textbook on causal designs.

Jaynes, E.T., and G. Larry Bretthorst. *Probability Theory: The Logic of Science*.
Cambridge University Press, 2003.
   A book about the connection between classical logic and probability theory.

About the Author

Max Shron runs a small data strategy consultancy in New York, working with many organizations to help them get the most out of their data. His analyses of transit, public health, and housing markets have been featured in the *New York Times*, *Chicago Tribune*, Huffington Post, WNYC, and more. Prior to becoming a data strategy consultant, he was the data scientist for OkCupid.

Colophon

The cover font is BentonSans Compressed, the body font is ScalaPro, the heading font is BentonSans, and the code font is TheSansMonoCd.

Have it your way.

Get even more for your money.

Join the O'Reilly Community, and register the O'Reilly books you own. It's free, and you'll get:

- $4.99 ebook upgrade offer
- 40% upgrade offer on O'Reilly print books
- Membership discounts on books and events
- Free lifetime updates to ebooks and videos
- Multiple ebook formats, DRM FREE
- Participation in the O'Reilly community
- Newsletters
- Account management
- 100% Satisfaction Guarantee

Signing up is easy:

1. Go to: oreilly.com/go/register
2. Create an O'Reilly login.
3. Provide your address.
4. Register your books.

Note: English-language books only

To order books online:
oreilly.com/store

For questions about products or an order:
orders@oreilly.com

To sign up to get topic-specific email announcements and/or news about upcoming books, conferences, special offers, and new technologies:
elists@oreilly.com

For technical questions about book content:
booktech@oreilly.com

To submit new book proposals to our editors:
proposals@oreilly.com

O'Reilly books are available in multiple DRM-free ebook formats. For more information:
oreilly.com/ebooks

Spreading the knowledge of innovators   oreilly.com

KELLEY TATRO is a writer and editor with a PhD in Music from Duke University. She lives in Chicago.

YAZ "PUNK" NÚÑEZ is a filmmaker and photographer with a degree in cinematography from the Universidad Nacional Autónoma de México. She lives in Mexico City.